2820

The New Italian Poetry

The New Italian Poetry

1945 to the
Present
A Bilingual
Anthology

Edited and
Translated by
Lawrence R. Smith

University of
California Press
Berkeley
Los Angeles
London

University of California Press
Berkeley and Los Angeles, California
University of California Press, Ltd.
London, England
© 1981 by
The Regents of the University of California
Printed in the United States of America

1   2   3   4   5   6   7   8   9

The New Italian poetry, 1945 to the present.

  Bibliography: p. 39
    1. Italian poetry—20th century.   2. Italian
poetry—Translations into English.   3. English
poetry—Translations from Italian.   I. Smith,
Lawrence R., 1945–
PQ4214.N4   851'.914'08   78-66014
ISBN 0-520-03859-2

To my wife, Vicki

Contents

The New Realism

Franco Fortini (b. 1917)

Pier Paolo Pasolini (1922–1975)

The New Hermeticism

The New Experimentalism

The New Avant-Garde

Antonio Porta (b. 1935)

Adriano Spatola (b. 1941)

Eugenio Montale's Nobel Prize for literature in 1975 stimulated new interest in modern Italian poetry throughout the world. Fortunately, English-speaking readers could find excellent translations of the works of Montale and his contemporaries, such as Umberto Saba, Salvatore Quasimodo, and Giuseppe Ungaretti. However, the poets of Montale's generation are not contemporary in the strict sense of the word. They rose to prominence in the twenties and thirties; many of them have died in recent years. Those English-speaking readers who have sought translations of the texts of the younger generation, poets who have made their reputations since 1945, have been largely disappointed. Aside from a scattered selection of translations in magazines and a brief representation in one or two anthologies devoted to the older poets, the works of these younger poets have been unavailable. This anthology attempts to fill that gap by assembling substantial samples of twenty-one of the most interesting and important contemporary Italian poets.

The history of Italian poetry since World War II has been characterized by divergent literary schools and their polemics. I have tried to represent all of these schools, from the neorealists to the neohermetics, from the new experimentalists to the new avant-garde. Nor have I ignored the outstanding independents: poets who have followed their own lights. I have also added poems written in dialect, by Pier Paolo Pasolini and Cesare Vivaldi, to represent that significant postwar literary phenomenon. For the aid of the reader, the author's translation into standard Italian has been printed beneath the dialect original. Above all, I have tried to select the best poems I could find, regardless of literary historical criteria.

Something should be said about the theory of translation which lies behind the poems in this anthology. My most important goal is that the end product be able to stand on its own as a good poem. An accurate transliteration is useless if the spirit of the original is lost. I have, however, worked for the highest degree of accuracy possible. Some modifications have been made where the conventions of colloquial American English differ substantially from the Italian, but those have been kept to a minimum. Aside from the normal difficulties of translation, many of these poems present unique problems. Syntax is particularly difficult in the work of many of the avant-garde poets, because they often intentionally distort conventional patterns of word order. In these cases I have tried to reproduce these ambiguities for the English-speaking reader. Finally, I have tried to approximate the original rhythm or cadence when possible, since many of these poets put strong emphasis on metrics.

I would like to acknowledge the kind assistance and encouragement of Professor Biancamaria Tedeschini Lalli, Professor Cristina Giorcelli, and Dottore Caterina Ricciardi, all of the University of Rome. The anonymous readers for the University of California Press also made a number of useful suggestions, for which I extend my thanks. Professor Glauco Cambon, a reader who allowed himself to be identified, made substantial and invaluable criticisms of the introduction. Its merits, whatever they may be, owe much to his help. Ms. Doris Kretschmer, editor at the University of California Press, has offered me vital guidance and encouragement. Without her generosity, this project would not have been possible. I would also like to thank the Commission for the International Exchange of Scholars for granting me the Fulbright-Hays Lectureship in American Literature for 1973–74 at the University of Rome. That year in Italy introduced me to the exciting Italian poetry of the postwar period.

Special thanks and deepest gratitude go to Emanuel Fenz, native of Florence and Professor of History at Eastern Michigan University, who has checked and rechecked this manuscript for accuracy. Professor Fenz has caught many errors, but I take full responsibility for any which may have slipped through. Most important, he has, as a critic and a friend, breathed life into this unwieldy mass and helped to make it a book.

L. R. S.
Ypsilanti, May 1979

Acknowledgments

For permission to reprint all works in this volume by each of the following poets, grateful acknowledgment is made to the holders of copyright, publishers, or representatives named below.

Giulio Einaudi Editore

Nanni Balestrini: "Senza lacrime per le rose," from *Poesie practiche, 1954–1969*. Franco Fortini: "Foglio di via," from *Foglio di via*. Alfredo Giuliani: "Resurrezione dopo la pioggia," "Il vecchio," "I giorni aggrappati alla città," "Predilezioni," "Azzuro pari venerdí," from *Povere Juliet e altre poesie*; "Chi l'avrebbe detto," from *Chi l'avrebbe detto*. Pier Paolo Pasolini: "Fevràr," "Il dí da la me muàrt," from *La nuova gioventù*; "Le ceneri di Gramsci," "Il pianto della scavatrice"—I, II, from *Le ceneri di Gramsci*.

Giangiacomo Feltrinelli Editore

Nanni Balestrini: "In questo modo," "L'istinto di conservazione," "Apologo dell'evaso," "Tape Mark," "De cultu virginis," from *Come si agisce*; "Ma noi facciamone un'altra," from *Ma noi facciamone un'altra*. Franco Fortini: "Camposanto degli inglesi," "Agro inverno," "Agli amici," "Lettera," "A Santa Croce," from *Poesia ed errore*. Alfredo Giuliani: "Lettera della terapia montana," "Il canto animale," from *Il tautofono*. Giancarlo Marmori: "Il tuo totem è la serpe opulenta," "Stava sempre medicando qualche sua umana ferita," "Ancora la tua traccia fine d'animale," "Nulla conosco del sonno che t'ammansisce," from *Poesie*. Elio Pagliarani: "Oggetti e argumenti per una disperazione," from *Lezioni di fisica e fecaloro*. Antonio Porta: "Europa cavalca un toro nero," "Dialogo con Herz," "Il vento soffia sul limite," "La pelliccia del castoro," *from* "Zero," "Aprire," *from* "Rapporti umani"—XII, XIII, XIV, XV, from *I rapporti*; "Utopia del nomade," from *Week-end*. Roberto Roversi: "Giorno di mercato," "La bomba di Hiroshima," "Le costumanze politiche," "Iconografia ufficiale," from *Dopo Campoformio*. Edoardo Sanguineti: "Laborintus"—1, 2, "Erotopaegnia"—3, 4, 5, 6, 7, "Purgatorio de l'inferno"—1, 2, 3, 14, 15, 16, 17, from *Catamerone*. Adriano Spatola: "Il boomerang," "Sterilità in metamorfosi," from *L'oblò*. Paolo Volponi: "La cometa," "Altra voce," "Stanze romane," from *L'antica moneta*; "La fine dell'estate," "Le mura di Urbino," "Domani è già marzo," from *Le porte dell'Appennino*.

Garzanti Editore

Pier Paolo Pasolini: "Il sole, il sole," "Un lungomare," from *Poesia in forma di rosa*; "L'anello," from *Trasumanar e organizzar*; Amelia Rosselli: from *Variazioni belliche*; "Neve," "Nessuno," "Dialogo con i morti," "Sciopero generale 1969," from *Documento (1966–1973)*.

Arnoldo Mondadori Editore

Bartolo Cattafi: "Antracite," from *Le mosche del meriggio*; "Qualcosa di preciso," "Apertura d'ali," from *Qualcosa di preciso*; "Al quinto piano," "Tabula rasa," from *L'osso, l'anima*; "Filo nero," "Il buio," "Vulnerabilità," from *La discesa al trono, 1972–1975*. Luciano Erba: "La Grande Jeanne," "Un equazione di primo grado," "Terra e mare," "Incompatibilità," "Lombardo-veneto," "Tabula rasa?," from *Il male minore*. Franco Fortini: "Il Comunismo," from *Una volta per sempre*; "Il presente," "Gli ospiti," from *Questo muro*. Giovanni Giudici: "Mi chiedi cosa vuol dire," "Se sia opportuno trasferirsi in campagna," "Epigramma romano," from *La vita in versi*. Giancarlo Majorino: "Strappo," "La miopia," "Anniversario," "Bisoccupato," "Paesaggio industriale," from *Lotte secondarie*. Elio Pagliarani: "Umilmente confesso che sono mortale," "Canto d'amore," "Narcissus pseudonarcissus," "Poème antipoème," from *La ragazza Carla e altre poesie*. Nelo Risi: "I meli i meli i meli," "L'altra faccia," from *Polso teso*; "Trinità dei Monti," from *Il contromemoriale*; "Tautologia," "Manovre," from *Pensieri elementari*; "Il teatro privato," from "Variazioni sul bianco," from *Amica mia nemica*. Rocco Scotellaro: "È un ritratto tutto piedi," "Alla figlia del trainante," "Camminano sulle zampe dei gatti," "Notte in campagna," "La luna piena," "Gli abigeatari," from *È fatto giorno*. Andrea Zanzotto, "Declivio su Lorna," from *Dietro il paesaggio*; "Da un'altezza nuova," from *Vocativo*; "Ecloga IV," "13 settembre 1959 (variante)," from *IX Ecloghe*; "La perfezione della neve," "Al mondo," from *La beltà*; "Subnarcosi," from *Pasque*.

Lamberto Pignotti

from "Vita zero"—3, 6, 8, 11, 15, 17, 22, *from* "Riduzioni"—IV, VII, VIII, IX, "Poesia e politica," from *Nozione di uomo*.

Cesare Vivaldi

"Viaggio," "Settembre," from *Il cuore di una volta*; "Madre non dimentico," "A Giovanni," from *Poesie liguri*; "Il muro," from *Dettagli*.

Some of these translations appeared for the first time in *Paris Review, Chicago Review, Small Moon, Laughing Bear, Poetry Now, Chariton Review,* and *Italian Poetry Today: Currents and Trends,* edited by Ruth Feldman and Brian Swann, and published by the New Rivers Press.

The literary landscape of twentieth-century Italy is filled with contrasts. Only a few need to be offered to illustrate the pattern. Because of its glorious heritage, Italy has long had an entrenched cultural traditionalism which, in its extreme manifestation, is simply a desire to live in the past. At the same time, another segment of the Italian literary and artistic community has been characterized by extreme radicalism. This group has produced innovations which have had international repercussions. Not only do the radicals not choose to live in the past, they often suggest destroying the past and its manifestations entirely. Part of Italy's literary community has carried on the tradition of internationalism, a continuous interaction—both give and take—with other European nations and the rest of the world. This is the spirit which made Italy the cradle of the Renaissance. On the other hand, there is also a tradition of fierce xenophobia, in which any sign of "non-Italic" influence is condemned as perverse and contaminating. This is the spirit of Benito Mussolini and the Fascists.[1] For many years the Italian universities have had an enormous influence on art and literature. Because of that elitist academic tradition, there is also a strong anti-academic tradition. The anti-academics have always struggled to counterbalance the power of the academy. Related to this contrast is another between linguistic traditions. The predominant Italian literary language over the centuries has been one of high diction enriched through the use of foreign and classical languages. The opposing tradition, which has become especially significant in the present century, has been characterized by a plain, colloquial

1. See Giorgio Luti, *La letteratura nel ventennio fascista* (Firenze: La Nuova Italia, 1972), esp. pp. 143–144.

literary language. In its extreme, the latter has become experimentation with street slang and dialect. Contrasting ideas of the purpose of literature exist as well. Some Italians have insisted on the autonomy of literature. For them poetry is a means of meditational self-exploration, a virtual retreat from the outside world. Others have seen poetry as a confrontation with the external world, an instrument of revolution which is only justified by its usefulness in bringing about a better society.

In political terms, the contrasts in Italy are as great as they are anywhere in the world. There is a powerful group of parties left of the Italian Communist Party including *Lotta Continua* and *Il Manifesto*. There is also a large and powerful neo-Fascist party, the *Movimento Sociale Italiano*. The conflicts between these extremists are not just abstract and philosophical; they are often carried to the streets with bloody results.[2]

Italy is a land of paradox as well as a land of violent extremes. Often the dialectic, which seems clearly defined in theory, becomes blurred and confused in actual practice. For instance, in Italy a large segment of the population considers the Communist Party too conservative. Another paradox within that framework: the Vatican-backed Christian Democrats, who have vowed never to compromise with the Italian Communist Party, have in fact been cooperating with them unofficially for years. There is also a large and influential group of Catholic Communists in Italy; their philosophy seems to be a contradiction in terms. Leaving the confusions of the political arena aside, we can see that literary battles have been just as paradoxical. One example from many possibilities will serve to illustrate. The new Italian avant-garde, which started out as a reaction to the hermetic school of poetry, has ended up writing poetry which is in many ways more difficult and obscure than that of the hermetics.

It is impossible to separate literature and politics in Italy because the penchant for factionalism governs both fields and inextricably mixes them. The intellectual impulse behind this political and literary factionalism in Italy is brilliantly summarized by Ninetta Jucker:

> What sort of people are the Italians? . . . it is sometimes hard to see the people for the parties. But that is how Italians see themselves. They hate empiricism. For them philosophy is the highest discipline and ideological theory and doctrine, however imperfectly assimilated, are matters of the first importance, determining not only how a man votes but how he lives and the people he consorts with. No one in Italy can fail to belong to one or other of the country's political traditions and if he did, the Italian passion for classification would soon find a place for him. A man may be a Catholic (integrationist or liberal) or an anti-clerical (liberal or radical) or a marxist (socialist or communist), or he may still be a fascist. Of course there are plenty of "qualunquists," that is people who sneer at democracy and claim to mind their own business without embracing any political creed, but they are usually bracketed as potential fascists and despised as

2. See Ninetta Jucker, *Italy* (New York: Walker, 1970). The last two chapters provide good historical background on these conflicts.

political outcasts. These divisions come naturally to Italians (the language itself can hardly refrain from adding an -ism to every concept) for they correspond to one of the very oldest Italian traditions, that of the factions whose partisan violence once destroyed the medieval communes and prepared the way for the tyranny of the *signorie*, just as today they are destroying Italy's post-war parliamentary democracy. To most Italians the party or the faction is a more vivid reality than the vaguer idea of nation. It even takes precedence of a man's sentimental attachment to his native region. Often it is stronger than class.[3]

Regardless of what stance a writer assumes, his choice of style always indicates a complex series of cultural and political choices. Even the writer who claims he is apolitical, as Jucker points out, is making a political statement. The literary traditionalist, for example, not only aligns himself with an elitist intellectual tradition, he also tends to support the political status quo: rule by the Christian Democrats. If he is a fanatical traditionalist, he might be a neo-Fascist.

The literary radical in Italy bases his approach to both literature and politics on the destruction of tradition. This destructive approach does not mean the Italian people are by nature intolerant, but is in some ways a practical and understandable reaction. Americans often express shock over the violence and stridency of Italian literary battles, but it is hard for an American to understand that history and tradition are by their very nature political in Italy. Tradition has often been the rationale for the repression of all expression not in line with official propaganda. Consider, for instance, the use to which Mussolini put Italian history. Even the monuments of ancient Rome became symbols for his regime. Perhaps the American preference for tolerance and peaceful coexistence in literary and cultural matters is the result of political stability and a general freedom from censorship. Italians have had neither. Even after the Fascist era, tradition and the past continued to symbolize oppression for many. There was then, and continues to be, a tacit assumption that to produce something new, you need to destroy something old. Considering the physical presence of so much Italian art and history, this has an undeniable logic. In order to build a subway in Rome or an office building in Florence, some masterpiece of a previous era must be sacrificed. The Italian artist does not compete with his predecessors simply for fame, but literally for space and survival in the scheme of things. When two Americans lamented the imminent collapse of the Coliseum because of vibrations from the heavy traffic around its base, a respected Italian scholar replied, "The sooner, the better." This reply was not entirely facetious. It has been said that the Italian intellectual's dream landscape is the American West, where everything must be created from absolute zero. One might add that the intellectual's nightmare landscape would be a Fellini-style scene of cluttered broken monuments, where the past reaches out to engulf you. Many modern Italians believe that the rubble must be cleared away in order to build a "new Italy."

3. Ibid., p. 167.

Even the word *politics* needs to be clarified in this discussion. It does not mean American-style, gentlemanly disagreements, such as those we continually witness between Democrats and Republicans. In twentieth-century Italy, politics has tended to be synonymous with violent confrontation. Even in the high schools of present-day Italy, there is a constant conflict between the students of extremist commitment, neo-Fascists on the one hand and the parties left of the Communists on the other. Not only do these students fight, they also kill each other—on a regular basis. The kidnapping and assassination of former premier Aldo Moro by the Brigata Rossa received extensive world publicity, but it was only one incident in a long list of violent acts perpetrated by extremists of the left and right.

Even though there are many differences between the American and Italian experiences in this century, there is one historical analogy which may help Americans understand what the Italians have gone through. The point from which all modern Italian history is measured is World War II: 1939 to 1945 and liberation. Although American soldiers fought and died in World War II, Americans did not experience the devastation of their homeland and the humiliation of their people, in Italy's case by both the Allies and the Germans. World War II for most Americans was just a four-year disruption of normalcy. Twenty years later, however, the United States underwent a period of internal upheaval. Just as all historical events of modern Italy are *prewar* and *postwar*, so we tend to use the terms *pre-sixties* and *post-sixties*. That is not to say that our national trauma was as severe as was Italy's during and after World War II. However, the violence of political disagreement, the cultural shock waves, the hopes for revolutionary change, and the eventual return to the status quo in our American experience reflect the pattern of the Italian experience. After the victory of the Christian Democrats in 1948, there was a virtual disenfranchisement of a large number of intellectuals and writers, perhaps even the majority. During the Vietnam War, American intellectuals felt a similar frustration and sense of impotency. It seemed impossible to affect the conduct of the nation's foreign policy. Neither national trauma has disappeared, because no aspect of life in either country has escaped the mark of its traumatic period.

In the area of literature, there is one significant common ground between American and Italian experience. Postwar poets from both countries have been obsessed with the question of language. American attitudes of the time were strongly influenced by William Carlos Williams, particularly by his long poem *Paterson* (1946–51), in which language is the main theme. Williams's ideas were developed and promulgated by Charles Olson in "Projective Verse," certainly the most influential American essay on poetics written after World War II.[4] The active Italian interest in language after World War II was nothing new; it was merely a continuation of the desire to purify language, which had its roots in the upheavals that occurred just after the turn of the century. Among the

4. See Karl Malkoff, *Escape from the Self* (New York: Columbia University Press, 1976), and Martin Duberman, *The Black Mountain School* (New York: Grove Press, 1975), for further discussion of Olson and his literary theory.

writers who had seriously pursued this objective were Sergio Corazzini, Filippo Tommaso Marinetti, Giuseppe Ungaretti, and Eugenio Montale. As much as these men disagreed on most matters, on one point they were unified: poetic language had to reflect more closely the contemporary reality they perceived. After 1945 both American and Italian writers reasserted their desire to find a "new language" which would break through sham and tradition, thereby unmasking and capturing truth. The postwar Italian realists looked to the works of Cesare Pavese and the philosopher Antonio Gramsci for guidance in this matter, just as the Americans looked to the works of Williams and Olson. Marxist ideology suggested to the Italians that getting closer to the language of the common man was the answer. Thus, Italian poets began to write more extensively in dialect. Later they even attempted to produce the language of the mass culture itself. American experiments, on the other hand, emphasized rhythm and delineation. That American writers stressed technical points while Italian writers concentrated on ideology is symbolic of the differences which distinguish them. However, the fact that they both had the same goal, the total reworking of poetic language, remains significant.

In both countries new theories of epistemology and linguistics were beginning to have their effects in literary circles after World War II. Neither these ideas nor the desire to rework poetic language were appearing for the first time; they were often echoes of modernist and surrealist experiments of the twenties and thirties. Phenomenology reasserted the relativity and autonomy of all linguistic constructs, as well as the limits of knowing and the impossibility of literary "content" as traditionally conceived.[5] Old linguistic theories which assumed a direct relationship between words as signs or pointers and outside reality were challenged. Languages were beginning to be seen as self-contained entities which created their own realities. Those realities did not necessarily refer to anything outside of themselves. A result of this new thinking in the United States was the idea of the poem as "process," as in Robert Creeley's work. Here there is no separable content, only an experience which is transmitted as the reader proceeds through the poem. Olson and his followers argued that this process reflects the way in which the mind works: we do not think in static abstracts. In Italy the new thinking on linguistics resulted in the avantgarde's experimentation with distorted or fragmented syntax, punctuation modification, and unconventional word meanings to create new language systems. Members of the avant-garde felt that these new systems would in turn change the reader's manner of perceiving things around him. The capitalist masters had manipulated traditional language in order to create a sense of "business as usual." New linguistic constructs would, the avant-garde believed, destroy that false surface and reveal the true crisis which lay beneath.[6]

---

5. See Luciano Anceschi, *Barocco e Novecento, con alcune prospettive fenomenologiche* (Milano: Rusconi e Paolazzi, 1960). Along with essays on Pascoli, D'Annunzio, and Ungaretti, Anceschi has an informative section entitled "Fenomenologia letteraria" in this text.

6. Alfredo Giuliani's introduction to *I novissimi: poesie per gli anni '60* (Torino: Einaudi, 1965) offers an excellent, thorough discussion of these ideas.

With all of these factors in mind, we can undertake a brief historical survey of the development of Italian poetry in the twentieth century, and see the poets included in this anthology within their proper historical context. The chronological survey naturally divides itself into three sections. First there will be a review of the main trends in Italian poetry from the turn of the century through World War II. Then the historical period covered by this anthology, 1945 until the present, will be divided into two sections: 1945 to 1956, and 1956 to the present. The first era was dominated by two groups: the neorealist poets, with their Marxist cultural experimentation, and the older hermetic poets, along with their younger followers. After the great crisis of European Marxism in 1956, sparked by the brutal Russian invasion of Hungary, there was a marked turn away from the neorealism of postwar Italy. The new Italian avant-garde, the final and most contemporary group covered in this anthology, then came into being.

ONE

Some years before Ezra Pound traveled to Europe and began his campaign to "modernize" poetry, Italian writers had begun to grapple with the same problem. For years they had lived in the shadow of three nineteenth-century literary giants: Giosuè Carducci, Giovanni Pascoli, and Gabriele D'Annunzio. As different as those three writers were, they were often considered together as the "triad." What the triad came to mean for many writers of that period was artificial language and diction, and the heavy use of rhetoric and classical literary convention. For those who disapproved of these tendencies, D'Annunzio, with his poetry of flamboyant rhetoric and grand gesture, became the *bête noire*. Other dissidents felt that the triad was keeping Italian poetry from developing along the lines of the new European movements. Carducci was the first Italian poet to be awarded the Nobel Prize, and D'Annunzio was an internationally known figure. However, as Walter Binni points out, the writers of the triad were not as much a part of European currents as it first might appear:

> Italian decadentism begins with Gabriele D'Annunzio and Giovanni Pascoli. But one must quickly add that, even with these two poets, Italian decadentism is still limited, confined in an atmosphere of provinciality which will in fact break up only in the twentieth century.[7]

This provinciality disturbed the literary dissidents as much as any aspect of the poetic triad. Although Italy had been politically unified, at least in theory, for thirty years at the turn of the century, it gave no signs of breaking through its literary and cultural isolation. Its literary tradition merely fed on itself; larger European trends were virtually unfelt at home.

It would be completely inaccurate, however, to suggest that the poetry of Pascoli and D'Annunzio ceased to be influential after the literary reaction set

7. Walter Binni, *La poetica del decadentismo* (Firenze: Sansoni, 1968). Another useful book on "decadentism" is Carlo Salinari, *Miti e coscienza del decadentismo italiano* (Milano: Feltrinelli, 1960).

in. On the contrary, the style and technique of Pascoli's *Myricae* (1891) and D'Annunzio's *Poema Paradisiaco* (1893) had significant effects on literary developments for many years. Pascoli's characteristic sentimentality and sense of the melodramatic are suppressed in *Myricae*. Here he depicts the rural countryside, with its peasants and farm animals, in great detail. The pathos of the poems comes from the atmosphere created by the images, rather than from a hyperbolic lament. *Myricae* exerted an important influence on the writing of Corazzini and his fellow *crepuscolari* or "twilight poets." Looking even farther ahead, these Pascoli poems seem to be heading in the direction of realism, the school which would become a powerful force after World War II. In the *Poema Paradisiaco*, D'Annunzio puts aside his nationalistic rant and his romantic excesses to write some moving poems. Rhetoric has not disappeared, but it is in control as he addresses these humanized poems to members of his family and others. This book by D'Annunzio served as a model for the penetrating self-exploration which became one of the main aspects of twentieth-century Italian poetry.

The apparent contradiction that new poets could rebel against the members of the triad and be influenced by them at the same time is one which we need to keep in mind. Literary developments and influences, reactions and cross-pollinations, of twentieth-century Italian poetry are much too complex to be forced into a neat critical pattern. Categorization and generalization are necessary evils in our attempt to evaluate the works of a period, especially in a brief survey of literary history such as this one. However, we must be wary of simplistic conclusions. Not only did writers have complex responses to their literary environments, but they often changed positions drastically over their careers. We see this pattern from the beginning of the century right through the latest literary turmoil and upheaval.

The first major reaction to the tradition represented by the triad came at the turn of the century from poets called *crepuscolari*. Sergio Corazzini and Guido Gozzano were the best known *crepuscolari*, but a number of other poets were identified with this group, some of whom were later involved with the futurists and *La Voce*. Among those poets were Corrado Govoni, Marino Moretti, Fausto Maria Martini, and Aldo Palazzeschi. It would be a mistake to call the twilight poets a school. There were no leaders among poets of this tendency; they did not operate collectively, issuing manifestoes like the futurists. Even the term *crepuscolari* was not their own invention; it was coined by an unsympathetic critic of the period. In spite of their general lack of organization, the twilight poets had one goal in common. They wanted to counteract what they considered to be the excessive romanticism and rhetoric of their predecessors, even though they were in some ways indebted to Pascoli and D'Annunzio. Alberto Frattini, in *Dai crepuscolari ai "novissimi,"* precisely defines the ideological nature of that reaction:

> The twilight poets represent, in lyric poetry, the first noteworthy current in
> our twentieth century. . . . One cannot speak of a "school" as much as of
> a sentimental convergence, an affinity of tastes, a new spiritual climate, a

reaction against the excesses of irrationalism, superhumanism, and the too facile and optimistic positivist and eudaemonistic *Weltanschauung* which characterized the period of transition between the two centuries.[8]

Aldo Vallone, in *I crepuscolari*, frames the contrast in a humorous perspective by comparing the twilight poets with each member of the triad:

> Next to the solemn austerity of Carduccianism, crepuscolarism would appear to be a degenerate and withered brat, a premature birth which repudiated the overflowing powers of the august forebear; in the presence of D'Annunzianism's magnificence it would appear to be a younger brother, dispirited by fortune and condition; next to Pascolism it would appear to be a poor relative, despoiled of every disguised richness and every learned simplicity.[9]

As Vallone implies, the poverty and humility of the twilight poets were their main strengths. They cultivated a quiet and understated style, one which intentionally focused on ordinary objects and emotions. Sergio Corazzini epitomizes this tendency in "Desolation of the Poor Sentimental Poet":

> My sorrows are poor common sorrows.
> My joys were simple,
> so simple that I should blush to confess them to you. . . .

Unlike the triad, the *crepuscolari* expressed neither optimism, nor wrath, nor moral indignation, nor passion of any sort. They created an atmosphere of "resignation, abandonment, that vague and consuming nostalgia, that almost morbid insistence on one's own misery. . . ."[10] The twilight poets wrote poems of overwhelming melancholy, but in their flashes of humorous self-deprecation and irony there are hints of the more active and forceful reactions to the tradition which were yet to come.

There were other poets who could not accept the solution of the *crepuscolari*, because they felt it never rose above its original status as a negative reaction to the triad and its followers. The twilight poets created a reverse image of their predecessors; they countered rhetoric with understatement, high emotion with noncommittal passivity, and commitment with irony. Many writers were looking for more active alternatives. In order to achieve that end, most chose to attack the provinciality of the Italian tradition. They wanted to rejoin the mainstream international movements of philosophy, literature, and the arts. The kind of internationalism they desired had not existed in Italy since the Renaissance, the last period when it had been the undisputed cultural center of Europe. Symbolic of that desire for a return to international cultural greatness, Giovanni Papini and Giuseppe Prezzolini founded a magazine called *Leonardo* in 1903. They wanted the spirit of the magazine to reflect the qualities of its namesake, a man who not only bridged national barriers but also bridged every

8. Alberto Frattini, *Dai crepuscolari ai "novissimi"* (Milano: Marzorati, 1969), p. 27.
9. Aldo Vallone, *I crepuscolari* (Palermo: Palumbo, 1965), pp. 5–6. Also see Panaro's *I crepuscolari* (Empoli: Edizioni del Calasanzio, 1962).
10. Frattini, p. 28.

barrier which divided the various disciplines of the arts and sciences. However, neither Papini, Prezzolini, nor their magazine could be called revolutionary. On the contrary, Giuliano Innamorati, in *Tra critici e riviste del Novecento*, calls *Leonardo* the symbol of the "nationalist anti-democratic intellectual" and the "bourgeois revival."[11]

Six years after the founding of *Leonardo*, the real cry of revolution was sent out. A young man named Filippo Tommaso Marinetti was traveling throughout Europe with a literary doctrine that was the most radical the world had ever seen. Most were astonished and amused by both theory and practice (Marinetti also delivered his poetry at multimedia events). Pound, however, and other literary notables were impressed and most certainly were influenced by the radical Italian movement.[12] Perhaps it would be more accurate to call it an international movement started by Italians, since Marinetti chose to publish the futurist manifesto in the February 22, 1909, edition of *Le Figaro*.[13] He suggested not only the end of Italian provincialism, but the total destruction of all literary tradition in order to make way for the future. In fact, Marinetti prescribed the destruction of all tradition, the entire past. It is too easy to smile condescendingly, from our contemporary viewpoint, at the uncompromising radicalism of the futurists, as well as at their passionate love for technology and their apocalyptic vision of a new order. We are more wary about putting our faith in technological progress; paeans to airplanes, cars, and gasoline seem absurd to us. However, the apocalypse the futurists predicted did, in many ways, come to pass. The two world wars, with all of their social, philosophical, and cultural ramifications, have changed us more than anyone could have imagined—anyone, that is, except Marinetti and the futurists. Nor has international literature been quite the same since the publication of the futurist manifesto. At a time when people were just beginning to debate the validity of *vers libre*, Marinetti pushed the debate to its logical extreme. His "free words," or *parole in libertà*, stripped of syntax and restored to a primitive and dynamic state of interaction, posed far-reaching questions about the nature of poetry itself. And as dissimilar as they may seem to be, it is unlikely that vorticism, surrealism, dadaism, or any other radical twentieth-century *ism* could have come into being if it had not been for the influence of these avant-garde Italians.[14]

The controversy set in motion by the futurists led to the birth of another poetic movement and another magazine. Giuseppe Prezzolini, who had been a co-founder of *Leonardo*, founded *La Voce* in 1909.[15] Whereas the futurist approach was based on military aggression and the complete destruction of the

11. Giuliano Innamorati, *Tra critici e riviste del Novecento* (Firenze: Vallechi, 1973), p. 135.
12. Louis Simpson, in *Three on the Tower* (New York: William Morrow, 1975), provides a thorough discussion of the influence of Marinetti and the futurists on Ezra Pound and the London literary world of the day (pp. 37–41). Pound took Marinetti to visit William Butler Yeats in 1913. Marinetti recited a poem in his usual manner, causing an uproar throughout the apartment building.
13. See R. W. Flint, ed., *Marinetti: Selected Writings* (New York: Farrar, Straus, and Giroux, 1972).
14. A good selection of futurist criticism is available in Mario Verdone, *Prosa e critica futurista* (Milano: Feltrinelli, 1973).
15. See Giuseppe Prezzolini, *Il tempo della "Voce"* (Milano: Longanesi, 1960).

social fabric (many futurists became conspicuous Fascists), the emphasis of the *La Voce* group, or *vociani*, was commitment to social reform. Some of the leading poets in the group were Camillo Sbarbaro, Clemente Rebora, Piero Jahier, Dino Campana, and Arturo Onofri. In direct opposition to the traditional view that poetry is a self-contained world, the *vociani* insisted that poetry interact with the real world around it. For *La Voce*, at least during the first years of its publication,[16] poetry by definition meant social commitment and moral responsibility. Rather than serve as a refuge for contemplation, they felt that poetry should lead to action outside the traditionally isolated world of intellectuals and literary men. Alberto Frattini summarizes the significance of the early years of *La Voce* as a dynamic force in twentieth-century Italian literary history:

> "La Voce" of Giuseppe Prezzolini (1908–1914) had a special position of importance, for the richness of cultural concerns which came together in it, for the assiduous and stimulating commitment to criticize, to erode, and to break down in its confrontations with stale and worn-out tradition, for its surprising ability to attract into its orbit the freshest and most fervent Italian intellectual energies of the time, beyond every ideological and political barrier. . . .[17]

Just as the futurists look forward to the Italian avant-garde of the sixties, the early *vociani* look forward to the strong social commitment of the postwar new-realists.

Radicalism, bursting out from time to time and in many different forms, is an integral part of twentieth-century Italian literary history. However, there is an opposing force of traditionalism or conservatism which also recurs with great regularity. One could argue that these two impulses create the dialectic which has characterized the Italian literary scene for the past seventy or eighty years. After the sweeping reconsiderations provoked by the futurists and the *vociani*, there was the predictable conservative reaction. In fact, there was a body of traditionalists who had never seen the need to challenge Carducci, Pascoli, and D'Annunzio at all. Others scorned even the tradition embodied by the triad; they looked even farther back to nineteenth-century poets like Giacomo Leopardi and Ugo Foscolo. One exponent of such a conservative reaction was Vincenzo Cardarelli. In the honored literary tradition for writers who want to sponsor new movements, and one which the Italians have always observed, he founded the magazine *La Ronda* in 1919.[18] It endorsed a return to classical formalism in style, language, and poetics. Giuliano Innamorati concedes that the editors of *La Ronda* (Cardarelli, Riccardo Bacchelli, Antonio Baldini, Bruno Barilli, Emilio Cecchi, and Lorenzo Montano) were and continued to be among the most talented and influential writers of the period. However, in their failure to take up the activist stance of the defunct *La Voce*, in their emphasis on classi-

---

16. Giuseppe Prezzolini edited *La Voce* from December 1908 until 1914. Under the editorship of Giuseppe De Robertis, from 1914 until 1916, the magazine had almost no concern with social issues.
17. Frattini, p. 16.
18. See Riccardo Scrivano, *Riviste, scrittori e critici del Novecento* (Firenze: Sansoni, 1965). Scrivano gives special attention to *La Ronda* in this text.

cal elegance and autonomous artistic principles, they epitomized the "unconscious collaboration" of the Italian middle class with the forces of Fascism.[19] The political and cultural ferment of that period simply could not be escaped. Cardarelli's classicist ideals, as reflected in La Ronda, were not destined to last. Nonetheless, a number of the writers who rose to prominence through La Ronda, particularly Cecchi and Bacchelli, retained a more lasting prominence. Even their ideals, or at least some of them, did not disappear entirely. The vision of art as an autonomous sphere became an important aspect of hermeticism, much to the chagrin of the Marxist-oriented realists.

Out of the confused and contradictory forces outlined above arose some truly extraordinary poets, whom Edoardo Sanguineti has termed the "new lyricists":[20] Umberto Saba, Giuseppe Ungaretti, and Eugenio Montale. Saba remained an isolated figure throughout his career. Like many of his contemporaries, Saba wanted to purify and renew poetic language. In one sense, he was even more conservative than the rondisti; his classical models went even farther back than Leopardi and Foscolo to Petrarch and Tasso. (His collected works are entitled Il Canzoniere.) But a comparison between Saba and the rondisti is misleading; he was never deeply involved in any group or movement. Although there are some similarities between Saba and the crepuscolari and Pascoli, especially the deep melancholy tone beneath his descriptions of everyday objects and people, there are also significant differences. There is an affirmation and celebration of life in the poetry of Saba that is not present in the earlier poets. In "To My Wife," where his wife Lina is compared to a number of ordinary animals which are "close to God," he expresses a profound and moving emotion through a deceptively simple poetic structure. Like St. Francis's "Cantico delle Creature," to which this poem has often been compared, Saba's work possesses a simplicity that is part of its powerful statement.

Neither Ungaretti nor Montale have the surface simplicity of Saba. Ungaretti studied in Paris and was a close friend of Guillaume Apollinaire. The French poets Rimbaud, Mallarmé, and Valéry also influenced his work significantly. In fact, it was the symbolic density and the linguistic difficulty of Ungaretti's work which led the critic Francesco Flora to coin the term hermetic to describe it. As that term became a cliché, finally a synonym for obscure, the original intent was forgotten. Silvio Ramat reminds us that it originally referred to Hermes Trismegistus and to the "remote but intuitively profound ascendance of his revelatory books."[21] It is true, however, that Ungaretti and many of the hermetic poets of a later generation turned deep within themselves for the subject matter of their poetry. This made their works hard to understand for much of the reading public. The hermetics reacted negatively to the kind of social involvement, from the futurists to the vociani, which had presented one of its uglier manifestations in the social programs of Mussolini and Fascism. Ungaretti and his followers saw the individual as the focus of literature; his struggles with

19. Innamorati, p. 168.
20. Edoardo Sanguineti, Poesia italiana del Novecento (Torino: Einaudi, 1969).
21. Silvio Ramat, L'ermetismo (Firenze: La Nuova Italia, 1969), p. 1.

and final alienation from a world without reason or morality were the true subjects of poetry.

Montale's approach to the struggle and anguish of the individual is even
more moral in its orientation than Ungaretti's. Furthermore, Montale's conclusions are more desperate and gloomy. His works reflect the same kind of
attitudes as those expressed by the early T. S. Eliot, a poet he admired. Like
Eliot, Montale, another hermetic, projected a vision of the modern world as a
desolate place, a sterile wasteland.

After the giant figures of Ungaretti and Montale, came a number of other
poets who were associated, at least for a time, with hermeticism. Among them
were Salvatore Quasimodo, Alfonso Gatto, Leonardo Sinisgalli, Sandro Penna,
Libero di Libero, Mario Luzi, and Vittorio Sereni. As different as these poets are
individually, they have in common the intensely subjective autobiographical
approach. Their worlds are illuminated by turning inward, rather than by con-
centrating on the social environment. It would be a mistake, however, to char-
acterize the hermetics as ivory tower escapists. Many of them made courageous
stands against Fascism in the thirties by publishing their works in the magazine
Solaria, which was considered dissident and anti-Fascist. Montale was severely
harassed because he would not join the Fascist party. Gatto became a well-
known partisan leader. Quasimodo, Luzi, and Sereni all modified their poetic
stances to incorporate a more rigorous sense of social commitment.

Nonetheless, after World War II, Marxist writers attacked the position of
the hermetics during the *ventennio*. Fabrizio Onofri articulates a widely felt
sense of bitterness and betrayal in his call for a complete rejection of the writers
of the Fascist era:

> Should one, therefore, completely condemn the Italian art, literature, and
> culture of the twenty years of Fascism? From the widest historical point of
> view, there can be no doubt about the answer. Italian art, literature, and
> culture did nothing to oppose Fascism.[22]

Writers like Cesare Pavese, who ended up in a prison camp, became heroes
after the war. Others who had suffered less, and who had perhaps done less,
were blamed. Salvatore Quasimodo, in the introduction to his anthology entitled *Poesia italiana del dopoguerra*, comments on the difficult lesson he, as a
hermetic poet, had learned from the war:

> We should say that the poet—man—now tries to place himself in the real
> world—not in an ideal one—so that he doesn't get hit over the head again
> while he watches the setting of the Pleiades.[23]

The bitterness which resulted from the Fascist period and World War II was not
soon to be forgotten. It became one of the most important factors in the development of Italian poetry during the postwar period.

22. Giuliano Manacorda, *Storia della letteratura italiana contemporanea, 1940–1965* (Roma:
Riuniti, 1967), p. 5.
23. Salvatore Quasimodo, *Poesia italiana del dopoguerra* (Milano: Schwarz, 1958), p. xxx. Also
see Salvatore Quasimodo, *Il poeta e il politico e altri saggi* (Milano: Schwarz, 1960).

TWO

It is easy to forget how different the American and Italian experiences of World War II were. The Americans traveled overseas to fight an essentially defensive war; they believed they were fighting to preserve the order in which they lived. They saw their four years of combat as a short interruption of the normal conduct of their lives, the Depression notwithstanding. In contrast to the American experience, the Italians were at the center of the storm: man, woman, and child. They all knew the horror of being physically trapped on some of the most bitterly contested ground in the war. The retreating Germans devastated the land and its people, and what the Germans didn't destroy, the Allied bombers did. For the Italians there was no return to normalcy; the old regime had collapsed, leaving the survivors to struggle for power among themselves. For many Italians, especially those who hated Fascism, the war was offensive rather than defensive. The Italian partisans were as active as any in Europe. Those men dreamed of a victory which would give their country a new start, a *vita nuova.*[24] For all of these reasons, the literature which comes out of the Italian experience is at the same time more optimistic about the future than American postwar literature and more shaken by the apocalypse which had been witnessed. Most important, their literature was—and continues to be—far more political in its orientation than American literature.

Immediately after the war, literary debate was set up along political lines. Among the anti-Fascists, there were two main groups: the Communists and the moderates. The dialectic which arose from this debate was similar to the one which went on between literary radicals and traditionalists earlier in the century. The moderates opted for the preservation of tradition and literary continuity, which in this case meant the hermetic school of poetry. The Communists, constituting a large number of the intellectuals and writers, attacked the moderates for their traditionalist stance. (There were, of course, real literary conservatives, who considered even the hermetics suspect.) They argued that it was precisely the kind of apolitical art which the hermetics produced which allowed the Fascists to take over and rule unimpeded. They even went a step further; they argued that the hermetics who had not protested openly against the regime had given it their tacit consent. The Communists were determined that such a betrayal would never happen again. These new radicals demanded a literature of social and moral responsibility; they wanted the artist to concern himself with more than his own internal vision.[25] It was this kind of thinking among the intellectuals of the political left which led to a new surge of realism in the late forties and early fifties.

The year of liberation marks a turning point in Italian history, a turning point by which all modern history is measured. The fact that all literary movements after World War II were dubbed with the prefix *neo (neoermetismo, neo-*

---

24. See Jucker, chapter 7.
25. Manacorda discusses this issue thoroughly in chapter 1.

realismo, neoavanguardia, neocrepuscolarismo, etc.) highlights not only the cyclical quality of Italian literary history, but the profound effect of the war. World War II's end also marked the emergence of a new kind of Italian writer. Previous to the war, Italian writers and artists were a privileged class. Protected and sheltered by universities and other institutions, they held remarkable social prestige. The tradition-oriented Italian culture has always accorded more honor to its intellectuals than its American counterpart. Even now, when most American writers make their livings teaching at universities, they do not—in general —hold the positions of social prestige held by Italian writers. The lofty status of the Italian intellectual encouraged him to ignore politics and to consider himself part of another world entirely. Most felt no need or desire to communicate with the people at large; in general they wrote, if not for themselves, at least for a very select group of educated people.

Regardless of their individual ideologies, World War II shattered the isolation of Italian writers and intellectuals. Even for those who were not politically inclined, there was no place to hide from the war and its consequences. For those who were political, or became politicized by what they saw, it became a question of trying to find a useful place in the cause of liberation. Most discovered that their intellectual tools would not serve them; knowledge of guns, explosives, and the terrain of the mountains was much more practical. The necessity of commanding men, or taking commands from men, from all walks of life was another shock. Never before had they found the need to communicate with people outside of their own elite groups. Those lessons, and the resulting sense of social duty, were not lost upon the Italian intellectuals who fought in the Resistance. They came away from their World War II experience convinced that a writer has a duty to his people, that he has no right to isolate himself from them. They also came to believe that politics and literature could not be separated without the disastrous effects they had witnessed. Finally, they realized the dangers a writer creates when he uses language or assumes intellectual stances which tend to separate him from his people. The experience of World War II and the Resistance had produced a generation of writers committed to social change.[26]

However, it would be misleading to claim that all Italian writers came to this conclusion. After the war, a raging battle of polemics went on for years between the new attitude and that of the traditionalists. Magazines representing the various viewpoints published attack and counterattack concerning the behavior of different groups of writers in the Fascist era. There was also lengthy discussion of the political-cultural consequences of that behavior. In 1944 *La Rinascita,* the official organ of the Italian Communist Party, published a statement on the necessary connection between politics and culture:

> We cannot raise artificial and hypocritical barriers between the various spheres of activity—economic, political, intellectual—of a nation. We do

26. See Paoluzi, *La letteratura della Resistenza* (Roma: 5 Lune, 1956), and Carlo Salinari, *Preludio e fine del realismo in Italia* (Napoli: Morano, 1967).

not separate and we cannot separate ideas from facts, intellectual history from the development of the relationships of real forces, politics from economics, culture from politics, individuals from society, art from real life. In this unitary and realistic conception of the entire world is our power, the power of the Marxist doctrine.[27]

On the basis of this kind of thinking, the leftist critics unleashed a merciless attack on the poets of the Fascist era, most of whom belonged to the hermetic school.[28] Their characteristic stance of personal isolation, existential anguish, and non-participation in the "real" or political world was now seen as their biggest liability. When some critics went to the extent of accusing the older writers of having actually collaborated with the Fascists, the hermetics reacted vigorously, in tones from hurt to outrage. Their reaction was not surprising; at a period in life when most poets are allowed to enjoy their reputations unharassed, these poets were fighting to keep their life work from total destruction. Some of the older poets claimed that the personal explorations they undertook were necessary and useful, for a man has to be understood as an individual before we can understand him as a social animal. They also pointed to their partial success in preserving some international currents in the midst of Mussolini's war on *esterofilia*, a part of his fanatical campaign for the development of a nationalistic culture. But the leftists were not satisfied. They replied that when the hermetics pretended they were above the turmoil, parading under the banner of Benedetto Croce's "autonomy of art," they were only trying to justify their betrayal of their fellow Italians. The leftists accused the hermetics of fighting on existential battlegrounds because they didn't have the courage to fight on real ones. Some of the older poets countered that a man would have been a fool if he had expressed his opposition to the regime openly. They admitted that the political conditions did indeed compromise the value of their work, but that there was nothing to be done about it. Of course, many writers, especially those in the camp of the realists, did express themselves more clearly than Mussolini liked. They found themselves in prisons and prison camps. Cesare Pavese himself, who was one of the victims of Fascist oppression, gave the more reticent hermetics at least partial justification. He claimed that the gloomy, neurotic quality of hermetic poetry was a result of its inability to speak directly. He added that even though that quality produced the poetic school's greatest moments, it was also a symbol of its greatest shame. Then the hermetics counterattacked by asserting that this postwar debate was just a renewal of the old conflict over style versus content, and had nothing to do with what anyone did before, during, or after the war. They also claimed that the leftists would pervert literature, in their destruction of its autonomy, in the same manner as Mussolini did. Therefore, they argued, literature had to remain above politics to retain its integrity. Alberto Moravia replied to that argument by pointing out that the debate was not between a depiction of real life and an interest in stylistic formalism; it was a

---

27. Cited in Manacorda, p. 5.
28. See Manacorda, chapter 1, for a more extensive treatment of this debate.

question of personal moral responsibility. Another writer added that if literature were really autonomous and separate from reality, then poetry would become calligraphy and mere wordplay. The hermetics countered that the new "popular literature" was just a philanthropic pose, and was in fact even farther from everyday reality than their own work had been.

Two magazines, Giovanni Battista Angioletti's *La Fiera Letteraria* (founded in 1925, publication was discontinued in 1936, and resumed in 1946) and Elio Vittorini's *Il Politecnico* (founded in 1945) became the main forum for this debate.[29] However, it was not long before it became evident to most that the debate had degenerated into mudslinging. Instead of concerning themselves with different kinds of literature and their relative merits, the combatants had stooped to *ad hominem* and *tu quoque* attacks. The entire debate could be reduced to a naive attempt to abolish tradition on the one hand and a rather naive attempt to deny history on the other. No critical terminology was being developed to deal with the problems which World War II had brought up. That problems had been raised was beyond denial. What was the theoretical relationship between literature and politics? What was culture? In order to have a rational debate, the opponents would have to agree upon the terminology. Most important of all, the debaters would have to stop avoiding the main point. The question was not whether or not tradition might be valuable, but where Italian literature was going in the future. That blindness to the most important issues seemed to be reflected ironically in the political events of the day. While the intellectuals, the existentialist hermetics on the one hand and the Marxist realists on the other, were fighting each other to carve up Italy's cultural future, the conservative Christian Democrats swept in and took control of the government in 1948. They have held it ever since that time. The conservative forces were destined to remain in control of Italy's culture; neither the cultural program of the moderates nor that of the leftists was destined to be put into action.

The debate, however, was not a complete loss. In his review of the period, Giuliano Manacorda emphasizes the gains derived from the extended dialogue: a stronger sense of social commitment and enthusiasm among the writers involved:

> In the passionate search for this conscience neither a certain ideological haziness nor a sometimes authentic confusion of terms and problems were lacking, but in compensation there was a fresh and often daring enthusiasm, and above all certain touchy issues which provoked harsh reactions and debates both quiet and violent were raised, which will undoubtedly enrich our cultural patrimony.[30]

Furthermore, both parties in the debate had been forced to refine their critical terms; both had become more sophisticated in their arguments. The hermetics had conceded the necessity of social responsibility. Salvatore Quasimodo, one

29. See Innamorati for a discussion of these two magazines.
30. Manacorda, p. 17.

of the most brilliant writers of the school during the thirties, made a public endorsement of the new poetics of social commitment. No one could go on writing as if Fascism and World War II had never occurred. The new realists also became more sophisticated, especially in their attitude toward the parties of the left. After the Italian Communist Party's *La Rinascita* criticized Vittorini for being an "ivory tower intellectual," and for failing to educate the masses, he countered with an angry reply.[31] He pointed out that *Il Politecnico* was a magazine run by Communists, not a Communist magazine. Vittorini stressed that culture must never become the propaganda instrument of any party, and that a cultural revolution is different from a political one. Ironically, political pressure from the Italian Communist Party had caused him to react as the hermetics had previously, proclaiming the autonomy of art.

One of the reasons why the debate had become clearer, and terms better defined, was that the works of Antonio Gramsci were agreed upon as the theoretical common denominator of the socially committed writers. In the introduction to the English translation of his *Letters from Prison*, Lynne Lawner summarizes the galvanizing effect Gramsci's works had on postwar Italian literature: "his *Letters* and what followed them had the effect of an electric shock, waking Italy out of the trauma of war and setting its brain in motion."[32] Gramsci's works on literary-political-cultural theory were written while he was imprisoned during the Fascist era. However, he anticipated the debate which would take place after the war and he spoke to the issues which would be raised. Gramsci proposed a "democratic philosophy," one which did not represent only a small group of intellectuals, but the entire society. He condemned the philosophies of the Catholics and Benedetto Croce as being elitist and reactionary. Gramsci claimed that Croce's universals were simply the ideals of a small elitist class projected on the whole society. Croce manifested absolutely no consciousness of Italian society at large. In reaction, Gramsci stressed that intellectuals should not be the servants of the ruling class, but should establish contact and rapport with the people. As some critics were later to point out, there are startling similarities between Gramsci's principles and those used by Mussolini in his attempt to construct a nationalistic culture.

Gramsci was, nonetheless, correct in his assessment of traditional Italian intellectuals. They were, in his terms, abstract, bookish, and aloof, more interested in style and eloquence than people. What was traditionally called Italian culture was determined by a very small group of men. Gramsci was out to change that culture, to make it more a reflection of the masses. His instructions to the writer were clear and explicit:

> The premise of the new literature must be historical, political, popular, it must tend to elaborate that which already exists, it doesn't matter whether

---

31. Ibid., p. 22.
32. Lynne Lawner, ed., Antonio Gramsci, *Letters from Prison* (New York: Harper and Row, 1973), p. 3.

it is done by polemic or by some other method; what matters is that it place its roots in the *humus* of popular culture as it is, with its tastes, its tendencies, etc., with its moral and intellectual world, even if they are backward and conventional.[33]

This pronouncement became the bible of the new-realist writers.

As we consider the Italian school of postwar neorealism, it is necessary to widen the focus of this discussion. Some critics have argued that there is no Italian school of poetic new-realism. They have claimed that only in fiction and in cinema were there legitimate movements. Even though most of the public's attention was focused on the novels and movies of the period, and the fiction writers and movie directors were more vocal on theoretical issues, that a poetic new realism existed cannot be denied. However, a brief look at the other two genres helps clarify some of the general tendencies this poetry shared with the fiction and cinema of the time.

Gramsci was not the only voice for social commitment in the thirties. The beginnings of Italian realist fiction also go back to the Fascist period. Works like *Gli indifferenti* by Alberto Moravia, *Tre operai* by Carlo Benari, *Un uomo provvisorio* by Francesco Jovine, and *Paesi tuoi* by Cesare Pavese depicted the Italian world as these writers saw it, not as the Fascists demanded that it be perceived. Such critical realism was not often as direct during the thirties as it was after World War II, but it was clear enough in its statement to draw vehement attacks from the Fascist literary establishment. In some cases the results were even more severe, as in the imprisonment of Pavese.

The Italian neorealist movie makers appeared immediately after the war.[34] In fact, Roberto Rossellini started filming *Città aperta* even before the Nazis had completed their retreat from the city of Rome. Along with Rossellini, other great neorealist directors of the postwar period were Vittorio De Sica, Alessandro Blasetti, Alberto Lattuada, and Giuseppe de Sanctis. These directors depicted Italian society, especially the lower echelons, in all of its squalor. They did not make the poor picturesque, as most Hollywood movies of the period did. The Italian directors were obsessed with the idea of presenting life exactly as it was. They usually cast non-actors in leading roles, employed many improvised scenes, and shot the film on location instead of using sets. That is not to say that the movies were objective; their social criticism and advocacy of reform were always clear. These directors wanted their audience to see that human misery was caused by an unjust social hierarchy. The poor were bestialized by the rich and the economic system they had created. Their final message was equally clear; conditions would not improve in Italy until the system was changed.

Carlo Salinari, in *Preludio e fine del realismo in Italia*, defines the neo-realistic literary movement from the point of view of a socially committed critic:

33. Antonio Gramsci, *Letteratura e vita nazionale* (Torino: Einaudi, 1950).
34. A good brief discussion of Italian cinematic realism, in its international context, appears in Gerald Mast, *A Short History of the Movies* (Indianapolis: Bobbs-Merrill, 1976). More thorough treatments of the subject can be found in Vernon Jarratt, *The Italian Cinema* (New York: Macmillan, 1951), and Gian Rondi, *Italian Cinema Today* (New York: Hill and Wang, 1965).

Neorealism in Italy arose—and everyone seems to agree about this now— as an expression of a profound historical break, that crisis of the war and the anti-Fascist struggle from 1940 to 1945, which exploded and shook everything down to its very roots, and changed the face of the entire Italian society. Neorealism nourished itself, above all, on a new way of looking at the world, a new morality and ideology which were actually based on the anti-Fascist revolution. There was an awareness of the failure of the old ruling class and of the position which, for the first time in our history, the popular masses had won on the social stage. There was a need for the *discovery* of the real Italy, with all its backwardness, its misery, its absurd contradictions, and a pure and at the same time revolutionary faith in our possibility of rebuilding ourselves and helping the progress of all mankind. The tone varied from the epic to the narrative to the lyric, but the ideologi- cal position remained the same. It's clear that a movement of this type presented itself as an authentic avant-garde movement, as opposed to other so-called *avant-gardes* which proposed only formalistic reforms, which didn't break the circle of the ruling class culture, and which, sometimes, created revolutions canonized by the Italian Academy. Authentic avant- garde, because it tended to reflect the points of view, the needs, the de- nunciations, the morality of a *real* revolutionary movement and not just a cultural one.[35]

What all of this ultimately meant was that the neorealists based their approach on Marxist dialectical materialism. They tried to reflect the reality of the world around them, both in its concrete particulars and in its ideological universals. There was to be no artistic intuition, fantasy, or elevation of the writer's subjec- tivity, but a mirroring of life as it actually was. The difficulty came when various writers tried to put these generalizations into practice. After all, what held the new realists together was more an amorphous humane impulse than a set of common principles, good intentions rather than a precise system of aesthetics. They agreed that fantasy and intellectualism had no place in literature. They also agreed that their writing should be politically practical and useful to the reader. However, there was a wide range of difference in the literature pro- duced by the new realists. It ranged from the pessimistic, anti-lyrical depiction of human misery to the lyrical and optimistic vision of a society changing for the better. Style, as well as tone, differed greatly from one writer to another. Some used slick, superficial techniques to produce "slice of life" works which would have wide popular appeal. Many of those works were little better than soap operas. Other new realists were so obsessed with producing a Marxist criticism of their society that literary concerns were virtually ignored. Finally, these writers were caught in what seemed to be a vicious circle. They were committed to depicting society as it was, in order to help it improve. However, Italian society was already changing rapidly, and in directions about which no one was sure. How could you accurately depict a society you couldn't under- stand? And if you couldn't understand it, how could you guide its change? In

35. Salinari, pp. 39–40.

spite of this theoretical problem, it must be conceded that the new realistic literature, as part of Italy's changing cultural face, was also a factor in forming its new reality.

As the fifties continued, the problems associated with the new-realist approach reached a crisis level. The new-realists' obsessive use of World War II almost exclusively as subject matter became inadequate to depict or explain the Italy of the postwar period. The extraordinary tensions and passions of war, which offer a convenient focus of interest, can become a literary crutch. The question was how to switch from war to peace, from abnormal to normal, and still maintain reader interest. Another problem was concerned with language. The realists all spoke of using a language which would be closer to the people. This desire on their part resulted in attempts to approximate the colloquial language of the streets, and it also led to the extensive use of dialect. Unfortunately, instead of having the desired effect, bringing the writer and reader closer together, these experiments often created artificial barriers. The theoretical purpose was at odds with the actual effect.

The new-realist poets had even more difficulty than the fiction writers of the school. First of all, they had a crisis of identity. The fiction writers had a tradition with recognized masters going at least as far back as the thirties. However, the masters of poetic realism, such as Cesare Pavese and the older Piero Jahier, did not receive as much attention and praise as the older hermetics, especially Ungaretti and Montale. With the exception of Pier Paolo Pasolini, none of the young neorealists had broken into the ranks of the major poets, as recognized by the Italian literary establishment. (Since that time, of course, other realists have risen to that high level of public acclaim.) However, the most basic and difficult problem of the neorealist poetic school lay in the very nature of poetry itself. Social concern and political polemic were much easier to carry off in prose than they were in verse. Instead of trying to develop new techniques and structures to accommodate this problem, they continued to spend too much time writing essays on the necessity of realism and the errors of the hermetic school. Unfortunately, their constant reversion to prose nearly constituted an admission of defeat; traditional poetic forms did not seem able to carry the political burden. When some of the neorealist poets began to employ the subjective and irrational, and to speak of alienation and isolation as aspects of modern life (without pointing out political solutions), the even more insidious problem of internal conflict arose. Hard-line Marxists began to accuse writers pursuing such explorations of "mystifying" reality. Figures as diverse as Pavese, Vittorini, Pasolini, and the movie director Federico Fellini became suspect. When a movement's greatest exponents are heretics, the movement cannot last.

The new-realist poets represented in this volume are seven of the most important figures in that movement: Pier Paolo Pasolini, Rocco Scotellaro, Cesare Vivaldi, Franco Fortini, Giovanni Giudici, Elio Pagliarani, and Paolo Volponi. Each one of these poets embodies the best principles of the larger movement, but at the same time distinguishes himself from it, through a unique ability or characteristic. In other words, each is a member of the general movement but, like all true artists, is an individual as well.

Pier Paolo Pasolini (1922–1975) was, without doubt, the most accomplished poet produced by the new-realist movement. He was also one of the most complex and enigmatic figures of twentieth-century Italian literature. Pasolini's poetry is full of paradoxes. The ideological content of his works is radical, but the forms he chose to write in were often classical, even archaic. For instance, "The Ditchdigger's Tears" and "Gramsci's Ashes" are written in a three line stanza which is a modification of *terza rima*. By employing this form, Pasolini defied the modernizing momentum of Italian poetry. Even more, he proclaimed the possibility of grand achievements in the old style, even in the manner of the master himself. Like Dante's *Divina Commedia*, "The Ditchdigger's Tears" recounts a spiritual journey. Unlike Dante, the spiritual journey leads to a communion with mankind through Marxist ideology. This leads us to another paradox in Pasolini's work. He was a Catholic Communist. The dichotomy implicit in that stance is always evident in his work; it is best articulated in the title of his long critical work on modern Italian poetry, *Passione e ideologia*. Giorgio Bàrberi-Squarotti, in *Poesia e narrativa del secondo Novecento*, describes the interplay of those two forces:

> But this stylistic contrast is not purely rhetorical; it constitutes the key to the . . . internal laceration from which Pasolini's poetry originates: if Pasolini has a rational (critical) faith in [Marxism], it contrasts with a much more pressing internal situation of the free play of the irrational, of excitation stirred up by the senses. . . .[36]

Like other new-realists, Pasolini experimented extensively with dialect. Most notable were his poems in the Friulano dialect, which were collected in a posthumous volume entitled *La nuova gioventù*. Rational and irrational at the same time, volatile and exuberant in all of his artistic work, Pasolini stirred many and various passions among his readers. Admirers and detractors alike felt that his death in 1975 was a major blow to Italian letters.

Rocco Scotellaro (1923–1953) was one of the most promising writers of the new realism, but he died at thirty, barely having begun his career. What he left behind, in the posthumous volume entitled *È fatto giorno*, are fascinating portraits of peasant life. There is no doubt about the social commitment of Scotellaro; he was a union organizer, a political activist, a Socialist mayor, and was ultimately harassed and imprisoned for his activities. But his commitment comes to the reader through the characters and scenes he creates, not through a polemical overlay. Scotellaro's poems always have a note of authenticity, because they are based upon his own experience. His eye for detail, the clumsiness of the shoes on a peasant laid out for burial or the sounds of the donkeys

---

36. Giorgio Bàrberi-Squarotti, *Poesia e narrativa del secondo Novecento* (Milano: Mursia, 1967), p. 102.

tied under the outside stairwells, prevents him from falling into the vague ideological platitudes which entrapped many other new-realists. Giuliano Manacorda summarizes the strength of Scotellaro and his powerful works:

> For Scotellaro the world of the peasants is neither a literary idea nor the object of indirect knowledge, of a merely ideological passion; it is the world in which he was born, which he studied and of which he gave us the unforgettable pictures. . . .[37]

Had Scotellaro lived, the course of the new-realist experience might have been significantly different.

Scotellaro's deep interest in the common people of his own region, and Pasolini's early and serious commitment to poetry written in dialect, are two manifestations of the new-realist insistence that poetry focus on real, specific people. Cesare Vivaldi (b. 1925) also wrote dialectal poems, in his native Ligurian. More than linguistic exercises, they have the power to move the reader's emotions. Vivaldi's poetry is always highly emotional, whether dealing with lovers, his mother, his fellow men, or his political ideology. Unlike Scotellaro, Vivaldi deals directly with the emotion, even as it is being fleshed out with imagery. It is as if the reader is joining the narrator in his personal and deeply private meditations. Like the other new realists, social commitment lies at the roots of Vivaldi's poetry. He himself describes the course of development which led him to that stance:

> . . . when very young I was "hermetic," afterwards a "realist" after the American and Pavesian models, then a "socialist realist," thus finding my way to safety in dialectal poetry, in a concrete adherence to the simplest things, the most elementary emotions. . . .[38]

The progress of Vivaldi's career reflects the thrust of the entire new realist movement: a rejection of the isolation of the hermetics and an affirmation of the communion of common men.

Franco Fortini (born Franco Lattes in 1917)—the literary senior statesman of socially committed poets—was also an apprentice to hermetic poets during his early career in Florence. However, he found the hermetic mode unsatisfying, and he continuously sought greater authenticity than he saw in that style of poetry. The result is a controversial poetic career based on a central paradox. Fortini was a committed Marxist, yet leftist critics found him to be disturbingly inconsistent. He could shift from optimism to desperate and inconsolable pessimism, from the choral voice of socialism to the intimate voice of the hermetics. His sense of literary history has also caused his critics problems. In spite of the modernity of his subject matter, the strong influence of Italian classicism is apparent in his verse. Silvio Ramat claims that Fortini uses "the rich and ambiguous vocabulary which the twentieth-century poet borrows from the Pe-

37. Manacorda, p. 61.
38. Giacinto Spagnoletti, ed., *Poesia italiana contemporanea* (Bologna: Guanda, 1959), p. 935.

trarchan-Leopardian tradition. . . ."[39] Pasolini, in *Passione e ideologia*, defines the paradox in Fortini's poetry as passion and ideology pulling in opposite directions. He schematizes this internal struggle by describing two mutually exclusive lines of development in Fortini's work:

1. The line of resistance against *"poeticità,"* product of literary apolitical attitudes and of the pseudoreligious and charismatic consciousness of twentieth-century Italian culture.
2. The line of temptation by *"poeticità,"* a marked residue of the middle class privilege of exquisite expressiveness, voluntarily rejected.[40]

Fortini's complex and paradoxical style has marked him as a maverick, and it has made all political and literary factions wary of him. This individualism, along with his spirit of humanity and commitment to poetic truth, is his greatest asset.

Giovanni Giudici (b. 1924) does, in much of his work, exactly what the theoreticians thought the new realist poetry should do. He describes, dissects, and criticizes the entire fabric of postwar Italian society, reproducing for the reader the prevalent feelings of frustration, alienation, and despair. A good example of this technique can be seen in "You Ask Me What It Means," where Giudici brings the lofty philosophical concept of alienation down to the objects and sensations that every human being experiences. Giudici makes quality of life the primary subject of his poetry. It is not that his poetry is abstract, since the quality of life is revealed through a series of mundane objects and events. In fact, even those things which are normally considered to be abstract, such as ideology and psychology, are treated as if they were concrete objects in Giudici's poetry. They become, therefore, the proper focus for his poetic realism.

Elio Pagliarani (b. 1927), like Franco Fortini, troubled his contemporaries. A nonconformist, his poetry never quite fits the guidelines of any school. Pagliarani's realism is not orthodox. It often verges on the surreal in his descriptions of contemporary Milanese life or in his wide-ranging meditations, as is the case in parts of "Subjects and Arguments for an Act of Desperation." Another quality of Pagliarani's poetry which differentiates him from most new realists is his critical distance. This quality places him at the polar extreme of Pasolini and his followers. Pagliarani's critical detachment also disturbed the committed ideologues, for there was nothing which escaped scrutiny in his poetry, even the leftist faith in the future of the revolution. Bortolo Pento defines this quality of Pagliarani:

> Between the writer and the elements of his construction there is disenchantment: a lucid condition of judgment bitingly put into play against himself and others. There is, insinuating itself with absolute naturalness into the fabric of the versification, irony and self-irony. There is a humor of an entirely different kind, in other words modern, generated by the crisis condition of the historical epoch, a twentieth century *mal du siècle.* . . .[41]

39. Silvio Ramat, *Storia della poesia italiana del Novecento* (Milano: Mursia, 1976), p. 573.
40. Pier Paolo Pasolini, *Passione e ideologia* (Milano: Garzanti, 1973), p. 469.
41. Bortolo Pento, *Letture di poesia contemporanea* (Milano: Marzorati, 1965), p. 92.

Pagliarani experimented with typography, delineation, and metrics throughout the fifties. Although he was a member of the older generation, he readily aligned himself with the sixties avant-garde, becoming one of the *novissimi* in Alfredo Giuliani's anthology of the same name.

The realism of Paolo Volponi (b. 1924) differs significantly from that of the poets discussed above. His poems deal almost entirely with the Apennine landscape, rather than the crowded industrialized cities of postwar Italy. But Volponi's mountain landscape is not a personal retreat from the crises of modern life. In this setting he creates a microcosm in which he can speak more clearly about the objects which interest the new realists: the war, social struggle, and the plight of the poor. For instance, in the beautiful and seemingly simple "Another Voice," Volponi implies that the war and the subsequent struggle for social justice color all human experience. Fortini, in *Il Menabò*, puts Volponi's apparent primitivism in its proper perspective:

> Volponi has a sense for the "representation" of objects, he lacks the dimension of time; it's all given; he puts only air between things and himself. As in the old landscapes of central Italian painting, a tree with its shadow, a flock and a shepherd.[42]

Although he has created a technique which differs entirely from that of his new-realist contemporaries, the poetry of Paolo Volponi manifests the same spirit.

The defection of Salvatore Quasimodo (1901–1968) to the ranks of the new realists provides an ironic footnote to our discussion of this poetic movement. After having established his reputation as a great hermetic poet, he shocked his old compatriots by coming out decisively for the poetry of social commitment. What was most surprising was the fact that he made the switch after the influence of the new realism was clearly on the wane. In fact, a new formalism or revival of the hermetic influence had already been set in motion. Not only did Quasimodo modify his writing style, he wrote polemical essays on the necessity of social responsibility as well. He claimed that it was the poet's duty to reconstruct the men who had been broken and fragmented by the experience of the war. He stressed the importance of content, ethical and political content, in poetry. Quasimodo also spoke of a new concrete literary language which would directly reflect the world of objects and objective reality. He even claimed that World War II was, at least in one sense, providential; it had forever broken down the provincialism and Arcadianism of the Italian poetic tradition. However, receiving a powerful ally like Quasimodo, just in time for the demise of the neorealist movement, takes its place as another one of the many ironies of twentieth-century Italian literary history.

THREE

The year 1956 marked the end of one era and the beginning of a new one in the history of modern Italian poetry. The new realism was on the wane as the

42. *Il Menabò* 2, 1960, cited by Manacorda, p. 364.

leading movement for writers committed to social and cultural change. There were also political rumblings among leftist intellectuals who were irritated by the constant pressure exerted on them to follow the doctrines of the Italian Communist Party to the letter. The freedom to experiment and to find individual solutions simply was not available within the ranks of the party. In the midst of this general discontent came the blow which forever changed the Italian intellectual and literary community: the Russian invasion of Hungary in 1956. That event produced a great awakening and a great sense of disillusionment. If Marxist optimism for a "new Italy" had sounded hollow before, it now sounded even more so. The theoretical basis for the new realist literature was discredited. Simultaneously, during this traumatic loss of ideals, the new middle class, under the leadership of the Christian Democrats, was creating another kind of "new Italy." It was the Italy of the "economic miracle,"[43] one which promised a greater distribution of material wealth for all those who were willing to join. Its rewards were cars and television sets, but its results were a conformity and homogenization of the society never before experienced. Other negative aspects of the new Italian society became evident. The ruling party was censorious and intolerant of innovation; it promoted uniformly bad taste on national television and radio. While insisting on a high level of public morality, the government itself was riddled with corruption. In spite of all the publicized progress, there were still huge numbers of very poor, unemployed Italians, especially in the South. In other words, the "new Italy" was disturbingly similar to the old Italy. The politicians seemed closer to the bureaucrats of Mussolini's regime than anyone would wish. Therefore, the writers, artists, and intellectuals of Italy were suddenly adrift. They certainly could not put their faith in what was rising around them, but then they also had lost faith in the force which had previously sustained them: Marxist idealism.

Pier Paolo Pasolini tried to salvage some of the good aspects of postwar concern by creating and naming a new movement: the "new experimentalism."[44] Since it was clear that the new realism's attempt to achieve its main goal, the political and cultural renovation of Italy, was a miserable failure, then its strident polemics could be safely ignored. Literature had to justify itself as literature now, not as a program of social reform. Pasolini realized that the imagination, as well as abstract critical theory, was necessary for a legitimate literary movement. In fact, he was trying to accommodate the recent reemergence of the hermetic school, or *neoermetismo*, which centered around the figure of Mario Luzi. By adding the imaginative and purely stylistic aspects of the hermetic school to the social commitment of the dying new realism, Pasolini hoped to save the best attributes of the latter. In his description of the "new experimentalism," Pasolini implied that the writer was free to do anything he wanted to do, without worrying about being an elitist, or not reaching the masses, or any other essentially non-literary concern. Not only was there now

43. See Jucker, chapter 11.
44. See Pasolini, pp. 470–492.

"official permission" to do the things the hermetics had been condemned for doing, there was also a new vision of the relationship between poetry and culture. The new realists had spoken of renovating Italian culture, but now it was obvious that Italian culture had gone its own way. It was now a question of trying to make literature responsive to the new culture and the new language it had produced. Culture was changing poetry, not poetry changing culture. This was the thrust that brought about the birth of the new avant-garde in the late fifties. Even before the emergence of this movement, some writers had already decided to use the language of the new capitalism and the new technology as an instrument to provide a more accurate reflection of the world as it existed. Lamberto Pignotti (b. 1926) argued for this change in the terminology of the market place.[45] He claimed that a reader wouldn't be interested in poetry that didn't communicate directly to him, relating specifically to the world he saw around him. If communication were the goal, then mass appeal was necessary. Therefore, the writer had to think of his work as a "product" on the market place. It is only a short step from this theory to the theories of the sixties avant-garde. They would suggest that poetry be constructed out of the "authentic fragments of the time." However, they insisted that those fragments remain fragments; no unitary political pattern was to be superimposed, as the new realists had done.

Reactions to the new realists in the fifties went in several different directions. The variety of those reactions is illustrated by six of the poets included in this anthology: Andrea Zanzotto, Luciano Erba, Nelo Risi, Bartolo Cattafi, Giancarlo Majorino, and Roberto Roversi. Zanzotto and Erba represent *neoermetismo*, or the hermetic revival; their works are clearly counterposed against the works of the new realists. But other reactions took other directions. Nelo Risi, Bartolo Cattafi, Giancarlo Majorino, and Roberto Roversi all fall into the category of the "new experimentalism," as Pasolini called it. They might also be called "post-realists," since the emphasis in their poetry is on disillusionment and alienation, rather than on social commitment. Although the stylistic techniques of these poets owe much to the older school, the spirit of their works is emphatically different.

Andrea Zanzotto (b. 1921), early in his career, was one of the most successful poets in the hermetic revival. His poetry, set in the countryside around Venice, creates one beautiful vision after another. But the title of his first book points to the metaphysical quality of what seem at first to be simple nature poems. *Dietro il paesaggio*, or *Behind the Landscape*, implies that external reality is a façade which must be penetrated. Thus, the world of these poems is inward rather than outward. As Fortini observed, Zanzotto uses the "modes of hermeticism . . . grafted on a theme of existential and cosmic titanism. . . ."[46] The search for that metaphysical realm goes on throughout Zanzotto's career, and his most important tool in that search is experimentation with language.

45. Manacorda, p. 232.
46. *Il Menabò 2*, 1960, cited by Manacorda, p. 342.

Ultimately language, or the search for the proper language, is the subject of these poems. Zanzotto wants to get back to a proto-language which is at the basis of human psychological experience: a *madre lingua*, as he calls it.[47] This belief that there is such a language, and that it has the power to destroy the false signs of external reality and penetrate to the truth within, anticipates the *novissimi* and the rest of the sixties avant-garde. Later in his career Zanzotto did, in fact, leave his hermetic roots and join with these literary radicals. His poems of that pivotal period, such as "September 13, 1959," use the same avant-garde techniques of language mixing (mainly Italian and Latin), fragmentary imagery, and broken syntax in order to explore the irrational "other reality."

Luciano Erba (b. 1922) started out his career as a socially committed poet, but he moved more and more in the direction of hermeticism as his career proceeded. He is a part of a group of Northern Italian poets dubbed the "*linea lombarda*."[48] They do not comprise a school; each member of this group has his own style and peculiarities. However, all of these poets share a common spirit, along with their sense of regionality. Like the *crepuscolari* of the first part of the century, the *linea lombarda* poets react against both the heroic anger and heroic optimism of the realists, replacing those passions with their more modest voices of disillusionment. High emotion was the mode of the new realists; the mode of the *linea lombarda* was irony. After the collapse of the reformist visions of new realism, these younger poets were unwilling to depict grand struggles, ideological or otherwise, and play the role of prophet. They felt that these things were poses, and that they contradicted the image of the society they saw around them. The collected works of Luciano Erba are entitled *Il male minore*, with the emphasis on *minore*. There is nothing titanic about Erba's poetry; it is focused on small things and small emotions. The prostitute of "La Grande Jeanne" and the kept woman of "A First-Rate Equation" are typical of the "heroes" of Erba's poems. Their small disappointments symbolize those of an entire society reduced to pointless and trivial lives. If there is any overall message to be carried away from Erba's poems, It Is that the contemporary world is confusing and exasperating, and that there seems to be little we can do to remedy the situation.

Nelo Risi (b. 1920) is another poet of the *linea lombarda*. His poetry is as full of irony as Erba's, but that is where the similarity ends. Risi's poetry is more in the mold of Giovanni Giudici; it is a poetry of protest based on a vision of moral judgment, even though there is little to indicate that reform can actually be achieved. In the long Milanese tradition, Risi assumes the stance of reason and civil concern, holding up to ridicule the frauds and hypocrites of contemporary society. However, his voice is finally more passive than aggressive. The best we can do in a world of impossibilities, as is clear in the poem entitled

47. See Ramat, pp. 606–612, and the discussion of Zanzotto's poetic theory by Glauco Cambon and Gino Rizzo, in *Selected Poetry of Andrea Zanzotto*, translated and edited by Ruth Feldman and Brian Swann (Princeton, N.J.: Princeton University Press, 1975).
48. See Luciano Anceschi, ed., *Linea lombarda* (Varese: Magenta, 1952).

"Tautology," is to perceive the bitter ironies of life and then simply to persist. Silvio Ramat speaks of Risi as being trapped in "the harshness of his own incorruptible judgment: which is the judgment of a victim, a loser. . . ."[49] The ultimate irony is that in Risi's state of alienation there are no footholds; not even the conscience of the writer himself will serve as an absolute.

Bartolo Cattafi (b. 1922), even though he was born in Sicily, is often considered part of the *linea lombarda*. With Risi he shares the disillusionment derived from great hopes which have never been fulfilled. A central idea in his work, reflected in the title of one of his books, is the search for *qualcosa di preciso*: something exact or precise which will serve as a point of reference in a chaotic modern world. Based on the experience of his own extensive world travel, Cattafi's poems create a spiritual odyssey, a quest for that "something" which would help to make sense out of the seemingly senseless, which would enhance man's best qualities and minimize his worst. But in the harshness and sterility of the landscape he portrays, or in the bitterness of his fables, it is clear that the search is never entirely successful. In one of those poetic fables, "Wingspan," the vision is one of unrelieved pessimism. All of nature and all of history seem to have conspired to bring us to the state of paralysis in which we currently exist. Although Cattafi believes that man must accept a responsible attitude toward his fellow man, his vision does not offer much hope for reform or amelioration.

Giancarlo Majorino (b. 1928) is also a Milanese, and the spirit of his poems is much the same as those of the *linea lombarda*. He can see all of the betrayals and disappointments of the new Italy, but he can do little but lament them. Majorino cannot even assume a stance of moral indignation (although he is often bitterly ironic), because he feels a personal complicity in the evil he sees around him. "Anniversary" is based on the assassination of Patrice Lumumba and the poet's inability to deal with the sense of guilt for his own culture's responsibility. Majorino recalls the Fascist period, thus condemning both himself and his country, and simultaneously raising Lumumba to the status of a martyr of the Resistance. Even more important, he expresses a kind of poetic impotence; he finds it impossible to sing of heroic social struggles. That he leaves to the more vital African poets. It is as if Majorino were describing the twilight of his own culture and looking elsewhere for a new one to replace it. "Anniversary" becomes an epitaph for the aspirations of the Italian postwar realists.

Roberto Roversi (b. 1923) has been compared to the Cesare Pavese of *Lavorare stanca*, but there is a significant difference between the two poets. Although Roversi's most important book, *Dopo Campoformio*, begins with Italian partisans in battle and proceeds through the postwar period, it is not part of the new realism. His poems are packed with images out of the political and historical context, but there is no attempt at making sense of the chaos and contradiction. Instead of social commitment, there is only anger, and finally resignation.

49. Ramat, p. 588.

Silvio Ramat sums up Roversi's stance in his judgment of *Dopo Campoformio*: "It is therefore the honest poem that doesn't know how to resolve, nor wants to pretend to have resolved, the conflict of poetry with history. . . ."[50] "Political Customs" offers an excellent example of Roversi's style. Lost in the morass of memories, philosophical meditations, events, and ghosts from the past, the narrator finds it difficult to make sense of anything. He can record these things, and react to them emotionally, but beyond that he cannot go.

In the midst of the resurgence of the hermetic school and the new experimentalism came the explosive appearance of the new avant-garde. Like the futurists at the beginning of the century, these new radicals wanted to shock and disrupt in order to clear away the clichés of the uninspired traditionalists. One of the most cogent spokesmen for the new group was Antonio Porta (b. 1935). He characterized the poetry of the hermetics as "exhibitions of *I*, continually recooked and served as first rate dishes, while [the people] have rejected them by instinct."[51] He spoke of his own "aversion for the *I-poet*, the one who is always telling his own story. For whatever happens to him is extremely interesting, just because it happens to him." But if Porta saw the hermetic tradition as a "desert of boneless forms," he also rejected the clichés into which the new realism and even the new experimentalism had slipped. Porta's ideal committed writer was one who reflected the world around him exactly as it was, not as it should be. Porta wanted a "poetry of objects," a poetry *in re* rather than *ante rem*. In this suggestion, he sounds very much like William Carlos Williams and his famous dictum: "No ideas but in things." The new Italian writers insisted that no ethical, political, or ideological content be forced into a text. In fact, Porta and his fellow *novissimi* rejected the idea of "content" entirely. It was the style of a poem, and the resulting dynamics of reader-writer interaction, which constituted the meaning of that poem. Nothing which could be extracted from the poem was valid. This theory has much in common with Charles Olson's idea of the poem as a field of action where the poet's mind works itself out spontaneously. The poetry which results is clearly more focused on experience than it is on thought. For both Italian and American poetry, these new theories revolutionized traditionally accepted ideas about the way poetry works and the way it is understood.

Having rejected political ideology in the disillusionment of the late fifties, the new avant-garde focused its attention on language. Alfredo Giuliani (b. 1924), one of the most frequent spokesmen for the new writers, spoke of the falsity of the "official" language, both in politics and literature.[52] This falsity in language created a schism between the word as sign and its actual meaning. The resulting "hypocrisy" reflected the hypocrisy of modern society, where stated values and actual values were at polar extremes. Instead of trying to cure the language by modifying it in some way, Giuliani suggested that it be held up

50. Ibid., p. 596.
51. *I novissimi*, p. 193.
52. The theories discussed here are presented in the introduction to *I novissimi*, written by Alfredo Giuliani.

to scrutiny, be stripped of its disguises, in order to reveal all its flaws, as well as the flaws of the schizophrenic society it reflected. Both philosophy and new linguistic theory could be rallied in support of this plan. Phenomenology, which enjoyed a great revival in Europe during the fifties, denied perceptual absolutes; any coherent system was essentially as valid as any other. New linguistic theories referred to languages as autonomous systems, with no necessary dependence on outside reality. Thus, the "languages" created by the avant-garde were suddenly liberated from the socio-political shackles of the new realists. The *novissimi* had ventured off into an autonomy of art which was even beyond that which Benedetto Croce had propounded. Indeed, the rebellion against "useful" literature by many of the young writers was very much in the spirit of the tradition of which the hermetics were a part. Yet there was great variance in approach to theoretical issues among these *novissimi*, as is the case in almost any literary movement. This was to become painfully clear when they met together in Palermo in 1963 to put together a literary manifesto.

Alfredo Giuliani was one of the early collaborators in Luciano Anceschi's *Il Verri*, founded in that pivotal year of 1956. Like many of the magazines which have already been mentioned, *Il Verri* became the heart of a new movement. Among its most important collaborators, aside from Giuliani, were Nanni Balestrini, Renato Barilli, Fausto Curi, Umberto Eco, Angelo Guglielmi, Antonio Porta, and Edoardo Sanguineti. The first undertaking of the magazine was a frontal attack on all rationalistic philosophers: Benedetto Croce, the soul of the hermetic movement, and Antonio Gramsci, the ideological center of the new realism. They argued that in a world characterized by irrationality, or schizophrenia in Giuliani's terms, rationalistic philosophy no longer pertained. The *Il Verri* group, echoing the surrealists of earlier years, felt that the reality of the modern world lay in the subconscious. That is what they wanted to capture in their poetry.

The first important national notice of this group came with the publication in 1961 of *I novissimi: poesie per gli anni '60*, edited by Alfredo Giuliani. Having been ignored for the most part by Italian critics, Giuliani felt it necessary to announce the arrival of the new movement with an aggressive and strident introduction. To a certain extent, his forcefulness was necessary. In historical terms the new writers were surrealists, and the Italian literary establishment of the fifties and early sixties felt about surrealism much as the American literary establishment did. They felt it didn't work. Giuliani not only asserted that it did work, but that it was the only literary approach which could accurately reflect the forces of the contemporary world.[53] The principles of the *novissimi* were delineated both in general theoretical terms and in specific definitions of those terms, in marked contrast with the vague polemics of the previous fifteen years. Giuliani said that the general effect of the new poetry would be shock and provocation. But then he explained that the specific means for attaining this effect would be: (1) discontinuity of the imaginative process; (2) a lack of tradi-

53. *I novissimi*, p. 18.

tional syntax; (3) a violence of images. All of these were the necessary stylistic correlatives of the schizophrenic society they were trying to depict. He also stated that there would be no preconstituted reality in the new poetry; that would be the goal, and perhaps an unreachable one, of the search. There would be no definitive ideology. Ideologies, like all other objects in the modern world, would be just another part of the *collage*. The new poetry would be a "naked poetry"; its only contents would be the words which constituted the poem. By denying the concept of poetic contents, Giuliani destroyed the traditional reader-writer relationship. However, he suggested a new relationship to replace the old one. The reader was to take on a new responsibility; he would no longer be "entertained," but would be "treated like an adult." The reader would have to complete the process of communication. In a sense, he would be completing the poem itself. This would lead to a better understanding of the problem which was to be the main focus of this poetry: the gap between official history and life as it was really being lived. The understanding which was supposed to result was termed a *"neo-contenuto"* of the poetry in question: content, but with a difference. With a greater understanding of the system, both writer and reader could work toward synthesizing a better system. Giuliani's expression of this ultimate social goal, in contrast with the Marxist optimism of new-realism, is worded with modesty. It is clear that he is more interested in the poetics of the movement than he is in any potential social benefits.

The five poets included in *I novissimi* were Nanni Balestrini, Antonio Porta, Edoardo Sanguineti, Elio Pagliarani, and Giuliani himself. Each one is an individual, and yet each one embodies the spirit of *Il Verri* and the new avant-garde. Nanni Balestrini (b. 1935) is probably the purest practitioner of the poetic theory which Giuliani advances in his introduction. He does not superimpose an order on his material. On the contrary, some of his poems appear at first reading to be pure nonsense. They certainly have no meaning in the traditional sense; they are closer to *collage*, or an assemblage of "authentic fragments of our time," in Giuliani's words. For example, "The Fugitive's Apologue" begins in the middle of one statement, ends at the beginning of another, and never connects the images which appear within. Although traditional syntax and continuity are missing, Balestrini develops a strange coherence in the linguistic world of his poems. Giuliani even claims that white spaces or gaps on the page in Balestrini's poems function as fragments themselves, thus taking part in the new linguistic order.[54] Balestrini splendidly fulfills one of the new movement's most emphatic goals: the reduction of the subjective *I*. It is impossible to identify a traditional "voice" in Balestrini's poetry; one cannot even be sure if he is being ironic, although one often suspects it. In his electronic and computer poetry (again, with a fascinating coherence of its own) he takes the new objectivity to its limit. If there is any purpose to his poetry, it is the revelation of the loss of meaning in modern language, and the implied loss of meaning in modern life. That revelation seems to be his main goal, although

54. Ibid., p. 399.

there is a hint that he believes some future synthesis can be produced from his "gutted" language.

Antonio Porta's poetry best exemplifies Giuliani's criteria of shock and provocation. His works, unlike Balestrini's, often make sense in the traditional meaning of the word. However, he also uses his own system of discontinuity: syntactically discrete fragments which piece together a narrative line. Porta's fragments are most often brief scenes of violence and degradation. In fact, when confronting poems like "To Open" and "Beaver Skin," many readers have been at a loss as to whether they were watching the hand of a sadist or the hand of a morally outraged critic of a brutal society. A reading of a substantial body of his work makes it evident that it is the latter, because Porta takes us on a Dantesque journey through an infernal modern world. The greatest horror of that world lies in the fact that its irrational brutality usually masquerades as order and reason. Unlike most of his contemporaries, Porta is extremely interested in the use of various metrical patterns to produce different effects, often varying them in a single poem. The most unique thing about Porta, however, is his Catholicism. Behind the fractured vision of a fallen world, there is a belief in the absolute. It is that absolute which he doggedly tracks in each of his poems.

Edoardo Sanguineti (b. 1930) is one of the very few modern poets who have taken the theory and methodology of Pound's *Cantos* seriously enough to attempt something similar themselves. In the early fifties, while the rest of the Italian poets were embroiled in the struggles between the hermetic school and new-realism, Sanguineti (as Pound said of Eliot) "modernized himself on his own." His own long work *Laborintus* anticipates the appearance of the avant-garde by almost a decade. Like Pound, Sanguineti uses classical Greek and Latin and a plethora of modern languages. This unabashed esotericism caused many contemporaries to suspect him of the same elitism that had always separated the Italian academy from the Italian public. However, Sanguineti was not trying to hide anything from his readers. Like Pound, he believed that the total effect of his poems would be "a rose in the steel dust" a subconscious pattern rising out of seeming chaos. Also similar to Pound is the strong political nature of Sanguineti's work, even though they are at opposite ends of the political spectrum. Sanguineti's Marxism always controls the form and movement of whatever he writes.

Elio Pagliarani, previously discussed in this essay, joined the *novissimi* as an older brother from another generation. Even though he was strongly connected with the new realists, his constant experimentation and his resistance to any simplistic ideology caused his contemporaries to view him with suspicion. It is that quality of nonconformity which allowed him to make the smooth transition into the ranks of the avant-garde.

Giuliani started his own career as a socially committed poet in the mold of Pasolini. Later on, he developed his central theme of schizophrenia and general psychological degeneration. Because of his concentration on this theme, Giuliani's poetry best exemplifies the movement's emphasis on the exploration of depth psychology. Unlike the other writers in the movement, Giuliani attempts to achieve his objectivity through total immersion in the subjective *I*. In "Who Would Have Said It," we are in a hallucinatory world, perhaps derived from an ether dream. However, even though the poem is clearly concerned with the internal struggles of the poet himself, rather than those of the outside world, it seems to shed light on the dilemmas of modern man. Like Sanguineti, he seems to believe that if you go deep enough into the psyche, you will discover universal truth.

Two years after the appearance of Giuliani's anthology, *I novissimi*, a group of thirty-four writers and nine critics met in Palermo for a six-day conference. It was the birth of the "Gruppo '63." The conference was composed of avant-garde writers from all over Italy, some in groups (like the *Il Verri* group) and some as individuals. Among those individuals are four writers who are also included in this anthology: Lamberto Pignotti, Adriano Spatola, Amelia Rosselli, and Giancarlo Marmori.

Lamberto Pignotti was the originator of the concept of "technological poetry." He wanted to use the languages and techniques of the mass media in order to reach a similar audience of "consumers":

> Pignotti suggested the diffusion of poems on match covers, over loud-speakers in stadiums, on records in juke-boxes or written in neon on the rooftops, etc. . . . he wanted to demonstrate how technological languages had already entered the field of poetry. . . .[55]

Pignotti uses languages, or more simply jargons, from every possible sphere of modern activity. It is hard to believe, however, that the general public would find his work palatable. Poems like those in *Vita zero* go around in logical circles; like the mobius strip, they always seem to be going somewhere, but always bring the reader back to the starting point. Rather than containing messages or communicating content, Pignotti's poems present linguistic artifacts. It is this tendency which led to Pignotti's interest in "*poesia visiva*," which he defines as "a poetry which searches for relationships between verbal and visual material. . . ." He edited the *Antologia della poesia visiva* (Bologna: Sampietro, 1965), the first book of its kind ever to appear.

Compared to Pignotti, Adriano Spatola is more in the mold of the *novissimi*, particularly Nanni Balestrini. His poems guide us through fragmentary visions of a dead, or near dead, contemporary society. As in the tour through the "necropolis" of "The Boomerang," we experience an emotional as well as a visual movement. The narrative tone varies, suddenly and without warning, from one of ironic amusement to raging anger or complete despair. Manacorda asserts that Spatola's work is close to the "technological poetry" of Pignotti.[56] It is true that Spatola presents a similar "pop art" vision of society, but unlike Pignotti, he does not refrain from becoming emotionally involved with his material.

55. Manacorda, p. 395.
56. Ibid., p. 399.

Amelia Rosselli, trained as a musician, specializes in the creation of irrational stories or parables out of syntactical fragments, using her fine sense of the rhythms of Italian as the glue. The title of one of her books, *Variazioni belliche*, indicates her methodology: producing rhythmic variations with her material just as a musical composer writes variations on a melodic theme. As irrational as they are, totally devoid of logical continuity, her poems always seem to have a strong emotional continuity. Amelia Rosselli's innovations are in keeping with the avant-garde interest in language; by manipulating rhythms and images as if they were musical notation, she introduces yet another kind of linguistic transformation to Italian poetry.

Giancarlo Marmori is known for the small, nightmarish worlds he creates in his poems. Like the works of Amelia Rosselli, Marmori's poems make no sense in traditional terms, but they still seem to communicate something about the people and things they portray. Manacorda sees the influence of Kafka in Marmori's works, carried to the extreme of creating an "absolutely gratuitous reality, in which by implication there remains, however, the symbolic and polemical enunciation of the dehumanized condition of today."[57] An example of this quality in Marmori can be seen in "Your Totem is the Opulent Serpent." Through the magical transformation of Marmori's poetic technique, the serpent becomes identified with some aspect of the human subconscious. Marmori implies that the snake-human is both passionate and cruel, and yet has a fascinating beauty. The poem could very well be directed to an individual, a woman perhaps. And yet, without ever making a rational statement to which the reader can point, the poem creates the impression that the snake represents a fundamental part of contemporary human life.

The purpose of all these writers, whether members of groups or individuals, in the "Gruppo '63" was to come together, express solidarity, and write a manifesto. All of them felt that unity would be necessary to displace the realist and hermetic writers who were then dominating the literary market place. It was soon obvious that the hoped-for unity was not to be. Rather than presenting a show of solidarity, the conference quickly became a heated ideological squabble.[58] Three figures, Angelo Guglielmi, Edoardo Sanguineti, and Renato Barilli, outlined three different theoretical approaches. In brief, they were as follows.

Guglielmi started with the premise that it was impossible to assert anything or explain anything. The world was chaos, without dignity, meaning, value system, or possibility of morality at all. Everything was equally good or bad; the world was a mass of "things" without value. Confronted with such a world, the writer would have to refrain from any judgment or ordering of his material. The best form would be a *pastiche* where the objects arranged themselves, thereby creating their own systems. This was Guglielmi's definition of "open form" po-

---

57. Ibid., p. 399.
58. For a full discussion of the conference, see Manacorda, pp. 382–390. A collection of "Gruppo '63" criticism, including the polemics of the first Palermo conference, can be found in *Gruppo 63: critica e teoria*, ed. Renato Barilli and Angelo Guglielmi (Milano: Feltrinelli, 1977).

etry. Since the world could not be thought about, only experienced, the writer could never interpret anything. Poetry was mimesis; the writer had to let the words become the objects to which they pointed. A poem was, therefore, a random series of neutral objects. When questioned, Guglielmi insisted that poetry was the total absence of vision, not the suggestion of a new one. Such an attempt to reform the contemporary situation would be falling into the fallacy of classical literature. Pressed further, Guglielmi conceded that the purest poetry, according to his theory, would be silence. The extremism of Guglielmi's stance was universally rejected by the conference.

Sanguineti counterattacked from an almost entirely opposite ideological stance. He insisted that the avant-garde had to function within history, not outside of it. The new literature would have to attack the corruption of the capitalistic literary market place in order to bring about constructive change. In support of this theory, which sounded suspiciously similar to the old postwar Marxist realism, Sanguineti advanced a clever argument. Understanding that all present would agree that language was the focus of avant-garde theory, he argued that language is by definition political. Sanguineti explained that class and class conflict determined each writer's language. The writer can never make language a neutral instrument, as Guglielmi suggested, because it can never be innocent of politics. In fact, Sanguineti asserted that neutral or "standard" language is a bourgeois myth, perpetuated to convince people that bourgeois ideals are reality and that everything else is distortion. The way to counteract that presumption is to create absurd, irrational poetic worlds and make them more "real" than bourgeois reality. However, it was pointed out to Sanguineti that the absurd and the irrational could not be politically subversive in the manner he described. Since both Marxism and capitalism were rational in basis, both would be subverted by the irrational.

Renato Barilli then stepped in to attempt to establish a more moderate position, hoping to effect a compromise between the extremes articulated by Guglielmi and Sanguineti. He claimed that both of those positions were incapable of dealing with the complex psychology which was the basis of the new literature. Barilli suggested that the chaos which the irrational world of their poetry appeared to be was merely a new order which was not yet understood. He emphasized that old orders and traditions were not broken down gratuitously, but in order to create a new system. The responsibility of the writer to help create such a system could not be denied. Barilli's position was immediately attacked, especially by Guglielmi and Sanguineti.

The great irony of the Palermo conference, aside from its obvious failure to bring unity to the movement, was that it contained the seeds of the eventual destruction of the "Gruppo '63." Both of the ideologies which dominated the conference, Guglielmi's and Sanguineti's, led to dead ends. Guglielmi's totally neutral poetry made poetry itself obsolete, as he himself admitted. Sanguineti's theory simply brought up the old problems of postwar realism, including its social ineffectiveness and its anti-imaginative bias. Those problems were the ones which had led to the demise of the earlier movement. One other irony, which was partially recognized by all, was that the bourgeois press was beginning to recognize the new avant-garde. In a few years, all of the principal members of the "Gruppo '63" would be published widely by important presses. Wasn't it inevitable that they would be absorbed by the capitalistic system they· abhorred? And as they were absorbed, wouldn't their strident attacks begin to soften? Young Turks do not remain young Turks forever. Not so many years later, in the early seventies, young political activists would accuse the members of the "Gruppo '63" of being reactionaries and sellouts to the establishment.

Another conference was held in November of 1964 at Reggio Emilia. The next year still another conference on the experimental novel was held at Palermo. Instead of coming closer together, the participants became more and more divided. Some pointed out the flaws that threatened the life of the movement. First, they could not agree on model texts for critical analysis. Many of the things they were talking about, apparently, did not yet exist. Even more serious, there was no consensus of critical approach or interpretation vis-à-vis the texts they did discuss. If this specialized group couldn't understand the texts produced by its own writers, then how could the public? That brought everyone back to the issue of communication. The esotericism and elitism of the hermetics were the prime reasons for the birth of the new avant-garde. Hadn't they now become even more obscure than the hermetics? The best answer to these questions is that it is theory, luckily, not poetry which is written at conferences. Although the critical theories presented were extreme, the poetry of these writers makes much more sense when we consider the works individually.

There were other meetings of the literary avant-garde: La Spezia in 1966 and Fano in 1967. The "Gruppo '63" was paralleled by other experimentalist groups. The "Gruppo '70," formed during a convocation in Florence in 1963 and led by Lamberto Pignotti, pressed its theories on the necessity of incorporating scientific and technological language into contemporary poetry. Pignotti's "Gruppo '70" also stressed interdisciplinary cooperation between the visual arts and literature; *poesia visiva* became the focus of their work.

In spite of the diversity of opinions and directions, a spirit of enthusiasm prevailed during much of the sixties. However, that spirit was suddenly challenged in the latter part of the decade. Ironically, the crisis was political rather than aesthetic. As Italy's boom, the "economic miracle," had begun to taper off, there was more and more unrest. The antagonism between political factions was greatly increased by the abortive right-wing *coup d'état* attempt in 1964 (the SIFAR affair). There was a widespread suspicion that some major industrialists had supported this venture. The stage was thus set for the serious student riots which broke out in 1967. The recent surge of student activism in the United States, particularly at the University of California, Berkeley, may have provided a catalyst, but the left-wing alliance of students and unions in Italy has a long and active tradition. One result of this escalating unrest was the formation of the Italian "1968 movement." But this movement was strictly political; cultural and literary matters were brushed aside. It was a mass movement, not a small intellectual clique. The avant-garde had been speaking of transforming society through disorientation and linguistic fragmentation. When the chaos in the streets offered a real opportunity for social change, they could neither suggest a direction nor adequately articulate the struggle.

It would be impossible to overestimate the seriousness of the crisis these events created for the sixties avant-garde. Some poets reacted by making a sharp turn back toward traditional Marxist ideology. In Balestrini's "Without Tears for the Roses," Rosselli's "General Strike 1969," and Porta's "Nomad's Utopia" we can see this change. Since these three writers had produced some of the most extreme experiments in the area of irrational linguistic fragmentation, this reversal is particularly significant. However, things could never be the same again. The ascendancy of the avant-garde groups had come to an end. After their stunning defeat in the moment of crisis, they seemed to break apart; various writers went in their own separate directions. What resulted was a vacuum. Philippe Sollers, a major poet in the French avant-garde "Tel Quel" group, commented on this change in 1976:

> I have seemed to note a cultural absence, the absence of those friends of ours who represented, when they were together, a strong, militant advance patrol. It seems to me that today that experience has gone back into the institutional system. . . . Yes, I'm talking about the avant-garde. I was amazed that during the period of our contacts with the "Gruppo '63," the Italians were perhaps even farther advanced than we were. Today I don't hear them anymore. . . .[59]

Sollers's lament underlines both the enormous influence of the Italian avant-garde in the sixties and the suddenness of their decline in the seventies. There have been subsequent attempts to start new groups, such as the "Gruppo '78," with its talk of "mao-dadaism, the liberation of desire, and schizophrenic activities. . . ."[60] However, these groups, who look back at the sixties avant-garde with disdain, have nothing of its vitality. A similar phenomenon has occurred in the United States. Coming after a decade of upheaval and experimentation, the seventies seem to have produced a cooling off period. Whether or not the seventies in Italy have actually created a literary vacuum will take at least another decade to ascertain. But literary history moves in cycles; we can be sure that the future holds still more conservative reactions and still more radical challenges. As long as the Italians write, there will be struggles on the literary battlefield.

59. Tommaso Chiaretti, "Che fine ha il Gruppo 63?", *La Reppublica*, 11 February, 1976, cited by Giorgio Luti, *Le idee e le lettere* (Milano: Longanesi, 1976), p. 55.
60. Umberto Eco, "Gli illuministi del sessantatrè," *Corriere della Sera*, 24 February, 1977.

Balestrini, Nanni and Alfredo Giuliani, eds. *Gruppo 63*. Milano: Feltrinelli, 1964.

Ballerini, Luigi. *La piramide capovolta*. Venezia: Marsilio, 1975.

Bàrberi-Squarotti, Giorgio. *Poesia e narrativa del secondo Novecento*. Milano: Mursia, 1967.

Feldman, Ruth, and Brian Swann, eds. *Italian Poetry Today: Currents and Trends*. New York: New Rivers Press, 1979.

Feldman, Ruth, and Brian Swann, eds. *Selected Poetry of Andrea Zanzotto*. Princeton: Princeton University Press, 1975.

Giuliani, Alfredo, ed. *I novissimi: poesie per gli anni '60*. Torino: Einaudi, 1965.

Golino, Enzo. *Letteratura e classi sociali*. Roma: Laterza, 1976.

Heiney, Donald. *America in Modern Italian Literature*. New Brunswick: Rutgers University Press, 1964.

Hughes, Serge. *The Fall and Rise of Modern Italy*. New York: Macmillan, 1967.

Jucker, Ninetta. *Italy*. New York: Walker, 1970.

Lind, Levi Robert. *Twentieth-Century Italian Poetry*. Indianapolis: Bobbs-Merrill, 1974.

Luti, Giorgio and Paolo Rossi. *Le idee e le lettere*. Milano: Longanesi, 1976.

Manacorda, Giuliano. *Storia della letteratura italiana contemporanea, 1940–1965*. Roma: Riuniti, 1967.

Modern Poetry in Translation, no. 26, *Italy* (Winter 1975), ed. Brian Swann and Ruth Feldman.

Pacifici, Sergio. *A Guide to Contemporary Italian Literature*. Carbondale: Southern Illinois University Press, 1972.

Pento, Bortolo. *Letture di poesia contemporanea*. Milano: Marzorati, 1965.

Raiziss, Sonia, and Alfredo de Palchi, eds. "Italian Poetry," in *Modern European Poetry*. General Editor Willis Barnstone, New York: Bantam, 1970.

Ramat, Silvio. *Storia della poesia italiana del Novecento*. Milano: Mursia, 1976.

Salinari, Carlo. *Preludio e fine del realismo in Italia*. Napoli: Morano, 1967.

Sanguineti, Edoardo. *Ideologia e linguaggio*. Milano: Feltrinelli, 1965.

Sanguineti, Edoardo, ed. *Poesia italiana del Novecento*. Torino: Einaudi, 1971.

Vanderbilt Poetry Review, Special Italian Issue (Summer 1974), ed. Frank Judge.

The New Realism

Born Franco Lattes in Florence in 1917, Fortini took his mother's name to avoid persecution as a Jew. As a young man, he was part of the Florentine literary scene, a friend of Alberto Carocci and Giacomo Noventa, and was involved with the magazine *Riforma Letteraria*. He fought as a partisan in World War II. After the war he was the editor of Vittorini's *Politecnico* and later the editor of *Avanti*. Fortini's poetry always manifests a sense of serious inquiry into human values and responsibility; that aspect of his work corresponds to his strong political convictions.

His books of poetry are:

Foglio di via ed altri versi.
    Torino: Einaudi, 1946.
Una facile allegoria.
    Milano: Edizioni della Meridiana, 1955.
In una strada di Firenze.
    Milano: Edizioni della Meridiana, 1955.
I destini generali.
    Caltanissetta: Sciascia, 1956.
Sestina a Firenze.
    Milano: Edizioni della Meridiana, 1957.
Poesia ed errore.
    Milano: Feltrinelli, 1959.
Una volta per sempre.
    Milano: Mondadori, 1963.
L'ospite ingrato.
    Bari: De Donato, 1966.
Questo muro.
    Milano: Mondadori, 1973.
Poesie scelte (1938–1973).
    Edited by Pier Vincenzo Mengaldo.
    Milano: Mondadori, 1974.

Foglio di via

Dunque nulla di nuovo da quest'altezza
dove ancora un poco senza parlare si guarda
e nei capelli il vento cala la sera.

Dunque nessun cammino per discendere
se non questo del nord, dove il sole non tocca
e sono d'acqua i rami degli alberi.

Dunque fra poco senza parole la bocca.
E questa sera saremo in fondo alla valle
dove le feste han spento tutte le lampade,

dove una folla tace e gli amici non riconoscono.

Deportation Order

So nothing new from up here
where you look around a bit longer without speaking
and wind in your hair the evening falls.

So there's no path down
except this one from the north, where sun never touches
and tree branches are water.

So very soon a mouth with no words.
And this evening we'll be at the bottom of the valley
where celebrations have burned out all the lamps,

where a crowd remains silent and friends don't know each other.

Camposanto degli inglesi

Ancora, quando fa sera, d'ottobre,
e pei viali ai platani la nebbia,
ma leggera, fa velo, come a quei nostri
tempi, fra i muri d'edera e i cipressi
del Camposanto degli Inglesi, i custodi
bruciano sterpi e lauri secchi.
                                        Verde
il fumo delle frasche
come quello dei carbonai nei boschi
di montagna.
                    Morivano
quelle sere con dolce strazio a noi
già un poco fredde. Allora m'era caro
cercarti il polso e accarezzarlo. Poi
erano i lumi incerti, le grandi ombre
dei giardini, la ghiaia, il tuo passo pieno e calmo;
e lungo i muri delle cancellate
la pietra aveva, dicevi, odore d'ottobre e il fumo
sapeva di campagna e di vendemmia.
Si apriva la cara tua bocca rotonda nel buio
lenta e docile uva.
                        Ora è passato
molto tempo, non so dove sei, forse vedendoti
non riconoscerei la tua figura. Sei certo
viva e pensi talvolta a quanto amore
fu, quegli anni, tra noi, a quanta vita
è passata. E talvolta al ricordare
tuo, come al mio che ora ti parla, vana
ti geme, e insostenibile, una pena;
una pena di ritornare, quale
han forse i poveri morti, di vivere
là, ancora una volta, rivedere
quella che tu sei stata, andare ancora
per quelle sere di un tempo che non esiste più,
che non ha più alcun luogo,

The English Cemetery

Still, when evening comes in October,
and on the boulevards the fog just lightly veils
the plane trees, as it used to in our day,
between the ivy-covered walls and the cypresses
of the English cemetery, the caretakers
burn twigs and dry laurel.
                              The smoke
from the branches is green,
like that of the charcoal makers in the forests
on the mountains.
                    Those evenings,
already a bit chilly for us, died with
sweet agony. I loved then to search
for your wrist and to caress it. Then
there were the dim lights, the huge shadows
in the gardens, the gravel, your steps full and calm;
the stone along the walls next to the gates
had, you said, the smell of October and the smoke
smelled of countryside and vineyards.
Your dear mouth opened round in the dark,
soft and submissive grape.
                            Now so much time
has passed, I don't know where you are, perhaps if I
saw you, I wouldn't recognize you. You're certainly
alive and you sometimes think of how much love
there was, during those years, between us, of how much
life has passed by. And sometimes in your reverie,
as in my own, the one who speaks to you now, a vain
and unbearable pain moans to you;
a painful desire to return, such as
perhaps the poor dead have, to live
there one more time, to see again
that which you were, to travel still
through those evenings of a time which no longer exists,
which no longer has any place,

anche se io scendo a volte per questi viali
di Firenze ove ai platani la nebbia,
ma leggera, fa velo e nei giardini,
bruciano i malinconici fuochi d'alloro.

even if I sometimes go down these Florentine
boulevards where the fog just lightly
veils the plane trees, and in the gardens
they burn the melancholy fires of laurel.

Agro inverno

Agro inverno crepiti il tuo fuoco
incenerisci inverno i boschi i tetti
recidi e brucia inverno.

Pianga chi piange chi ha male abbia più male
chi odia odii più forte chi tradisce trionfi:
questo è l'ultimo testo è il decreto del nostro inverno.

Non abbiamo saputo che cosa fare per noi
della verde vita e dei fiori amorosi.
Per questo la scure è alla radice dei cuori

e come stecchi che si divincolano saremo arsi.

Bitter Winter

Bitter winter, you crackle your fire
winter, you consume the woods, the roofs
winter, you slash and burn.

Whoever mourns, let him mourn; whoever suffers, let him suffer more
whoever hates, let him hate more; whoever deceives, let him triumph:
this is the ultimate text and decree of our winter.

We didn't know what to do with
green life and the loving flowers.
That's why the ax is at the root of our hearts

and like writhing twigs we shall be burnt.

Agli amici

Si fa tardi. Vi vedo, veramente
eguali a me nel vizio di passione,
con i cappotti, le carte, le luci
delle salive, i capelli già fragili,
con le parole e gli ammicchi, eccitati

e depressi, sciupati e infanti, rauchi
per la conversazione ininterrotta,
come scendete questa valle grigia,
come la tramortita erba premete
dove la via si perde ormai e la luce.

Le voci odo lontane come i fili
del tramontano tra le pietre e i cavi.
Ogni parola che mi giunge è addio.
E allento il passo e voi seguo nel cuore,
uno qua, uno là, per la discesa.

To Friends

It's getting late. I see you, just
like me in your weakness for emotion,
with overcoats, papers, sputtering
lamps, hair already thin,
with words and winks, excited

and depressed, wasted and yet children, hoarse
from uninterrupted conversation,
as you go down into this gray valley,
as you press down the stunned grass
where the way and the light by now are lost.

The voices I hear distant as the wires
beyond the mountains between rocks and hollows.
Every word that reaches me is farewell.
And I slow down my pace and follow you in my heart,
one here, one there, on the downward path.

Franco Fortini

Lettera

Padre, il mondo ti ha vinto giorno per giorno
 come vincerà me, che ti somiglio.

Padre, i tuoi gesti sono aria nell'aria,
 come le mie parole vento nel vento.

Padre, ti hanno umiliato, tradito, spogliato,
 nessuno t'ha guardato per aiutarti.

Padre di magre risa, padre di cuore bruciato,
 padre, il più triste dei miei fratelli, padre,

il tuo figliuolo ancora trema del tuo tremore,
 come quel giorno d'infanzia di pioggia e paura

pallido tra le urla buie del rabbino contorto
 perdevi di mano le zolle sulla cassa di tuo padre.

Ma quello che tu non dici devo io dirlo per te
 al trono della luce che consuma i miei giorni.

Per questo è partito tuo figlio; e ora insieme ai compagni
 cerca le strade bianche di Galilea.

Letter

Father, the world conquered you day by day
as it will conquer me, the one who resembles you.

Father, your gestures are air in the air,
as my words are wind in the wind.

Father, they humiliated, betrayed, robbed you,
no one looked out to help you.

Father of meager laughter, father of burnt out heart,
father, the saddest of my brothers, father,

your boy still trembles with your trembling,
as in that childhood day of rain and fear

pale, your hand tossed, between the dark howls
of the contorted rabbi, lumps of dirt on your father's coffin.

But what you don't say I must say for you
at the throne of the light which consumes my days.

For this your son departed; and now with comrades
searches for the white roads of Galilee.

A Santa Croce

A Santa Croce, dove le strade
han fiato d'aglio e di vino a digiuno,
e dalle soglie dei pizzicagnoli
i soriani covano, se cade
dal cielo stretto il sole e rade
archi, rigagnoli, stemmi di sasso,
e non passa nessuno;

a Santa Croce, dove dai cortili
gridano donne senza seni lunghi guai,
e nei testi di basilico
non c'è che fil di ferro e i fili
di ferro dei campanelli lontani sottili
che dagli anditi assassini e i corridoi
non smettono mai . . .

In Santa Croce

In Santa Croce, where the streets
smell of garlic and heartless wine,
and tabbies curl up in
delicatessen doorways, if the sun
falls from the narrow sky and skims
arches, gutters, stone coats of arms,
and no one passes by;

in Santa Croce, where breastless women
shout long sorrows from the courtyards,
and in the drying bunches of basil
there's only iron wire and the iron
wires of distant slender bells
because assassins never stop coming
from the passages and corridors . . .

Franco Fortini

Il Comunismo

Sempre sono stato comunista.
Ma giustamente gli altri comunisti
hanno sospettato di me. Ero comunista
troppo oltre le loro certezze e i miei dubbi.
Giustamente non m'hanno riconosciuto.

La disciplina mia non potevano vederla.
Il mio centralismo pareva anarchia.
La mia autocritica negava la loro.
Non si può essere comunista speciale.
Pensarlo vuol dire non esserlo.

Così giustamente non m'hanno riconosciuto
i miei compagni. Servo del capitale
io, come loro. Più, anzi: perché lo dimenticavo.
E lavoravano essi, mentre io il mio piacere cercavo.
Anche per questo sempre ero comunista.

Troppo oltre le loro certezze e i miei dubbi
di questo mondo sempre volevo la fine.
Ma la mia fine anche. E anche questo, più questo,
li allontanava da me. Non li aiutava la mia speranza.
Il mio centralismo pareva anarchia.

Com'è chi per sé vuole più verità
per essere agli altri più vero e perché gli altri
siano lui stesso, così sono vissuto e muoio.
Sempre dunque sono stato comunista.
Di questo mondo sempre volevo la fine.

Vivo, ho vissuto abbastanza per vedere
da scienza orrenda percossi i compagni che m'hanno piagato.
Ma dite: lo sapevate che ero dei vostri, voi, no?
Per questo mi odiavate? Oh, la mia verità è necessaria,
dissolta in tempo e aria, cuori più attenti a educare.

Communism

I have always been a communist.
But other communists have distrusted me,
and rightly so. I was a communist
too far beyond their certainties and my doubts.
They did not acknowledge me, and rightly so.

They could not understand my doctrine.
My centralism seemed anarchic.
My self-criticism undermined theirs.
One cannot be a special communist.
To think you were would mean you weren't.

Therefore my comrades didn't acknowledge me,
and rightly so. I, a slave of capitalism,
like them. Even more: because I forgot about it.
And they worked, while I pursued my pleasure.
Because of this as well, I was always a communist.

Too far beyond their certainties and my doubts
I always wanted the end of this world.
But my end as well. And this also, especially this,
estranged them from me. My hope was no help to them.
My centralism seemed anarchic.

Like the one who wishes more truth for himself
so he can be truer to others, since the others
might have been him, so I have lived and will die.
Therefore I have always been a communist.
I always wanted the end of this world.

I am living, I have lived long enough to see
the comrades who bent me beaten by horrible science.
But tell me: you knew I was one of yours, didn't you?
You hated me for this? Oh, my truth is necessary,
it melts in time and air, hearts more set on instructing.

Franco Fortini   59

Il presente

Guardo le acque e le canne
di un braccio di fiume e il sole
dentro l'acqua.

Guardavo, ero ma sono.
La melma si asciuga fra le radici.
Il mio verbo è al presente.
Questo mondo residuo d'incendi
vuole esistere.
            Insetti tendono
trappole lunghe millenni.
Le effimere sfumano. Si sfanno
impresse nel dolce vento d'Arcadia.
Attraversa il fiume una barca.
È un servo del vescovo Baudo.
Va tra la paglia d'una capanna
sfogliata sotto molte lune.
Detto la mia legge ironica
alle foglie che ronzano, al trasvolo
nervoso del drago-cervo.
Confido alle canne false eterne
la grande strategia da Yenan allo Hopei.
Seguo il segno che una mano armata incide
sulla scorza del pino
e prepara il fuoco dell'ambra dove starò visibile.

The Present

I look at the water and reeds
in a river branch and the sun
in the water.

I looked, I was but I am.
The mud dries between the roots.
My verb is in the present tense.
The residual world of fires
wants to exist.
                    Insects lay traps
for long millennia.
Mayflies vanish. They disappear
imprinted on the soft breeze of Arcadia.
Across the river a boat.
It's Bishop Baudo's servant.
He goes through the straw of a hut
weathered under many moons.
Proverbial my ironic law
to the buzzing leaves, to the nervous
flitting of the dragon beetle.
I whisper to the false eternal reeds
about the great strategy from Yenan to Hopei.
I follow the sign that an armed hand cuts
into the pine tree's bark
and prepares the amber's fire where I'll be visible.

Gli ospiti

I presupposti da cui moviamo non sono arbitrari.
La sola cosa che importa è
il movimento reale che abolisce
lo stato di cose presente.

Tutto è divenuto gravemente oscuro.
Nulla che prima non sia perduto ci serve.
La verità cade fuori della coscienza.
Non sapremo se avremo avuto ragione.
Ma guarda come già stendono le loro stuoie
attraverso la tua stanza.

Come distribuiscono le loro masserizie,
come spartiscono il loro bene, come
fra poco mangeranno la nostra verità!
Di noi spiriti curiosi in ascolto
prima del sonno parleranno.

The Guests

The premises we work from are not arbitrary.
The only thing that matters is
the true movement which destroys
the present state of things.

Everything has become gravely unclear.
Nothing serves us unless first it is lost.
Truth falls outside consciousness.
We won't know if we were right.
But look how they're already spreading their mats
across your room.

How they distribute their houseware,
how they divide up their goods, how
they will soon eat up our truth!
They will speak of us, curious
listening spirits, before sleep.

Pier Paolo Pasolini

Born in Bologna in 1922, Pasolini lived in Rome until his death in 1975. He was editor of *Officina*, *Paragone*, and *Nuovi Corrente*. As a Catholic and a Communist, he was perhaps the most successful poet of the neorealist school. His ideal of popular art led him to write many of his early poems in dialect. It also led to his work in the cinema, as an outstanding screenwriter and director. His style in poetry and film was stark, but compassionate, emotional, but never sentimental. Pasolini's murder, at the age of fifty-three, was a tragedy for Italy's artistic community.

His books of poetry are:

Le ceneri di Gramsci.
 Milano: Garzanti, 1957.
L'usignolo della chiesa cattolica.
 Milano: Longanesi, 1958.
La religione del mio tempo.
 Milano: Garzanti, 1961.
Poesia in forma di rosa.
 Milano: Garzanti, 1964.
Trasumanar e organizzar.
 Milano: Garzanti, 1971.
Le poesie.
 Milano: Garzanti, 1975.
La nuova gioventù: poesie friulane 1941–1974.
 Torino: Einaudi, 1975.

Fevràr

Sensa fuèjs a era l'aria,
sgivíns, ledris, moràrs . . .
Si jodèvin lontàns
i borcs sot i mons clars.

Strac di zujà ta l'erba,
in tai dis di Fevràr,
i mi sintavi cà, bagnàt
dal zèil da l'aria verda.

I soj tornàt di estàt.
E, in miès da la ciampagna,
se misteri di fuèjs!
e àins ch'a son passàs!

Adès, eco Fevràr,
sgivíns, ledris, moràrs . . .
Mi sinti cà ta l'erba,
i àins son passàs par nuja.

FEBBRAIO. Senza foglie era l'aria, canali, pianelli, gelsi. Si vedevano lontani i borghi sotto i chiari monti.

Stanco di giocare, sull'erba, nei giorni di Febbraio, mi sedevo qui, bagnato dal gelo dell'aria verde.

Sono tornato di estate. E in mezzo alla campagna, che mistero di foglie! e quanti anni sono passati!

Adesso, ecco Febbraio, canali, pianelli, gelsi . . . Mi siedo qui sull'erba, gli anni sono passati per nulla.

February

The air, canals, plane trees,
mulberries were without leaves . . .
Far away you saw
towns under the clear mountains.

Tired of playing on the grass,
in those February days,
I sat here, bathed
in the green air's chill.

I went back in summer.
And in the middle of the countryside,
what a mystery of leaves!
and so many years have gone by!

Now February is here,
canals, plane trees, mulberries . . .
I sit on the grass,
the years have gone by for nothing.

Il dí da la me muàrt

> . . . se il chicco di grano, caduto in terra, non morirà,
> rimarrà solo, ma se morirà darà molto frutto.
> San Giovanni, *Vangelo* 12.24 (citato da Dostoevskij)

Ta 'na sitàt, Trièst o Udin,
  ju par un viàl di tejs,
di vierta, quan' ch'a múdin
    il colòur li fuejs . . .
      un al à vivút,
cu' la fuàrsa di un zòvin omp
        tal còur dal mond,
e al ghi deva, a chej pucs
òmis ch'al cognosseva, dut.

Po', par amòur po' di chej ch'a erin zuviníns
    cu'l suf tal sorneli
coma lui fin a puc prin
    che tal so ciaf li stelis
      a cambiàssin la so lus—
al vorès vulút dà la so vita par dut
        il mond scunussút,
lui, scunussút, píssul sant,
gragnèl pierdút tal ciamp.

E invessi al à scrit
    poesiis di santitàt
crodínt che cussí
    il còur al doventàs pí grand.

IL GIORNO DELLA MIA MORTE. In una città, Trieste o Udine, per un viale di tigli, quando cambiano colore le foglie . . . uno è vissuto, con la forza di un giovane uomo, nel cuore del mondo, e dava, a quei pochi uomini che conosceva, tutto.

Poi, per amore di quelli che erano ragazzetti, come lui—fino a poco prima che sul suo capo le stelle cambiassero la loro luce—avrebbe voluto dar la sua vita per tutto il mondo sconosciuto—lui, sconosciuto, piccolo santo, granello perduto nel campo.

E invece ha scritto poesie di santità, credendo che cosí il cuore gli si ingrandisse. I giorni sono passati a un lavoro che ha rovinato la santità del suo cuore: il granello non è morto, e lui è restato solo.

The Day of My Death

Except a corn of wheat fall into the ground and die, it
abideth alone: but if it die, it bringeth forth much fruit.

John 12 : 24 (cited by Dostoevsky)

In a city, Trieste or Udine,
    down in a valley of lime trees,
when the leaves
    change color . . .
    a person lived,
with the strength of a young man
            in the heart of the world,
and he gave, to those few men
he knew, everything.

Then, for love of those
    who were boys
like him—until shortly before
    the stars changed
    their light on his head—
he would have wanted to give his life
            for the whole unknown world,
he, unknown, little saint,
seed fallen in the field.

And instead he wrote
    poems of holiness
believing that in this way
    his heart would become larger.

Pier Paolo Pasolini   69

I dis a son passàs
a un lavoru ch'al à ruvinàt
            la santitàt dal so còur:
il gragnèl a no'l è muàrt
e lui al è restàt bessòul.

      The days have passed
in a labor which ruined
            the holiness of his heart:
the seed hasn't died
and he has remained alone.

Le ceneri di Gramsci

I

Non è di maggio questa impura aria
che il buio giardino straniero
fa ancora piú buio, o l'abbaglia

con cieche schiarite . . . questo cielo
di bave sopra gli attici giallini
che in semicerchi immensi fanno velo

alle curve del Tevere, ai turchini
monti del Lazio . . . Spande una mortale
pace, disamorata come i nostri destini,

tra le vecchie muraglie l'autunnale
maggio. In esso c'è il grigiore del mondo,
la fine del decennio in cui ci appare

tra le macerie finito il profondo
e ingenuo sforzo di rifare la vita;
il silenzio, fradicio e infecondo . . .

Tu giovane, in quel maggio in cui l'errore
era ancora vita, in quel maggio italiano
che alla vita aggiungeva almeno ardore,

quanto meno sventato e impuramente sano
dei nostri padri—non padre, ma umile
fratello—già con la tua magra mano

delineavi l'ideale che illumina
(ma non per noi: tu, morto, e noi
morti ugualmente, con te, nell'umido

giardino) questo silenzio. Non puoi,
lo vedi?, che riposare in questo sito
estraneo, ancora confinato. Noia

Gramsci's Ashes

I

It's not of May this impure air
which the dark foreign garden
makes even darker, or dazzles

with blind clearings . . . over yellowish
attics this sky of breezes
which veil the bends of the Tiber

in huge semi-circles, to the deep blue
mountains of Lazio . . . The autumnal May
spreads a deadly peace, indifferent

as our destinies, between the old
walls. The world's grayness is in there,
the closing of the decade when, it seems,

the profound and naive effort to remake life
came to an end in rubble;
the silence, decayed and barren . . .

You were young, in that May when the error
was still life, in that Italian May
which at least added passion to life,

so much less frustrated and impurely sane
than our fathers—not father, but humble
brother—already with your thin hand

you traced the ideal which lights up
(but not for us: you, being dead, and we
just as dead, with you, in the damp

garden) this silence. Don't you see?
You can't do anything but lie in this foreign
place, still imprisoned. Patrician

patrizia ti è intorno. E, sbiadito,
solo ti giunge qualche colpo d'incudine
dalle officine di Testaccio, sopito

nel vespro: tra misere tettoie, nudi
mucchi di latta, ferrivecchi, dove
cantando vizioso un garzone già chiude

la sua giornata, mentre intorno spiove.

II

Tra i due mondi, la tregua, in cui non siamo.
Scelte, dedizioni . . . altro suono non hanno
ormai che questo del giardino gramo

e nobile, in cui caparbio l'inganno
che attutiva la vita resta nella morte.
Nei cerchi dei sarcofaghi non fanno

che mostrare la superstite sorte
di gente laica le laiche iscrizioni
in queste grige pietre, corte

e imponenti. Ancora di passioni
sfrenate senza scandalo son arse
le ossa dei miliardari di nazioni

piú grandi; ronzano, quasi mai scomparse,
le ironie dei principi, dei pederasti,
i cui corpi sono nell'urne sparse

inceneriti e non ancora casti.
Qui il silenzio della morte è fede
di un civile silenzio di uomini rimasti

uomini, di un tedio che nel tedio
del Parco, discreto muta: e la città
che, indifferente, lo confina in mezzo

a tuguri e a chiese, empia nella pietà,
vi perde il suo splendore. La sua terra
grassa di ortiche e di legumi dà

boredom is all around you. And only
a faint anvil blow from Testaccio
workshops, muffled in the evening,

reaches you: among miserable roofs, naked
heaps of tin, scrap iron, where
a boy singing badly brings his day

to a close, as the rain around him ceases.

II

Between the two worlds, the truce, we're not in.
Choices, devotions . . . they have no sound other
than the one in this wretched and noble

garden, where the deceit which mitigated
life stubbornly remains in death.
In the rings of sarcophagi the secular

inscriptions, short and imposing,
on these gray stones do nothing
but show the surviving destinies

of secular people. The bones of thousands
in larger nations are still burnt
with wild passions and without

shame; the ironies of princes, of pederasts
buzz, almost never having vanished,
their burnt bodies are in the scattered

urns and still not chaste.
Here the silence of death is true
to a civil silence of men who have remained

men, to a tedium which changes discreetly
in the tedium of the Park: and the city
which—indifferent, cruel in its compassion,

banishing him in its midst to hovels and churches—
loses its splendor there. Its land
fat with nettles and legumes sends forth

questi magri cipressi, questa nera
umidità che chiazza i muri intorno
a smorti ghirigori di bosso, che la sera

rasserenando spegne in disadorni
sentori d'alga . . . quest'erbetta stenta
e inodora, dove violetta si sprofonda

l'atmosfera, con un brivido di menta,
o fieno marcio, e quieta vi prelude
con diurna malinconia, la spenta

trepidazione della notte. Rude
di clima, dolcissimo di storia, è
tra questi muri il suolo in cui trasuda

altro suolo; questo umido che
ricorda altro umido; e risuonano
—familiari da latitudini e

orizzonti dove inglesi selve coronano
laghi spersi nel cielo, tra praterie
verdi come fosforici biliardi o come

smeraldi: « And O ye Fountains . . . » —le pie
invocazioni . . .

III
Uno straccetto rosso, come quello
arrotolato al collo ai partigiani
e, presso l'urna, sul terreno cereo,

diversamente rossi, due gerani.
Lí tu stai, bandito e con dura eleganza
non cattolica, elencato tra estranei

morti: Le ceneri di Gramsci . . . Tra speranza
e vecchia sfiducia, ti accosto, capitato
per caso in questa magra serra, innanzi

alla tua tomba, al tuo spirito restato
quaggiú tra questi liberi. (O è qualcosa
di diverso, forse, di piú estasiato

these thin cypresses, this dark
dampness which stains the walls round about
with pale arabesques of boxwood, which the clearing

evening extinguishes in homely
scents of seaweed . . . this new grass
stunted and unscented, where violets absorb

the atmosphere, with a shiver of mint,
or rotten hay, and tranquility is foreshadowed
by diurnal melancholy, the extinguished

anxiety of the night. Harsh
in climate, most sweet with history, between
these walls there is a soil from which another

soil oozes: this damp which
recalls another dampness; and they sing out
—relatives from latitudes and

horizons where English woods crown
lakes scattered in the sky, among grasslands
as green as phosphoric billiard tables or as

emeralds: "And O ye Fountains . . ."—the pious
invocations . . .

III

A red strip of cloth, like the one
the partisans put around their necks
and, near the urn, on the pale ground,

a different red, two geraniums.
There you stand, exiled and with a hard
non-Catholic elegance, listed with the foreign

dead: Gramsci's Ashes . . . Between hope
and old distrust, I approach you, having arrived
by chance in this meager greenhouse, before

your tomb, your spirit having remained
down here among these free ones. (Or it's something
different, perhaps, more enraptured

e anche di piú umile, ebbra simbiosi
d'adolescente di sesso con morte . . .)
E, da questo paese in cui non ebbe posa

la tua tensione, sento quale torto
—qui nella quiete delle tombe—e insieme
quale ragione—nell'inquieta sorte

nostra—tu avessi stilando le supreme
pagine nei giorni del tuo assassinio.
Ecco qui ad attestare il seme

non ancora disperso dell'antico dominio,
questi morti attaccati a un possesso
che affonda nei secoli il suo abominio

e la sua grandezza: e insieme, ossesso,
quel vibrare d'incudini, in sordina,
soffocato e accorante—dal dimesso

rione—ad attestarne la fine.
Ed ecco qui me stesso . . . povero, vestito
dei panni che i poveri adocchiano in vetrine

dal rozzo splendore, e che ha smarrito
la sporcizia delle piú sperdute strade,
delle panche dei tram, da cui stranito

è il mio giorno: mentre sempre piú rade
ho di queste vacanze, nel tormento
del mantenermi in vita; e se mi accade

di amare il mondo non è che per violento
e ingenuo amore sensuale
cosí come, confuso adolescente, un tempo

l'odiai, se in esso mi feriva il male
borghese di me borghese: e ora, scisso
—con te—il mondo, oggetto non appare

di rancore e quasi di mistico
disprezzo, la parte che ne ha il potere?
Eppure senza il tuo rigore, sussisto

and also more humble, drunken adolescent
symbiosis of sex and death . . .)
And, from this country where your tension had no

resting place, I feel that guilt
—here in the quiet of the tombs—and that
rationality as well—in our restless

fate—you had drafting the last
pages in the days of your assassination.
Here I am to bear witness to the still

unscattered seed of the old regime,
these dead attached to a property
which sinks its abomination and grandeur through

the centuries: and along with it, obsessed,
that ringing of anvils, in a minor key,
stifled and mournful—from the poor

district—to bear witness to the end.
And here I am myself . . . poor, dressed
in clothes that poor people covet in shopwindows

for their cheap splendor, and who has lost
the filthiness of the most secluded streets,
of the tram benches, from which my day

is alienated: while I have ever more
harbor in this vacation; in the torment
of staying alive; and if it happens

that I love the world it isn't with a violent
and naive sensual love
like the one, embarrassed adolescent, you once

hated, if in it I wounded the bourgeois
sickness of my bourgeois self: and now, the world
—with you—divided, doesn't the part

which power played in it seem an object
of rancor and almost mystical contempt?
However, without your rigor, I keep going

Pier Paolo Pasolini

perché non scelgo. Vivo nel non volere
del tramontato dopoguerra: amando
il mondo che odio—nella sua miseria

sprezzante e perso—per un oscuro scandalo
della coscienza . . .

IV

Lo scandalo del contraddirmi, dell'essere
con te e contro te; con te nel cuore,
in luce, contro te nelle buie viscere;

del mio paterno stato traditore
—nel pensiero, in un'ombra di azione—
mi so ad esso attaccato nel calore

degli istinti, dell'estetica passione;
attratto da una vita proletaria
a te anteriore, è per me religione

la sua allegria, non la millenaria
sua lotta: la sua natura, non la sua
coscienza; è la forza originaria

dell'uomo, che nell'atto s'è perduta,
a darle l'ebbrezza della nostalgia,
una luce poetica: ed altro più

io non so dirne, che non sia
giusto ma non sincero, astratto
amore, non accorante simpatia . . .

Come i poveri povero, mi attacco
come loro a umilianti speranze,
come loro per vivere mi batto

ogni giorno. Ma nella desolante
mia condizione di diseredato,
io possiedo: ed è il più esaltante

dei possessi borghesi, lo stato
più assoluto. Ma come io possiedo la storia,
essa mi possiede; ne sono illuminato:

ma a che serve la luce?

because I don't make choices. I live in the lack of will
of the faded postwar period: loving
the world I hate—in its misery

scornful and lost—through a dark shame
of consciousness . . .

IV

The shame of contradicting myself, of being
for you and against you; for you in my heart,
in the light, against you in the darkness of my guts;

betrayer of my fatherland
—in thought, in a shadow of action—
I know I'm devoted to him in the heat

of instincts, of aesthetic passion;
attracted to a proletarian life
which came before you, it's his joy

which is religion for me, not his ancient
struggle: his nature, not his
consciousness: it's man's primary

strength, which has become lost in the act,
to give them the drunkenness of nostalgia,
a poetic light: and I don't know what to say

beyond that, which may not be
right, but at least not sincere, abstract
love, not grieving sympathy . . .

Poor like the poor, I devote myself
like them to humiliating hopes,
like them I struggle every day

to live. But in grieving
my condition as one of the disinherited,
I possess something: and it is the most exalted

of the bourgeois possessions, the most
absolute state. But as I possess history,
it possesses me; I am illuminated by it:

but whom does the light serve?

V

Non dico l'individuo, il fenomeno
dell'ardore sensuale e sentimentale . . .
altri vizi esso ha, altro è il nome

e la fatalità del suo peccare . . .
Ma in esso impastati quali comuni,
prenatali vizi, e quale

oggettivo peccato! Non sono immuni
gli interni e esterni atti, che lo fanno
incarnato alla vita, da nessuna

delle religioni che nella vita stanno,
ipoteca di morte, istituite
a ingannare la luce, a dar luce all'inganno.

Destinate a esser seppellite
le sue spoglie al Verano, è cattolica
la sua lotta con esse: gesuitiche

le maníe con cui dispone il cuore;
e ancor piú dentro: ha bibliche astuzie
la sua coscienza . . . e ironico ardore

liberale . . . e rozza luce, tra i disgusti
di dandy provinciale, di provinciale
salute . . . Fino alle infime minuzie

in cui sfumano, nel fondo animale,
Autorità e Anarchia . . . Ben protetto
dall'impura virtú e dall'ebbro peccare,

difendendo una ingenuità di ossesso,
e con quale coscienza!, vive l'io: io,
vivo, eludendo la vita, con nel petto

il senso di una vita che sia oblio
accorante, violento . . . Ah come
capisco, muto nel fradicio brusio

del vento, qui dov'è muta Roma,
tra i cipressi stancamente sconvolti,
presso te, l'anima il cui graffito suona

V

I'm not talking about the individual, the phenomenon
of sensual and emotional fervor . . .
he has other vices, his sin

has another fate and name . . .
But in him are mixed such common,
inborn vices, and such

objective sin! The internal and external acts,
which flesh it out into life,
are not immune from any

of the religions which exist in life,
mortgage of death, set up
to deceive the light, to give light to deception.

His remains destined to be
buried in Verano, his battle with them
is Catholic: the manias with which

he handles his heart, Jesuitic;
and even deeper; his consciousness
has political cunning . . . and ironic liberal

fervor . . . and crude light, in the midst of the aversions
of a provincial dandy, of provincial
healthiness . . . Right down to the smallest trivialities

where Authority and Anarchy vanish
in the sensual depths . . . Well protected
from impure virtue and drunken sin,

defending an obsessive naiveté,
and with such a consciousness! the I lives: I,
I live, eluding life, with the feeling in my breast

of a life which might be grieving, violent
oblivion . . . Ah, just as I
understand, silent in the rotten whispering

of the wind, here where Rome is silent,
among the wearily disturbed cypresses,
near you, the soul whose inscription calls out

Shelley . . . Come capisco il vortice
dei sentimenti, il capriccio (greco
nel cuore del patrizio, nordico

villeggiante) che lo inghiottí nel cieco
celeste del Tirreno; la carnale
gioia dell'avventura, estetica

e puerile: mentre prostrata l'Italia
come dentro il ventre di un'enorme
cicala, spalanca bianchi litorali,

sparsi nel Lazio di velate torme
di pini, barocchi, di giallognole
radure di ruchetta, dove dorme

col membro gonfio tra gli stracci un sogno
goethiano, il giovincello ciociaro . . .
Nella Maremma, scuri, di stupende fogne

d'erbasaetta in cui si stampa chiaro
il nocciòlo, pei viottoli che il buttero
della sua gioventú ricolma ignaro.

Ciecamente fragranti nelle asciutte
curve della Versilia, che sul mare
aggrovigliato, cieco, i tersi stucchi,

le tarsie lievi della sua pasquale
campagna interamente umana,
espone, incupita sul Cinquale,

dipanata sotto le torride Apuane,
i blu vitrei sul rosa . . . Di scogli,
frane, sconvolti, come per un panico

di fragranza, nella Riviera, molle,
erta, dove il sole lotta con la brezza
a dar suprema soavità agli olii

del mare . . . E intorno ronza di lietezza
lo sterminato strumento a percussione
del sesso e della luce: cosí avvezza

Shelley . . . Just as I understand the whirlpool
of emotions, the freak accident (Greek
in the patrician's heart, Nordic

vacationer) which swallowed him in the blind
azure of the Tyrrhenian; the carnal
joy of adventure, aesthetic

and childish: while Italy prostrate
as if inside the belly of an enormous
cicada, opens white coasts,

scattered through Lazio with its veiled swarms
of pine trees, baroque, yellowish
clearings of rocket, where a Goethian dream,

the Roman peasant boy, sleeps
with his swollen organ in his rags . . .
In the Maremma, dark, with stupendous drains

of arrow grass where the hazel tree
clearly leaves its imprint, along paths which the cowherd,
unaware, fills to the brim with his youth.

Blindly fragrant in the dry
bends of the Versilia, which—on the
blind, tangled sea, the terse stucco works,

the light inlays of its Easter
countryside, totally human,
—it displays, darkened on the Cinquale,

unraveled under the torrid Apuane,
glassy blues on the rose . . . Of rocks,
landslides, overturned, as in a panic

of fragrance, in the Riviera, soft,
steep, where the sun struggles with the breeze
to give supreme sweetness to the oils

of the sea . . . And round about the enormous
percussion instrument of sex and light
buzzes lightly: Italy is so used

ne è l'Italia che non ne trema, come
morta nella sua vita: gridano caldi
da centinaia di porti il nome

del compagno i giovinetti madidi
nel bruno della faccia, tra la gente
rivierasca, presso orti di cardi,

in luride spiaggette . . .

Mi chiederai tu, morto disadorno,
d'abbandonare questa disperata
passione di essere nel mondo?

VI

Me ne vado, ti lascio nella sera
che, benché triste, cosí dolce scende
per noi viventi, con la luce cerea

che al quartiere in penombra si rapprende.
E lo sommuove. Lo fa piú grande, vuoto,
intorno, e, piú lontano, lo riaccende

di una vita smaniosa che del roco
rotolío dei tram, dei gridi umani,
dialettali, fa un concerto fioco

e assoluto. E senti come in quei lontani
esseri che, in vita, gridano, ridono,
in quei loro veicoli, in quei grami

caseggiati dove si consuma l'infido
ed espansivo dono dell'esistenza—
quella vita non è che un brivido;

corporea, collettiva presenza;
senti il mancare di ogni religione
vera; non vita, ma sopravvivenza

—forse piú lieta della vita—come
d'un popolo di animali, nel cui arcano
orgasmo non ci sia altra passione

to it that it doesn't tremble, like
death in its life: the sweating boys,
soaked in the brownness of their faces,

call out the names of their friends
from hundreds of ports, among the coast
people, near gardens of chard,

in dirty strips of beach . . .

Will you ask me, homely death,
to give up this desperate
passion to be in the world?

VI

I'm going now, I'm leaving you in the evening
which, even though sad, descends so sweetly
for us the living, with its waxen light

that congeals into dusk in the quarter.
And rouses it. It makes it larger, empty,
round about, and, farther away, it catches fire

once again from a restless life which creates
a hoarse and absolute concerto from dialectal
human shouts and the raucous rolling

of the trams. And you feel how in those distant
beings who shout and laugh in life,
in those vehicles of theirs, in those wretched

tenements where one consumes the fickle
and expansive gift of life—
that life is nothing but a shiver;

physical, collective presence;
you feel the absence of every true
religion; not life, but survival

—maybe happier than life—of
a population of animals, in whose mysterious
orgasm there isn't any passion other than

che per l'operare quotidiano:
umile fervore cui dà un senso di festa
l'umile corruzione. Quanto piú è vano

—in questo vuoto della storia, in questa
ronzante pausa in cui la vita tace—
ogni ideale, meglio è manifesta

la stupenda, adusta sensualità
quasi alessandrina, che tutto minia
e impuramente accende, quando qua

nel mondo, qualcosa crolla, e si trascina
il mondo, nella penombra, rientrando
in vuote piazze, in scorate officine . . .

Già si accendono i lumi, costellando
Via Zabaglia, Via Franklin, l'intero
Testaccio, disadorno tra il suo grande

lurido monte, i lungoteveri, il nero
fondale, oltre il fiume, che Monteverde
ammassa o sfuma invisibile sul cielo.

Diademi di lumi che si perdono,
smaglianti, e freddi di tristezza
quasi marina . . . Manca poco alla cena;

brillano i rari autobus del quartiere,
con grappoli d'operai agli sportelli,
e gruppi di militari vanno, senza fretta,

verso il monte che cela in mezzo a sterri
fradici e mucchi secchi d'immondizia
nell'ombra, rintanate zoccolette

che aspettano irose sopra la sporcizia
afrodisiaca: e, non lontano, tra casette
abusive ai margini del monte, o in mezzo

a palazzi, quasi a mondi, dei ragazzi
leggeri come stracci giocano alla brezza
non piú fredda, primaverile; ardenti

that necessary for daily functioning:
humble fervor which gives a sense of festivity
to humble corruption. How much more futile

—in this vacuum of history, in this
buzzing pause in which life remains silent—
is every ideal, clearly better is

the stupendous, sunburnt almost
Alexandrian sensuality, that illuminates
and impurely ignites everything, when there

in the world, something breaks down, and the world
drags itself along, in the twilight, going back
into empty piazzas, depressed workshops . . .

The lights are already coming on, spangling
Via Zabaglia, Via Franklin, the entire
Testaccio, homely between its grand

lurid mountain, the Tiber drives, the black
background, beyond the river, which Monteverde
accumulates or evaporates invisible on the sky.

Diadems of light which fade,
dazzling, and cold with an almost
oceanic sadness . . . He lacks little at dinner;

the rare buses of the quarter gleam,
with bunches of workers at the ticket windows,
and groups of soldiers walk, unhurriedly,

toward the mountain which, at the center of rotten
loose dirt and dry heaps of garbage
in shadow, conceals hidden clumps

that wait irritably on the aphrodisiac
filth: and, not far away, among cottages
which protrude along the edges of the mountain, or among

palaces, almost worlds in themselves, boys
light as rags play in the no longer cold
springtime breeze; burning

di sventatezza giovanile la romanesca
loro sera di maggio scuri adolescenti
fischiano pei marciapiedi, nella festa

vespertina; e scrosciano le saracinesche
dei garages di schianto, gioiosamente,
se il buio ha resa serena la sera,

e in mezzo ai platani di Piazza Testaccio
il vento che cade in tremiti di bufera,
è ben dolce, benché radendo i capellacci

e i tufi del Macello, vi si imbeva
di sangue marcio, e per ogni dove
agiti rifiuti e odore di miseria.

È un brusio la vita, e questi persi
in essa, la perdono serenamente,
se il cuore ne hanno pieno: a godersi

eccoli, miseri, la sera: e potente
in essi, inermi, per essi, il mito
rinasce . . . Ma io, con il cuore cosciente

di chi soltanto nella storia ha vita,
potrò mai piú con pura passione operare,
se so che la nostra storia è finita?

their Roman May evening with youthful
recklessness, dark adolescents
hoot along the sidewalks in the evening

holiday; and the rolling garage doors
roar to a crash, joyously,
if the darkness has made the evening serene,

and in the midst of Piazza Testaccio's plane trees
the wind that falls in the quivers of a gale,
is sweet enough, even though grazing your hair

and Macello tufa; one is overwhelmed there
with rotten blood, and stirred garbage and
smells of poverty all over the place.

Life is a buzzing sound, and these lost
in it, they lose it serenely,
if their hearts are full: here they are

in their poverty, to enjoy the evening: and powerful
in them, vulnerable, for them, the myth
is reborn . . . But will I, with my conscious heart

which has life only in history,
ever again be able to act with pure passion,
if I know that our history has ended?

DA Il pianto della scavatrice

I

Solo l'amare, solo il conoscere
conta, non l'aver amato,
non l'aver conosciuto. Dà angoscia

il vivere di un consumato
amore. L'anima non cresce piú.
Ecco nel calore incantato

della notte che piena quaggiú
tra le curve del fiume e le sopite
visioni della città sparsa di luci,

echeggia ancora di mille vite,
disamore, mistero, e miseria
dei sensi, mi rendono nemiche

le forme del mondo, che fino a ieri
erano la mia ragione d'esistere.
Annoiato, stanco, rincaso, per neri

piazzali di mercati, tristi
strade intorno al porto fluviale,
tra le baracche e i magazzini misti

agli ultimi prati. Lí mortale
è il silenzio: ma giú, a viale Marconi,
alla stazione di Trastevere, appare

ancora dolce la sera. Ai loro rioni,
alle loro borgate, tornano su motori
leggeri—in tuta o coi calzoni

di lavoro, ma spinti da un festivo ardore—
i giovani, coi compagni sui sellini,
ridenti, sporchi. Gli ultimi avventori

FROM The Ditchdigger's Tears

I

Only loving, only knowing
matters, not having loved,
not having known. Living

a spent love brings
anguish. The soul no longer grows.
Here in the enchanted heat

of the night—which flooded down there
between the bends of the river and the drowsy
visions of the city scattered with lights,

it still echoes with a thousand lives—
indifference, mystery, and misery
of the senses, make the forms of the world

into my enemies, which until yesterday
were my reason for living.
Bored, tired, I go home through darkened

market piazzas, sad
streets around the river port,
between stalls and warehouses interspersed

with the last fields. Silence is deadly
there: but farther over, on Viale Marconi,
at the Trastevere Station, the evening

still seems sweet. In their districts,
in their villages, they're returning on motor
scooters—in overalls or work

pants, but driven by a holiday fervor—
the young men, with their pals on the back seats,
smiling, dirty. The last customers

chiacchierano in piedi con voci
alte nella notte, qua e là, ai tavolini
dei locali ancora lucenti e semivuoti.

Stupenda e misera città,
che m'hai insegnato ciò che allegri e feroci
gli uomini imparano bambini,

le piccole cose in cui la grandezza
della vita in pace si scopre, come
andare duri e pronti nella ressa

delle strade, rivolgersi a un altro uomo
senza tremare, non vergognarsi
di guardare il denaro contato

con pigre dita dal fattorino
che suda contro le facciate in corsa
in un colore eterno d'estate;

a difendermi, a offendere, ad avere
il mondo davanti agli occhi e non
soltanto in cuore, a capire

che pochi conoscono le passioni
in cui io sono vissuto:
che non mi sono fraterni, eppure sono

fratelli proprio nell'avere
passioni di uomini
che allegri, inconsci, interi

vivono di esperienze
ignote a me. Stupenda e misera
città che mi hai fatto fare

esperienza di quella vita
ignota: fino a farmi scoprire
ciò che, in ognuno, era il mondo.

Una luna morente nel silenzio,
che di lei vive, sbianca tra violenti
ardori, che miseramente sulla terra

chat on their feet with voices loud in
the night, here and there, at the tables
of the bars still lit up and half-empty.

Stupendous and poor city,
you have taught me what fierce and happy
men teach their children,

the little things in which the grandeur
of a peaceful life is discovered, like
going along in the street crowd ready and

tough, turning around to another man
without trembling, not being ashamed
to look at the money counted out

by the sluggish fingers of the errand boy
who sweats along the façades while running
in an eternal color of summer;

to defend myself, to offend, to keep
the world before my eyes and not
just in my heart, to understand

that few know the passions
in which I have lived:
that they aren't brotherly to me, yet they are

real brothers in having
the passions of men
who happy, conscious, whole,

live experiences
unknown to me. Stupendous and poor
city, you who made me

experience that unknown
life: making me discover
what, in everyone, was the world.

A moon dying in the silence,
from which it lives, bleaches among violent
passions, which—miserably on the mute

muta di vita, coi bei viali, le vecchie
viuzze, senza dar luce abbagliano
e, in tutto il mondo, le riflette

lassú, un po' di calda nuvolagliá.
È la notte piú bella dell'estate.
Trastevere, in un odore di paglia

di vecchie stalle, di svuotate
osterie, non dorme ancora.
Gli angoli bui, le pareti placide

risuonano d'incantati rumori.
Uomini e ragazzi se ne tornano a casa
—sotto festoni di luci ormai sole—

verso i loro vicoli, che intasano
buio e immondizia, con quel passo blando
da cui piú l'anima era invasa

quando veramente amavo, quando
veramente volevo capire.
E, come allora, scompaiono cantando.

II

Povero come un gatto del Colosseo,
vivevo in una borgata tutta calce
e polverone, lontano dalla città

e dalla campagna, stretto ogni giorno
in un autobus rantolante:
e ogni andata, ogni ritorno

era un calvario di sudore e di ansie.
Lunghe camminate in una calda caligine,
lunghi crepuscoli davanti alle carte

ammucchiate sul tavolo, tra strade di fango,
muriccioli, casette bagnate di calce
e senza infissi, con tende per porte . . .

Passavano l'olivaio, lo straccivendolo,
venendo da qualche altra borgata,
con l'impolverata merce che pareva

soil of life, with beautiful avenues, the old
back streets—dazzle without giving light
and, throughout the world, some warm mass

of clouds reflects up there.
It's the most beautiful night of the summer.
Trastevere, with a smell of straw

from old stables, empty
inns, still doesn't sleep.
The dark corners, the peaceful walls

echo with enchanted sounds.
Men and boys go home
—by this time alone under festoons of light—

toward their alleys, which darkness
and garbage choke, with that gentle step
which more fully possessed my soul

when I truly loved, when
I truly wanted to understand.
And, as before, they disappear singing.

II

Poor as a Colosseum cat
I lived in a village all lime
and dust, far from the city

and far from the country, jammed each day
into a rattletrap bus:
and every trip, every return

was a calvary of sweat and nerves.
Long strolls in the hot smog,
long twilights in front of a table

heaped with papers, between streets of mud,
low walls, cottages washed in lime
and without plumbing, with curtains for doors . . .

The olive man and the rag vendor passed through,
coming from some other village,
with dusty stuff that seemed to be

frutto di furto, e una faccia crudele
di giovani invecchiati tra i vizi
di chi ha una madre dura e affamata.

Rinnovato dal mondo nuovo,
libero—una vampa, un fiato
che non so dire, alla realtà

che umile e sporca, confusa e immensa,
brulicava nella meridionale periferia,
dava un senso di serena pietà.

Un'anima in me, che non era solo mia,
una piccola anima in quel mondo sconfinato,
cresceva, nutrita dall'allegria

di chi amava, anche se non riamato.
E tutto si illuminava, a questo amore.
Forse ancora di ragazzo, eroicamente,

e però maturato dall'esperienza
che nasceva ai piedi della storia.
Ero al centro del mondo, in quel mondo

di borgate tristi, beduine,
di gialle praterie sfregate
da un vento sempre senza pace,

venisse dal caldo mare di Fiumicino,
o dall'agro, dove si perdeva
la città fra i tuguri; in quel mondo

che poteva soltanto dominare,
quadrato spettro giallognolo
nella giallognola foschia,

bucato da mille file uguali
di finestre sbarrate, il Penitenziario
tra vecchi campi e sopiti casali.

Le cartacce e la polvere che cieco
il venticello trascinava qua e là,
le povere voci senza eco

the fruit of theft, and had the cruel faces
of youths grown old around the vices
of those who'd had tough and hungry mothers.

Renewed by the new world,
free—a blaze, a breath
I can't explain, by reality

which, humble and dirty, confused and immense,
was seething in those southern outskirts,
and gave me a sense of serene compassion.

A spirit in me, which was not mine alone,
a tiny spirit in this limitless world,
grew, nourished by the happiness

of a man who loved, even if not loved in return.
And everything was illuminated by this love.
Maybe still boyish, heroically boyish,

but also matured by the experience
which was born at the feet of history.
I was at the center of the world, in that world

of sad villages, cheap women,
of yellow plains beaten down
by a wind that was never at peace,

coming from the tidal waters of Fiumicino,
or from the countryside, where the city loses itself
in rambling shacks; in that world

which could only oppress,
a spectral painting in faded yellow
on a faded yellow haze,

pierced by a thousand equal lines
of barred windows, the Penitentiary
in the middle of old fields and dozing farmhouses.

The paper scraps and dust which the blind
gusts of wind dragged here and there,
the thin voices without echo

di donnette venute dai monti
Sabini, dall'Adriatico, e qua
accampate, ormai con torme

di deperiti e duri ragazzini
stridenti nelle canottiere a pezzi,
nei grigi, bruciati calzoncini,

i soli africani, le piogge agitate
che rendevano torrenti di fango
le strade, gli autobus ai capolinea

affondati nel loro angolo
tra un'ultima striscia d'erba bianca
e qualche acido, ardente immondezzaio . . .

era il centro del mondo, com'era
al centro della storia il mio amore
per esso: e in questa

maturità che per essere nascente
era ancora amore, tutto era
per divenire chiaro—era,

chiaro! Quel borgo nudo al vento,
non romano, non meridionale,
non operaio, era la vita

nella sua luce piú attuale:
vita, e luce della vita, piena
nel caos non ancora proletario,

come la vuole il rozzo giornale
della cellula, l'ultimo
sventolio del rotocalco: osso

dell'esistenza quotidiana,
pura, per essere fin troppo
prossima, assoluta per essere

fin troppo miseramente umana.

of peasant women from the Sabine
mountains, from the Adriatic, and
camped here, by this time with hordes

of tough and scrawny kids
screeching in their ragged undershirts
and in their gray, scorched shorts,

the African suns, the downpours
which turned the streets into torrents
of mud, the buses at the end of the line

sunk into their terminal stops
between a final strip of whitish grass
and some seething, acid heap of garbage . . .

this was the center of my world, since it was
the center of the history of my love
for it: and in this

maturity which because it was still being born
was still love, everything was
about to become clear—it was

clear! This village naked in the wind,
not Roman, not Southern,
not working class, it was life

in its most real light:
full life, and the light of life,
in chaos not yet proletarian,

as the crude newspaper of the local
cell, the latest flapping of the lithopress,
would like it to be: the bare bones

of daily existence,
pure, finally becoming too
close, absolute, finally becoming

too miserably human.

Il sole, il sole

Il sole, il sole. Come già in fondo a Marzo,
nei meandri d' Aprile. Corri, mia macchina azzurra,
dove vuoi, per le strade segnate da altro sole,
il Monteverde dei poveri, tra sfondi straripanti
di case a strati, riarse—un pino sull'asfalto—
file di bar e macellerie con sola cliente la luce—
e un altro versante del quartiere, con la luce di striscio—
una strada in salita—il Sanatorio, coi giardini neri—
la Portuense . . .
Al Trullo il sole, come dieci anni fa.
« Fèrmete, a Pa', dà du' carci co' noi! »
Giorgio, Giannetto, Carlo, il Moro,
e gli altri, i pigri venticinquenni,
già un po' stempiati, con qualche annetto di galera;
i fratelli minori di primo pelo, chi
come un lieto pagliaccio dentro i panni del padre,
chi elegante nella sua miseria, gli occhietti
come due foglioline umide colpite dal sole.
La partitella, nel cuore della borgata,
tra i lotti che oltre al sole, e a qualche figura
di sorella, di madre, coi golf dei giorni di lavoro,
non hanno nulla da offrire alla nuova primavera . . .
Correndo Giorgio ha la faccia di Carlo Levi,
divinità propizia, facendo una rovesciata,
Giannetto ha l'ilarità di Moravia, il Moro
rimandando, è Vigorelli, quando s'arrabbia o abbraccia,
e Coen, e Alicata, e Elsa Morante, e i redattori
del Paese sera o dell' Avanti, e Libero Bigiaretti,
giocano con me, tra gli alberetti del Trullo,
chi in difesa, chi all'attacco. Altri,
con Pedalino dal maglione arancione
o Ugo coi blu-jeans dell'anno scorso bianchi sul grembo,
stanno appoggiati lungo il muro color miele della prigione
delle loro case, Benedetti, Debenedetti, Nenni,
Bertolucci con la faccia un po' sbiancata dal sole,
sotto la fiacca falda del cappello, e il dolce ghigno
della certezza sacra degli incerti.

The Sun, the Sun

The sun, the sun. As it already is at the end of March,
the meanderings of April. Run, my blue car,
wherever you want, through streets marked by another sun,
the poor people's Monteverde; among backgrounds overflowing
with houses in layers, parched—a pine tree on the asphalt—
rows of bars and butcher shops with only light as a customer—
and another section of the quarter, with light in stripes—
a rising street—the Sanatorio, with its black gardens—
the Portuense . . .
In Trullo the sun, just as it was ten years ago.
"Hey Pasolini, why don't you stop and play soccer with us?"
Giorgio, Giannetto, Carlo, the Moor,
and the others, lazy twenty-five year olds,
already starting to bald, with some time in jail;
the younger brothers of first puberty, the one
like a happy clown in his father's clothes,
and the other elegant in his poverty, little eyes
like two tiny moist leaves struck by the sun.
The little game, in the heart of the quarter,
in the lots which, other than sun, and some figures
of sister, mother, with work-day sweaters,
have nothing to offer to the new Spring . . .
While running Giorgio looks like Carlo Levi,
gracious divinity, making a back-kick,
Giannetto has Moravia's good humor, the Moor
throwing in, is Vigorelli, when he gets mad or hugs,
and Coen, and Alicata, and Elsa Morante, and the editorial
staff of *Paese Sera* or *Avanti*, and Libero Bigiaretti,
play with me, among the little trees of Trullo,
one defending, the other on the attack. Others,
with Pedalino in the orange sweater
or Ugo with last year's blue jeans white in the lap,
they stand leaning against the honey-colored wall of the prison
of their houses, Benedetti, Debenedetti, Nenni,
Bertolucci with his face a bit bleached out by the sun,
under the sagging brims of their hats, and the soft grin
of the sacred certainty of those who are uncertain.

Pier Paolo Pasolini   103

E accanto ad un dorato immondezzaio c' è Ungaretti, che ride.
E i giovani, che, ai giovani del Trullo, son fratelli,
Siciliano, Dacia, Garboli, Bertolucci figlio; e come Sordello,
disapprovante e innamorato, Citati. E chi è là,
su quella terra con un barattolo rosa e un torsolo giallo?
Baldini e Natalia. E dentro un cortile tagliato
dalla luce come in un caravaggesco senza neri, Longhi,
la Banti, con Gadda e Bassani. Roversi e Leonetti
e Fortini, 'scendono alla fermata dell'autobus,
con i saluti di Contini e non so che sociologo tedesco.
E, con questi, la Bachman, Uwe Johnson, Enzensberger . . .
e un gruppo di angeli londinesi e di fotografi americani
con gli occhi rossi dei nevrotici, e, dalla Russia,
Ciukrai, come venisse alle crociate, e Sartre,
come un sordo, che si fa tradurre, mentre ha capito tutto . . .
Chi ha detto che il Trullo è una borgata abbandonata?
Le grida della quieta partitella, la muta primavera,
non è questa la vera Italia, fuori delle tenebre?

And there, next to a golden garbage heap is Ungaretti, who's smiling.
And the young guys who are the brothers of the young Trullo guys,
Siciliano, Dacia, Garboli, Bertolucci junior; and like Sordello,
disapproving and in love, Citati. And who's there,
on that bit of ground with a pink can and a yellow core?
Baldini and Natalia. And inside a courtyard sliced
by the light as in a Caravaggio painting without blacks, Longhi,
the Banti woman, with Gadda and Bassani. Roversi and Leonetti
and Fortini get off at the bus stop,
with the greetings of Contini and some German sociologist.
And, with these, the Bachman woman, Uwe Johnson, Enzenberger . . .
and a group of angels from London and American photographers
with the red eyes of neurotics, and, from Russia,
Ciukrai, as if he had come to the crusades, and Sartre,
like a deaf man, who makes you translate when he has understood
                                            everything . . .
Who said Trullo is a deserted quarter?
The shouts of the peaceful little game, the silent Spring,
isn't this the true Italy, brought out of the shadows?

Un lungomare . . .

Un lungomare. Lumi bianchi, schiacciati.
Vecchi lastrici, grigi d'umidità tropicale.
Scalette, verso la sabbia
nera; con carte, rifiuti.
Un silenzio come nelle città del Nord.
Ecco ragazzi con blu-jeans color carogna,
e magliucce bianche, aderenti,
sudice, che camminano lungo le spallette
—come algerini condannati a morte.
Qualcuno più lontano nell'ombra calda
contro altre spallette. E il rumore del mare,
che non fa ragionare . . . Dietro il largo
d'un marciapiede scrostato (verso il molo),
dei ragazzi, più giovani; pali; cassette
di legno; una coperta, stesa sulla sabbia nera.
Stanno lì sdraiati; poi due si alzano;
guadagnano l'opposto marciapiede,
lungo luci di bar, con verande di legni marci
(ricordo di Calcutta . . . di Nairobi . . .)
(Una musica da ballo, lontana,
in un bar di hôtel, di cui arriva
solo un zum-zum profondo, e lagni
cocenti di frasi musicali d'oriente).
Entrano in un negozio, tutto aperto . . .
tanto più pieno di luce quanto più povero,
senza un metallo, un vetro . . . Riescono,
ridiscendono. Mangiano, in silenzio,
contro il mare che non si vede,
ciò che hanno comprato. Quello
disteso sulla coperta non si muove; fuma,
con una mano sul grembo. Nessuno
guarda chi li guarda (come gli zingari,
perduti nel loro sogno).

A Sea Promenade

A sea promenade. White lights, crushed.
Old paving stones, gray from tropical dampness.
Steps, down to the black
sand; with papers, trash.
A silence like that of the Northern cities.
Here are boys with blue jeans the color of carrion,
and white, clinging, filthy
sweaters, who walk along the parapets
—like Algerians condemned to death.
Someone farther away in the hot shadow
against other parapets. And the sound of the sea,
which stops you from thinking . . . Behind the open space
of chipped sidewalk (toward the pier),
some younger boys; piles, wooden
boxes; a blanket, also on the black sand.
They're stretched out there; then two get up;
they get to the sidewalk on the opposite side,
along the lights of the bars, with porches of rotten wood
(memory of Calcutta . . . of Nairobi . . .)
(Dancing music, far away,
in a hotel bar, from which only
a deep humming arrives, and bitter
lamentations of oriental musical phrases).
They go into an open air shop . . .
the poorer they are the more full of light,
without metal, without a window . . . They go out again,
go down again. They eat, in silence,
in front of the sea you can't see,
what they've bought. That guy
stretched out on the blanket doesn't move; he smokes,
with a hand on his lap. No one
watches to see who's watching them (like gypsies,
lost in their dream).

L'anello

Da dove il vento, che inanellata pria
viene, e dove finirà—
contro esso ergiamo—di comune accordo tacendolo—
fisicità colme di dolore, abbandonate sul mare;
la gemma che disposa!
Consapevoli della sua provenienza e della sua meta
le Petalis si tenevano dentro
quel loro sapere, tragico, perché in ogni affetto
ritorna il senso che ha per noi la nostra intera vita;
questa cosa che si muove al vento—
senza temperatura esso inanella
corpi e cose e li abbandona,
intento a raggiungere con complicità
quei luoghi che alla vita son tolti;
e la vita ne è svuotata;
l'affetto si veste di sentimenti non suoi;
gli occhi guardano l'invisibile gemma che scorre—
di comune accordo essi nascondono
o manifestano—
le parole si fanno bugiarde; e la complicità
che c'è tra le isole deserte e il vento
viene imitata da una complicità ipocrita
in cui il non detto si finge non conosciuto;
non cesserà il vento col calare della notte;
anzi inanellando bracci di mare abbandonati nel mondo—
la gemma scorre con le sue tante anime riunite
in un solo soffio che passa alto
sfiorando dolori—
ma tu dirai ciò che dicono le ragazze
selvagge, su quel molo umile, abitato da soli due corpi
parole che non hanno nessuna risonanza nella realtà;
nei luoghi dei banditi non s'intende ciò che si dice
a Tragonissi
col sorriso beato della finta sicurezza
e le mani strette sulle ginocchia come le bambine
che nascondono il tremore dietro una furba finta spigliatezza
e le parole gaie hanno radici che, strappandosi

The Ring

Where does she come from, the wind who comes first
adorned with rings, and where will she end—
we rise against it—keeping it quiet by mutual consent—
physicalities brimming with pain, abandoned on the sea;
the jewel she displays!
Conscious of her origin and destination
the Petalis stayed inside
what they knew, tragic, because in every love
the sense our whole life has for us returns;
this thing which moves in the wind—
without temperature it rings
bodies and objects and abandons them,
intent on reaching with complicity
those places which are taken away from life;
and life is emptied of them;
love dresses in feelings not its own;
eyes watch the invisible jewel which glides—
by mutual consent they hide
or reveal—
words become lies; and the complicity
that exists between desert islands and the wind
is imitated by a hypocritical complicity
in which the unsaid pretends to be the unknown;
the wind will not cease with nightfall;
on the contrary, ringing arms of sea abandoned in the world—
the jewel glides with all its spirits reunited
in a single gust which passes high over
skimming pains—
but you will say what rough
girls say, on that humble pier, inhabited only by two bodies
words which have no resonance in reality;
in the bandit lairs you don't mean what you say
to Tragonissi
with the blissful smile of false security
and hands wrapped around knees like children
who hide their trembling behind a cunning false ease
and cheerful words have roots which, getting torn

nella delusione, strappano l'anima dal suo fondo;
così riappare il corso del vento
che dà vita
e va, volontà inanimata, nell'oscurità dell'Egeo.

in delusion, tear the soul from its foundation;
then the path of the wind which gives life
and goes
reappears, inanimate will, in the darkness of the Aegean.

Rocco Scotellaro

Born in 1923 at Tricarico (Matera), Scotellaro died in 1953. He was a labor organizer, unionist, and mayor, as well as a brilliant young poet of the neorealist school. Few Italian writers have been able to portray peasant life with such moving authenticity, and yet without sentimentality. A posthumous collection of his poems, edited by Carlo Levi, won the Premio Viareggio for 1954.

His books of poetry are:

È fatto giorno.
   Milano: Mondadori, 1954.
La poesia di Scotellaro.
   Edited by Franco Fortini. Roma-Matera:
   Basilicata, 1974.

È un ritratto tutto piedi

Nella grotta in fondo al vico
stanno seduti attorno la vecchia morta,
le hanno legate le punte
delle scarpe di suola incerata.
Si vede la faccia lontana sul cuscino
il ventre gonfio di camomilla.
E' un ritratto tutto piedi
da questo vano dove si balla.

The Portrait's All Feet

In the grotto at the end of the alley
they sit around the dead old woman,
they've tied her shoes with oilcloth soles
together at the toes.
You see the distant face on the pillow
her stomach puffed up with camomile.
The portrait's all feet
seen from this place where you dance.

Alla figlia del trainante

Io non so piú viverti accanto
qualcuno mi lega la voce nel petto
sei la figlia del trainante
che mi toglie il respiro sulla bocca.
Perché qui sotto di noi nella stalla
i muli si muovono nel sonno
perché tuo padre sbuffa a noi vicino
e non ancora va alto sul carro
a scacciare le stelle con la frusta.

To the Wagoner's Daughter

I don't know how to live next to you anymore
somebody's tied up my voice in my chest
you're the wagoner's daughter
who takes the breath right out of my mouth.
Because the mules stir in their sleep
here in the stable beneath us
because your father snorts close by
and has yet to go up on his wagon
to drive away the stars with his whip.

Camminano sulle zampe dei gatti

Improvvisa la sera ci ha toccati
me, le mie carte, la pezza di luce
sui mattoni della stanza.
E' tanto imbrunito
che mi sento addosso paura.
Ha ripreso la vita
dei piccoli rumori.
Sono sui tetti le anime
dei morti del vicinato,
camminano sulle zampe dei gatti.

They Walk on Cats' Paws

Suddenly the evening touched us
me, my papers, the piece of light
on the room's brick wall.
It's gotten so dark
I feel fear within me.
The life of small noises
has started up again.
The spirits of the neighborhood dead
are on the rooftops,
they walk on cats' paws.

Rocco Scotellaro

Notte in campagna

Coricati ai piedi dell'olmo,
il cielo ha meno stelle per il vento.
Le Pleiadi sono incenerite,
l'Orsa è sgangherata
sull'orizzonte pulito.

Io voglio te, niente boccali di vino forte
né l'origano e il sale sul pane.
Tu distesa rimani
ferita da non so chi ti ha giocato a sorte.

Country Night

Lie down at the foot of the elm,
the sky has fewer stars because of the wind.
The Pleiades were burned to ashes,
the Bear was smashed
on the clean horizon.

I want you, not gulps of strong wine
or oregano and salt on bread.
You're still lying there
wounded by some guy who shot craps with you.

La luna piena

La luna piena riempie i nostri letti,
camminano i muli a dolci ferri
e i cani rosicchiano gli ossi.
Si sente l'asina nel sottoscala,
i suoi brividi, il suo raschiare.
In un altro sottoscala
dorme mia madre da sessant'anni.

The Full Moon

The full moon fills our beds,
the mules step along quietly
and the dogs gnaw bones.
You hear the donkey in the stairwell,
its shudders, its snore.
In another stairwell
my mother has been sleeping for sixty years.

Gli abigeatari

Chi non dorme nel mare sonnolento
delle ristoppie unite, sulle spoglie
dei calanchi, gli abigeatari.
Scansàti alle tamerici,
sulla sabbia accolta del fiume,
gettano i mantelli neri,
amano il loro mestiere,
uomini sono gli abigeatari,
spiriti pellegrini della notte,
si cibano all'alba.

The Rustlers

The ones who don't sleep in the drowsy sea
of bound wheat chaff, in the washed out
gullies: the rustlers.
Having escaped to the tamarisks,
on the sand gathered by the river,
they throw down black cloaks,
they love their trade,
men are cattle thieves,
wandering spirits of the night,
they eat at dawn.

Giovanni Giudici

Born in Le Grazie (near La Spezia) in 1924, Giudici now lives in Milan and works for Olivetti as a copywriter. Early in his career he was influenced by Eugenio Montale and T. S. Eliot. He also translated books by Ezra Pound, Robert Frost, and John Crowe Ransom. As he developed his characteristic style, Giudici emerged as one of the most important poet-critics of modern industrial society and its problems.

His books of poetry are:

Fiorì d'improvviso.
    Roma: Il Canzoniere, 1953.
La stazione di Pisa.
    Urbino: Istituto Statale d'Arte, 1955.
L'intelligenza col nemico.
    Milano: Scheiwiller, 1957.
L'educazione cattolica.
    Milano: Scheiwiller, 1963.
La vita in versi.
    Milano: Mondadori, 1965.
Autobiologia.
    Milano: Mondadori, 1969.
O Beatrice.
    Milano: Mondadori, 1972.

Mi chiedi cosa vuol dire

Mi chiedi cosa vuol dire
la parola alienazione:
da quando nasci è morire
per vivere in un padrone

che ti vende—è consegnare
ciò che porti—forza, amore,
odio intero—per trovare
sesso, vino, crepacuore.

Vuol dire fuori di te
già essere mentre credi
in te abitare perché
ti scalza il vento a cui cedi.

Puoi resistere, ma un giorno
è un secolo a consumarti:
ciò che dài non fa ritorno
al te stesso da cui parte.

È un'altra vita aspettare,
ma un altro tempo non c'è:
il tempo che sei scompare,
ciò che resta non sei te.

You Ask Me What It Means

You ask me what
the word alienation means:
it is to die from the moment of birth
in order to live in a master

who sells you—it is to hand over
the things you carry—power, love,
total hate—in order to find
sex, wine, a broken heart.

It means to live outside yourself
while you believe you reside within
because the wind you yield to
knocks you off your feet.

You can fight it, but one day
is a century of dissipation:
the things you give away never
return to you, their source.

Waiting is another life,
but there is no other time:
the time which is you disappears,
what remains isn't you at all.

Se sia opportuno trasferirsi in campagna

Gli scherzi, le meraviglie della natura,
i nani, i nidi, le uova con due tuorli,
scoprirli come ti piace—più sicura
ti fanno che un miracolo è possibile,

non qui, ma altrove, dove attraversano
la strada tra bosco e bosco gli scoiattoli,
e la vita è vicina, il tiranno invisibile,
e gli uomini, senza fretta, conversano.

Se sia opportuno trasferirsi in campagna
spesso pensiamo: qui ci tiene il lavoro
che non manca, il civico decoro
di cui partecipiamo, la cuccagna

delle vetrine addobbate, dei cinema aperti,
dello stadio, dei dancing, dell'ippodromo,
di ciò che vuoi pronto a tutte le ore
della voglia improvvisa . . . Ti diverti

anche tu nella festa cittadina,
ma se una sera d'estate troppo calda
l'afa della pianura ti stagna in cuore,
t'affanna il respiro, ti fa meschina,

per noi è facile andare in Brianza,
una mezzora di macchina se è sgombra
la via da chi ritorna, se la danza
dei fari non è cominciata. E l'ombra

è chiara, il giorno ancora non si perde,
la strada sale appena e più lontana
la città più veri si fanno i paesi:
Desio, Seregno e la musica verde

Is It Right to Move to the Country?

The tricks, the wonders of nature,
the dwarfs, nests, eggs with two yolks,
how delighted you are to find them—they help you
believe that a miracle's possible,

not here, but elsewhere, where the squirrels
cross the road from wood to wood,
and life is close by, the tyrant invisible,
and men converse without hurry.

Is it right to move to the country
we often think: the plentiful work
keeps us here, the civic obligation
in which we share, the abundance

of decorated shopwindows, open moviehouses,
the stadium, dances, hippodrome,
whatever you want ready at all hours
at your sudden whim . . . Even you

enjoy yourself at the city festival,
but if on one overhot summer evening
the sultriness of the plain congeals in your heart,
makes you gasp for breath, makes you miserable,

it's easy for us to go to Brianza,
a half an hour by car if the road
is clear of returning traffic, if the dance
of headlights hasn't started. And the shadows

are sharp, the day is not yet lost,
the road rises slightly and the farther away
the city the more real the villages are:
Desio, Seregno and the green music

Giovanni Giudici   131

dei cipressi che avvolgono Inverigo;
bianche, grige, celesti ville, austere
o d'una grazia semplice, un intrigo
settecentesco invitano o severe

meditazioni nel cortile interno:
il sabato una visita in città
e a primavera una festa in giardino
per chi le abiterà nel lungo inverno.

Se sia opportuno trasferirsi in campagna,
se tanto costa pagare la vita,
mangiare, amare, respirare l'aria
viziata dallo smog che fa patita

anche una piccola pianta sul balcone:
qui, dove accampa prigioniera un'orda
per un settimo giorno d'evasione
sei giorni cupa, e su strade a raggera

domenicale un allegro padrone
emula e crede liberarsi—sorda
alla voce di rabbia che ogni sera
strozza un singulto assonnato . . . Se sia

giusto appassire qui tutta la vita
in attesa di trasformarla oppure
rassegnarsi ai perduti, dar partita
vinta ai traffici, al corso degli onori,

e scegliere il treno del mattino,
la corriera alle sette da Bosisio
sulle rive del vago Eupili—fuori
la notte almeno da questa città,

dove un me stesso a un tavolo, a uno scranno
servile insegue vana libertà
di giorno in giorno rinviata, e spera
ritrovare per sé l'ultima luce dell'anno

l'ultimo anno di vita con forza intera . . .

of the cypress which wind around Inverigo;
white, gray, sky blue villas, austere
or with a simple grace, they invite
an eighteenth century intrigue or stern

meditations in the inner courtyard:
on Saturday a visit to the city
and in Spring a garden party
for those who will live in them through the long winter.

Is it right to move to the country,
if it costs so much to make a living,
to eat, make love, breathe air
ruined by smog which has made even

a small plant on the balcony suffer:
here, where an imprisoned horde camps
six days in gloom for a seventh day
of escape, and on the roads for a

Sunday spin a happy boss
conforms and thinks he's getting away—deaf
to the angry voice which strangles
a drowsy sob every evening . . . Is it

right to wither your whole life here
waiting to change it or instead
resign yourself to the losses, give up
on the traffic, the procession of honors,

and take a train in the morning,
the seven o'clock bus from Bosisio
on the shores of the graceful Eupili—to spend
at least the night outside this city,

where one part of me at a table, on a lowly
bench pursues vain freedom
postponed from one day to the next, and hopes
to find the year's last light for himself again

the last year of life with full force . . .

Giovanni Giudici   133

Sarà opportuno trasferirsi in campagna,
una piú salubre aria c'invita:
questo chiedono il tempo, le migliori
condizioni che allietano la vita,

il progresso, i miracoli, i conforti
della tecnica nostri servitori,
questo l'industria dei semplici cuori
che ci apparecchia le felici morti

delle poche letture, pochi amici,
pochi giuochi serali, pochi storti
ribelli umori . . . Cosí ci vuole il mondo
che invecchia delle nostre vecchie sorti:

e anch'io, vinto pudore, mi dispongo
nei numeri d'attente previsioni,
coltivo fiori, inchiodo legni, rispondo
con lagrime a elette commozioni

pubbliche—e sono là, cosí diverso,
chiudo un cancello, sciolgo un cane
guardia al piccolo mondo d'un disperso
villino nella fitta schiera uguale

dei simili, depreco il tempo avverso:

« quello che sono è bene, il resto è male »
penso nel coro—e un'altra libertà
benedico, riposo domenicale.

. . .

Qui di me si perdeva la miglior parte,
che maledice e spacca la noce tra i denti,
e a quel minuscolo crac ancora prossima spera
la fine di ormai remoti stenti.

It will be right to move to the country,
a healthier air invites us:
this they ask of the time, the best
conditions which make life happy,

progress, miracles, the comforts
of technology our servants,
this the industry of simple hearts
which prepare us for the happy deaths

of a little reading, a few friends,
a little evening entertainment, a few twisted
rebellious humors . . . This is how it wants us,
the world which ages with our old destinies:

and even I, having overcome reserve, prepare myself
with a number of careful provisions,
I grow flowers, I nail boards, I respond
with tears to selected public

upheavals—and I am there, so different,
I close a gate, I unleash a watchdog
in the small world of a cottage
lost in a crowded group

of similar ones, I complain about the bad times:

"what I am is good, the rest are bad"
I think in the chorus—and I bless
another freedom, Sunday rest.

. . .

Here the better part of me was lost,
which curses and breaks the walnut in his teeth,
and at that tiny crack he hopes even closer
the end of privations by now remote.

Giovanni Giudici   135

Epigramma romano

Tutto ignorate come a Weimar Goethe:
ma troppo grande è Roma per essere Weimar
e voi (perchè dirlo?) troppo piccoli siete.

Potevano ben dire la grassa redditiera,
a Weimar, lo stalliere, la guardia, la ragazza:
'Siamo al centro del mondo,' perchè con essi c'era
uno che senza il mondo poteva vivere.

Ma noi siamo noi soli nel mezzo d'una piazza.

Roman Epigram

Like Goethe at Weimar you ignore everything:
but Rome's too big to be Weimar
and you're (why even say it?) too small.

The fat landlady, the stable boy, the guard,
the girl at Weimar could very well say:
"We're at the center of the world," because there was
a man with them who could live without the world.

But we're only ourselves in the middle of a piazza.

Paolo Volponi

Born in Urbino in 1924, Volponi now lives in Ivrea. He received a degree in law from the University of Urbino. Currently he works for Olivetti. Volponi's poetry is characterized by a studied simplicity; there is seldom the immediate and shocking impact of his avant-garde contemporaries. However, there are deep and complex resonances in his poems. Since the publication of his last book of poetry, Volponi has concentrated on writing fiction. Volponi won the Premio Carducci in 1954 and the Premio Viareggio in 1960.

His books of poetry are:

Il ramarro.
>   Urbino: Istituto Statale d'Arte, 1948.
L'antica moneta.
>   Firenze: Vallecchi, 1955.
Le porte dell'Appennino.
>   Milano: Feltrinelli, 1960.

La cometa

Tu sei donna
d'arioso giardino
e di terrazza,
donna del mio paese
affacciata ai torrioni.
Gli uccelli recano i tuoi occhi
nel becco alle vallate,
come il vento di maggio
che ti ruba un nastro.
Per te colorata cometa
io svolgo la mia anima
in filo.

The Comet

You are the lady
of airy garden
and terrace,
lady of my birthplace
studded with castles.
The birds carry your eyes
to the valleys in their beaks,
like the May wind
which steals a ribbon from you.
For you, blushing comet,
I unravel my soul
like a spool of thread.

Paolo Volponi

Altra voce

1

Seppure è triste
il canto della fanciulla
che scaccia le cornacchie
dal dorso dei bovi,
facile è restare
sugli orli delle grotte,
cedere ai richiami del falco,
illudersi di scoprire
il covaccio delle volpi;
la lunga neve
m'indulge a una capanna,
ai dolci sapori
di ghiande e di castagne.
Oracoli porta il letargo.

2

Quando a specchio della luna
tra gli odorosi cespugli
filtrerà la corrente
e colma sarà
l'orbita dei fossi
e il mio cavallo
vagherà libero;

quando affioreranno i cimiteri
d'antiche guerre ai valichi
e infido alla foce
sarà il canneto;

e tra i sassi
trepiderà l'allodola
nuda e chiara
come un seno di sposa,

Another Voice

1

Even if the song
of the girl who drives
the crows from the backs
of the oxen is sad,
it's easy to linger
at the rims of the caves,
to yield to the falcon's calls,
to deceive yourself that you've found
the wolves' den;
the long snow
treats me to a cabin,
to the sweet smells
of acorns and chestnuts.
Lethargy brings oracles.

2

When in the moon's mirror
the stream filters
through the fragrant bushes
and the ring of trenches
is full
and my horse
wanders freely;

when the graveyards of ancient wars
surface at the mountain passes
and the canebrake turns traitor
at the stream's mouth;

and the skylark trembles
among the stones
naked and bright
as the breast of a bride,

nel mio diletto campo
altra voce avrà
come un canto di coturnice
la fanciulla dei bovi.

in my beloved field
the oxherd girl
will have another voice—
like a quail song.

Stanze romane

Come le donne
in vicolo del Lupo
si chiamano con nomi di città
hanno piazze
e sguardi di fontane.
Portano bende
d'aceto sulla fronte,
questi antichi guerrieri
amputati sui banchi d'osteria.

A Mario dei Fiori,
capellute,
cingono collane d'oro;
il seno e la cintura
dolci come ginestre.
L'uomo è un fante di giuoco
con la coppa sulla spalla,
il volto nascosto.

Un cavaliere bussa
alla Fontanella Borghese
ma la sua muta di cani
disperde le giovani
tutte di vene celesti.

Le meretrici di via Fontanella
giacciono come sponde
e sulla loro sabbia
s'accovaccia
l'anatra colorata.

Tristi canzoni
a Capo le Case
hanno le spose dei marinai
con le terrazze del Sud
e gli spari dei finanzieri.

Roman Rooms

Since the women
in the Vicolo del Lupo
call themselves by city names
they have piazzas
and views of fountains.
They wear bands
of vinegar on their foreheads,
these ancient amputee
warriors on tavern benches.

At Mario dei Fiori,
long-haired,
golden necklaces encircle;
the breasts and waist
sweet like juniper.
The man is a jack
with a cup on his shoulder,
his face hidden.

A knight knocks
at the Fontanella Borghese
but his pack of dogs
disperses the young women
all of celestial blood.

The prostitutes of Via Fontanella
lie like banks
and on their sand
the colored duck
nestles.

The sailors' wives
at Capo le Case
have sad songs
with southern terraces
and gunshots from customs officials.

Paolo Volponi   147

A via del Pellegrino
materne
allattano i figli dietro le porte
e chiedono ai carrettieri
notizie dei paesi.

Quante gli storni
a Torre Argentina,
in via dei Giubbonari
e via de' Coronari
ricche di denti,
portano l'uomo in barca
ma con le mani
toccano la sponda fresca del fiume
e con gli occhi
seguono gli alberi
vestiti da soldati.

Agli Avignonesi
hanno viso di tabacco
e ventre di marengo;
cantano canzoni
mai udite per le strade
scendendo dalla scala
col tacco d'oro.

At Via del Pellegrino
motherly
they nurse children behind doors
and ask cart-haulers
for news from the villages.

So many, starlings
at Torre Argentina,
in Via dei Giubbonari
and Via de' Coronari
rich with teeth,
they lie under men in boats
but with their hands
they touch the fresh riverbank
and with their eyes
they follow the trees
dressed like soldiers.

On the Avignonesi
they have tobacco faces
and Marengan vaginas;
they sing songs
never heard on the streets
coming down the stairs
on golden heels.

Paolo Volponi   149

Le mura di Urbino

La nemica figura che mi resta,
l'immagine di Urbino
che io non posso fuggire,
la sua crudele festa,
quieta tra le mie ire.

Questo dovrei lasciare
se io avessi l'ardire
di lasciare le mie care
piaghe guarire.

Lasciare questo vento collinare
che piega il grano e l'oliva,
che porta sbuffi di mare
tra l'arenaria viva.

Lasciare questa luna tardiva
sul diamante degli edifici,
questa bianca saliva
su tutte le terrazze,
dove amici e ragazze
stendono le soffici tele
del loro amore infedele.

Lasciare il caldo respiro
del sole sulle mura,
la lunga tortura delle case,
lo stesso temporale
che ritorna da anni,
pur se la vita non è uguale nel giro
e s'abbandona ogni ora.

Antica sulle mura
è la mia casa;
immobile e non sicura
sembra veleggiare
tra le nuvole come riviere

The Walls of Urbino

The hostile picture which stays with me,
the image of Urbino
that I cannot escape,
its cruel festival,
calms down between my rages.

I would let this go
if I had the nerve
to let my dear
wounds heal.

To let this wind which bends the grain
and the olive, which carries sprinkles
from the sea to the living sandstone,
disperse on the hills.

To leave this backward moon
on the diamond of the buildings,
this white saliva
on all the terraces,
where friends and young girls
lay the soft threads
of their unfaithful love.

To leave the hot breath
of the sun on the walls,
the long torture of the houses,
the same thunderstorm
which has returned for years,
even if life isn't equal in its turning
and loses heart every hour.

My house stands
ancient on the walls;
motionless and insecure
it seems to sail
through the clouds like coasts

Paolo Volponi   151

nel fluviale nembo
delle selvagge sere.

Il cielo a forma di grembo
divora la città;
allora si sente morire
ogni cosa d'intorno
e ognuno sta per sortire
dal proprio cuore.

È il vento, al confine del giorno,
che mormora tra i colli,
che a me di fronte sgombra la campagna
o con la nera ombra delle nubi
la fa sparire;
che con me giuoca
fingendo di fuggire
e poi con aria fioca
torna a imbiancare i colli,
il vento d'incerta natura
che passa come un ragazzo
dietro le siepi o le mura,
senza niente,
come chi si allontani d'un passo
o per sempre;
niente più d'un rimorso
e d'un sorso d'acqua nei campi.

La città trema nel cuore dei suoi cortili,
apre il suo dorso alle congiure vili
del tempo, e giace morente
sopra di noi.

Allora i giardini pensili
piegano l'ombra ostile dei pini
verso quel punto dell'orizzonte,
nuovo ogni sera,
dove io non giungerò mai
libero dai miei cattivi pensieri,
dalla sorte nemica
che il mio amore castiga.

in the fluvial storm
of savage nights.

The womb-shaped sky
devours the city;
then you hear everything
around you die
and everyone is ready to leave
his own heart.

It's the wind, at the end of the day,
that murmurs in the hills,
that clears the countryside before me
or with the black shadow of clouds
makes it disappear;
that plays with me
pretending to run away
and then returns with a whistling
draught to whiten the hills,
the unpredictable wind
which passes like a boy
behind bushes or walls,
without anything,
like one who went away for a moment
or forever;
nothing more than a feeling of remorse
and a gulp of water in the fields.

The city trembles in the heart of its courtyards,
it opens its back to time's cowardly
plots, and it lies dying
on top of us.

The roof-gardens
bend the hostile shadows of the pines
toward that point on the horizon,
new every night,
where I will never arrive
free from my evil thoughts,
from the hostile fate
that my love inflicts on me.

Paolo Volponi

Domani è già marzo . . .

Domani è già marzo e la strada
scopre tra i frutteti il petto della contrada.
A marzo il contadino
riordina gli attrezzi e libera i confini.
A marzo i contadini
scendono verso i paesi;
si fermano nelle piazze mercatali
davanti alle osterie, ai forni, ai falegnami
che odorano sotto i portali di pietra fiorita,
davanti ai negozi di ferramenta,
davanti a tutti gli spacci
con un sentore d'acqua muffita.
I vecchi si fermano alle porte;
i giovani salgono le vie cittadine.
Ormai li mischia aprile,
mese senza paura,
e salgono insieme i mezzadri e i garzoni,
i mietitori, i braccianti, i legnaioli,
i muratori di campagna, gli innestatori,
gli scavatori di pozzi e di vigna,
i cercatori d'acqua e i cacciatori.
Il giorno nella città non ha paura,
stretto tra le mura è sempre luminoso,
e sempre vive di qualche cosa, ora per ora;
preso alla mattina presto nei mercati,
nella profonda luce che rispecchiano
le facciate nobiliari o i porticati;
guidato per le vie al suono dei selciati
sino ai vertici gentili dei rioni;
alzato a mezzogiorno in fronte alle chiese
su tutte le piazze, una sopra l'altra,
di mattone o di pietra;
non è vinto dalla foglia incerta,
non predato dalle fratte di spini,
non morto nella morte degli insetti;
non arato, seminato, sarchiato,
faticato ora per ora,

Tomorrow Is March Already . . .

Tomorrow is March already and the road
between the orchards reveals the bosom of the countryside.
In March the farmer
cleans up his tools and clears the boundaries.
In March the farmers
come down to the towns;
they stop in the market squares
in front of taverns, at bakeries, carpenter shops
that smell of flowering stone under their doorways,
in front of hardware stores,
in front of all the shops
with a scent of musty water.
The old people stop at the doors;
the young ones go up the streets of the town.
Now April mixes them,
month without fear,
and sharecroppers and apprentices go up together,
reapers, farm-hands, woodcutters,
country bricklayers, grafters,
the diggers of wells and vineyards,
the water-searchers and the hunters.
The day in town holds no fear,
packed between the walls it's always light,
and something's always happening, hour after hour;
taken in the markets in the early morning,
in the deep light which reflects
the noble façades or arcades;
guided through the streets by the pavement's sound
to the gentle summits of the quarters;
raised at noon in front of the churches,
on all the piazzas, one on top of another,
in brick and stone;
it isn't conquered by the uncertain leaf,
nor plundered by the thickets of thorns,
nor does it die an insect's death;
nor is it plowed, seeded, hoed,
laboriously worked hour after hour,

dalla mattina alla sera.
Il giorno gira nella città il suo dolce sole,
muove il ventaglio alto delle nubi,
e chiama dal mare l'amorosa luce serale
che si stende su tutte le terrazze,
sui giardini pensili, sull'arcate
dalle quali soffia l'Appennino.
Si congiunge alla notte per le strade,
quando vicino s'odono risate di ragazze
e verso i torrioni e voci da tutti i portoni.

from morning to evening.
The day moves its sweet sunshine through the city,
moves the high wind of the clouds,
and calls from the sea the amorous evening light
which spreads out on all the terraces,
on the roof-gardens, on the archways
through which the Apennine wind blows.
At night they come together on the streets,
when close by you hear the laughter of girls
from the direction of the towers, and voices from all the doorways.

Paolo Volponi

La fine dell'estate

Muoiono stasera
gl'insetti che recavano lampade
alle mie chiare notti
lungo il fiume;
ahimè che li uccide
in agonia segreta tra il fogliame
il primo ritornello di vento.

Cosí lo scorpione rubino
che il tetano d'agosto
rizzava sulla pietra
è un gioiello appannato
e il grillo porta la notte
d'innumeri stelle graffita
al meriggio della cicala.

La fine dell'estate
mi sorprende antico;
come la roccia immobile
sopporto il trapasso,
essa ch'altro non muta
che un occhio di muschio
e un'ombra di colore.
Sul mio sguardo
fisso nella corrente
come per uno scoglio
l'acqua s'increspa;
(vi dondola un ragno
l'ultime acrobazie).

Ogni istante in silenzio
nel cielo si completa
un astro dalla coda velenosa.

Ormai i guardiani delle vigne
preparano per me
i loro colpi di sale.

Summer's End

This evening
the insects who've brought lamps
to my clear nights along the river
are dying;
ah, the first refrain of wind
kills them in the foliage
in secret agony.

Thus the ruby scorpion
that the tetanus of August
raised on the rock
is a tarnished jewel
and the cricket carries the night
of innumerable stars scratched
on the cicada's back.

Summer's end
catches me ancient;
like the motionless rock
I endure the passing,
in which nothing changes
but a bit of moss
and a shadow of color.
The water ripples
around my fixed
glance in the current
as if around a rock;
(a spider dangles
its final acrobatics there).

Every instant
in the sky's silence
adds a star to the venomous tail.

Now the vine-tenders
prepare their volleys
of wit for me.

Paolo Volponi

Cesare Vivaldi

Born in Imperia in 1925, Vivaldi now lives in
Rome. He is one of the few modern Italian
poets who has attempted an historical epic, as
he did in *Ode all'Europa*. In his early career,
Vivaldi was associated with the neorealists,
but in later periods he became involved with
experimentation in language and technique.
He was part of the "Gruppo '63." He has
written many poems in Ligurian dialect, and
they are among the most successful of modern Italian dialectal poems.

His books of poetry are:

I porti.
    Modena: Guanda, 1945.
Otto poesie nel dialetto ligure di Imperia.
    Roma: Il Canzoniere, 1951.
Il cuore di una volta.
    Caltanissetta: Sciascia, 1956.
Dialogo con l'ombra.
    Roma: Grafica, 1960.
Poesie liguri.
    Milano: Rizzoli, 1964.
Dettagli.
    Milano: Rizzoli, 1964.
A caldi occhi, 1964–1972.
    Milano: All'insegna del pesce d'oro,
    1973.
Lo zodiaco.
    Modena: Cooperativa tipografi, 1973.
Una mano di bianco.
    Milano: Guanda, 1978.

Madre non dimentico

A nun me sun scurdàu de ti, che ti me
disgevi, o màe, che « u ventu u nasceva
da e muntagne e u caàva in t'e maíne,
cu u ventu ti sei nasciüu ti ». Fasgeva

freidu, in ütubre frèidu: u gh'èa in fine-
strun darè au letu, e u ventu u ghe batteva,
e sensa fin nívue gianche. Dimme
se au ventu ti sei morta ti! Cureva

troppu u me cö cu u ventu. In t'e maíne
trövu a to faccia, e au so che ti sei morta.
Trövu u to cö duse e amaru in te st'agri

àsgini d'üga, e toe man sensa fin
in t'e nívue, e (so che ti sei morta)
in t'u me cö u diamante d'ina lagrima.

Non mi sono dimenticato di te, che mi diveci, o madre, che « il vento nasceva dalle
montagne e calava nelle marine, col vento sei nato tu ». Faceva

freddo, un ottobre freddo: c'era un finestrone dietro al letto, e il vento ci batteva, e senza
fine nuvole bianche. Dimmi se al vento sei morta tu! Correva

troppo il mio cuore col vento. Nelle marine trovo la tua faccia, e lo so che sei morta.
Trovo il tuo cuore dolce e amaro in questi agri

acini d'uva, le tue mani senza fine nelle nuvole, e (so che sei morta) nel mio cuore il
diamante d'una lagrima.

Mother, I Won't Forget

Mother, I haven't forgotten you who told
me that "the wind was born
in the mountains and came down to the sea;
you were born with the wind." It was

cold, a cold October: there was a big
window behind the bed, and the wind battered it,
and endless white clouds. Tell me
if you died in the wind! My heart

has run with the wind too much. I find your face
in the sea and I know that you are dead.
I find your heart, bitter and sweet, in these bitter

grape seeds, and your endless hands
in the clouds, and (I know you are dead)
the diamond of a teardrop in my heart.

Cesare Vivaldi

A Giovanni

U ma u l'è verde cume ti u dipinzi,
e au mattin, s'u l'è nettu, u gh'è in te l'aia
fresca u criu d'i fiöi che i fan brinsi,
e i pan vöi, gaggiài da a vusge ciàia.

Ti hai rasgiùn ti: e i pesci, e e barche e e cà,
e ancúa a fatiga che a turmenta i scöggi,
u ventu d'a misèia u l'ha cargài
de curúi forti che i te sciàppa i öggi.

U to mundu u l'è onestu, nettu. A sèia
i omi i sta in riga cu ina canna in man,
ün fiö u i mia mangiandu ina mèia,
e a barca d'u carbún passa luntan.

Il mare è verde come lo dipingi, e al mattino, se è limpido, c'è nell'aria fresca il grido dei ragazzi che fan salti, e sembrano voli, gabbiani dalla voce chiara.

Hai ragione tu: e i pesci, e le barche, e le case, e ancora la fatica che tormenta gli scogli, il vento della miseria li ha caricati di colori forti che ti spaccano gli occhi.

Il tuo mondo è onesto, pulito. A sera gli uomini stanno in fila con una canna in mano, un ragazzo li guarda mangiando una mela, e la barca del carbone passa lontano.

To Giovanni

The sea is as green as you paint it,
and in the morning, if the weather's nice,
there are shouts of leaping boys in the cool air,
and they seem to fly, seagulls with clear voices.

You're right: the fish, the boats, the houses,
and even the strain which torments the rocks,
the wind of misery that has filled them
with bright colors which cleave your eyes.

Your world is honest, clean. In the evening
the men sit in a row with canes in hand,
a boy eating an apple watches them,
and a coal boat passes in the distance.

Cesare Vivaldi   165

Settembre

Otto settembre: odo i treni fischiare
a tarda notte sulla ferrovia.
Io me ne stavo a guardarli passare

nell'aria tremante di spari fiochi,
ma avrei voluto fuggirmene via,
via, sotto il cielo stellato di fuochi.

September

September eighth: I hear trains whistling
late at night on the tracks.
I stood there watching them pass by

in the air trembling with faint gunshots,
but I would have liked to run away,
far away, under the sky sprinkled with fire.

Viaggio

Il « Cavaliere d'Occidente » oscilla
nella stanza deserta, screpolato
dal vento. E c'è una luna alta e veloce
come lassú qualcuno
lungo i greti stellari desse sprone
a un Vegliantino di neve e ricordi.

Ulisse cieco d'affanni, io, solo
dalle rotte polari
queste figure strappo alla memoria.
S'accavallano i mondi intorno a me,
astri s'accendono e spengono. Brontola
squallido, lontanissimo
un mare ostile, cupo di cipressi
lividi e di compassi
aperti e chiusi in alternanza, i flutti
accidiosi e puntuti:
e l'aereonave scivola leggera
dove un fiume galattico
di mostri e cani di fuoco m'insegue,
alzando lingue che mute ricadono
nell'oscuro groviglio d'onde herziane
che senz'orma precede
quest'ultimo avamposto sull'abisso.

                    · · ·

L'universo lavora
per segni colorati.
Pesa, trigonometrica
come fonda lavagna, questa notte
senza confini, fitta di pianeti
ronzanti e vitree stelle che si muovono
con movimenti oliati
e secchi.

Voyage

The "Cavaliere d'Occidente" wavers
in the deserted room, cracked
by the wind. And there is a moon high and swift
as if someone up there
along the stellar gravel-bed were spurring on
a Vegliantino of snow and memories.

Ulysses blind from worries, alone
along the polar route,
I tear these figures from my memory.
The worlds around me overlap,
stars light up and go out. Bleak,
in the far distance, a hostile sea
grumbles, gloomy with pale
cypresses and compasses
alternately open and closed, the waves
indolent and pointed:
and the flying ship skims along smoothly
where a galactic river
of monsters and fire dogs follows me,
raising tongues which fall mute again
in the dark tangle of Hertzian waves
that this last outpost on the abyss
precedes without a trace.

                    . . .

The universe struggles
for colored signs.
This limitless night,
trigonometric like a deep blackboard,
weighs heavily, shower of hovering
planets and glass stars which move
with oiled and dry
motions.

Solo, rinchiuso in questo
duro guscio, argonauta
dell'avvenire e naufrago
del passato, ben poche cose ho preso
da sbrigativo viaggiatore,
Il remo che con me porto, votato
nella speranza a farsi ventilabro,
sprigiona dal suo legno
l'odore agro dei boschi;
cosí la cella misera risuona
d'uno stormire d'alberi, d'un canto
magro di pettirosso.

E il sale sterile, l'arido amico
delle greggi, che verso
parcamente nel cibo,
chiama il porto spinoso
di molte voci, di lumi, di battiti,
con il giorno che cade
in tonfi d'acque, e reti, e bastimenti
oltre l'ultimo molo
avviati, tra rade
luci che forano il nebbione: armenti
di rugiade e di fumi.

Alone, enclosed in this
hard shell, argonaut
of the future and shipwrecked sailor
of the past, I have taken few things
from the hasty traveler.
The oar I carry with me, consecrated
in the hope of becoming a winnowing fan,
gives off from its wood
the sour odor of the forest;
thus the poor cell echoes
with the rustling of trees, with the thin
song of the robin redbreast.

And sterile salt, the dry friend
of the herds, that I pour
sparingly on food,
calls the spiny port
of many voices, lights, heartbeats,
with the day which ends
in splashes of water, nets, merchant ships
beyond the last thriving
pier, among harbors
lights which pierce the thick fog: herds
of dew and vapors.

Il muro

1

Il muro calcinato si copre di rovi. A perdita d'occhi è solo muro rovente di sole: screpolato da miliardi di zampe di lucertole in corsa. Fiutato sa solo d'intonaco cotto e di parietarie appassite.

Murato in uno spazio immenso. Sigillato nel tempo. Il muro sta: resiste.

La bianca pozza di lacrime non lo corrode. Hallalí hallalí. Trapassa una muta corsiva di cani sul fianco del colle che odora di lepre.

Si schiaccia contro il muro. Piano rientra nell'ombra: nell'orbita. Macchie abrasioni graffiti nel silenzio rovente.

2

Nell'immenso tempo resiste. Il muro sta. Murato: sigillato nello spazio.

Hallalí hallalí. Bianca muta di cani trapassa in corsiva pozza di lagrime sul fianco del colle che l'odore di lepre non corrode.

Piano rientra nel muro. Si schiaccia nel silenzio rovente: nell'orbita. Macchie graffiti abrasioni dell'ombra.

Solo intonaco cotto: il muro rovente di rovi a perdita d'occhi si copre di sole. Solo fiutato da parietarie lucertole: calcinato da miliardi di corse di zampe appassite.

3

Odore di bianca lepre non corrode la muta dei cani. Trapassa una pozza di lagrime sul fianco corsivo del colle. Hallalí hallalí.

Piano si schiaccia nell'orbita: nel silenzio rovente dell'ombra del muro. Rientra in graffiti macchie abrasioni.

Cotto muro di rovi. Intonaco solo rovente d'occhi appassiti di lucertole: fiutato da miliardi di parietarie calcinate dal sole. Screpolato in perdita di zampe.

Muro murato in un immenso muro. Resiste: sta sigillato nello spazio il tempo.

The Wall

1

The whitewashed wall is covered with blackberries. As far as the eye can see it's only wall red-hot from the sun: cracked by the feet of a billion lizards. Sniffed it knows only of baked plaster and of withered pellitory.

Walled in an immense space. Sealed in time. The wall stands: it endures.

The white pool of tears doesn't corrode it. Tirraa tirraa. A running pack of hounds passes on the flank of the hill which smells of jackrabbit.

It gets crushed against the wall. Slowly it returns to shadow: in the orbit. Stains scrapes graffiti in the red-hot silence.

2

In immense time it endures. The wall stands. Walled in: sealed in space.

Tirraa tirraa. White pack of hounds passes through running pool of tears on the flank of the hill that the smell of jackrabbits doesn't corrode.

Slowly it returns into the wall. It gets crushed in the red-hot silence: in the orbit. Stains graffiti scrapes of the shadow.

Only baked plaster: the red-hot wall of blackberries as far as the eye can see is covered with sun. Only sniffed by pellitory lizards: whitewashed by billions of runs by withered feet.

3

Smell of white jackrabbit doesn't corrode the pack of hounds. A pool of tears passes on the running flank of the hill. Tirraa tirraa.

Slowly it gets crushed in the orbit: in the red-hot silence of the wall's shadow. It returns into graffiti stains scrapes.

Baked wall of blackberries. Plaster only red-hot with withered lizard eyes: sniffed by billions of pellitory whitewashed by the sun. Cracked by the loss of feet.

Wall walled in an immense wall. It endures: time is sealed in space.

Cesare Vivaldi

4

L'ombra si schiaccia nell'orbita d'un rovente silenzio. Abrasioni graffiti macchie rientrano piano nel muro.

Il muro di solo intonaco cotto si copre a perdita d'occhi di sole screpolato di rovi roventi e parietarie appassite. È muro fiutato da miliardi di zampe di lucertole calcinate dalla corsa.

Muro resiste nell'immenso spazio. Murato sta nel tempo: sigillato.

Un hallalí corsivo non corrode lagrime. Hallalí bianca pozza. Trapassa la lepre sul fianco del colle se odora la muta dei cani.

5

Solo muro a perdita d'occhi calcinato da miliardi di rovi appassiti: coperto di zampe di parietarie lucertole. Fiutato sa solo di sole rovente che screpola in corsa l'intonaco cotto.

Sta nello spazio. Resiste sigillato. Muro murato in un immenso tempo.

Hallalí hallalí. Corsiva la pozza dei cani non lo corrode. Bianca trapassa una muta di lepri sul fianco del colle che odora di lagrime.

Rientra piano nell'orbita del muro. Si schiaccia nell'ombra. Nel silenzio rovente macchie abrasioni graffiti.

4

The shadow gets crushed in the orbit of a red-hot silence. Scrapes graffiti stains quietly come back into the wall.

The wall of only baked plaster is covered as far as the eye can see with sun cracked by red-hot blackberries and withered pellitory. It's a wall sniffed by billions of lizard feet whitewashed from running.

Wall endures in immense space. Walled it stands in time: sealed.

A running tirraa doesn't corrode tears. Tirraa white pool. The jackrabbit passes on the flank of the hill if it smells the pack of hounds.

5

Only wall as far as the eye can see, whitewashed by billions of withered blackberries: covered by feet of pellitory lizards. Sniffed it knows only of red-hot sun which cracks the baked plaster while running.

It stands in space. It endures sealed. Wall walled in an immense time.

Tirraa tirraa. The running pool of hounds doesn't corrode. A white pack of jackrabbits passes on the flank of the hill which smells of tears.

Slowly it returns into the orbit of the wall. It gets crushed in the shadow. In the red-hot silence stains scrapes graffiti.

Born in Viserba (near Rimini) in 1927,
Pagliarani now lives in Rome. Pagliarani's
degree is in political science, and he taught
for some time in professional schools. He also
served as the editor for a political newspaper.
Pagliarani has been involved with a number
of Italian literary magazines, including *Il
Verri*, *Il Menabò*, *Nuovi Argomenti*, and
Nuova Corrente. He was a member of the
"Gruppo '63" and "i novissimi." His poetry is
a strange cross between neorealism, with its
stress on common language and the colloquial, and the new experimentalism, with its
concern about forging a new language and
style. The result is a poem which produces a
series of revelations through dramatic mono-
logue. As important as his individual contri-
bution is his official encouragement of
experimental writers. He edited an important
and influential anthology entitled *Manuale di
poesia sperimentale*.

His books of poetry are:

Cronache ed altre poesie.
    Milano: Schwarz, 1954.
Inventario privato.
    Milano: Veronelli, 1959.
La ragazza Carla e altre poesie.
    Milano: Mondadori, 1962.
Lezione di fisica.
    Milano: Scheiwiller, 1964.
Lezione di fisica e fecaloro.
    Milano: Feltrinelli, 1968.

Umilmente confesso che sono mortale

Umilmente confesso che sono mortale
atteggiato come bambino avanti al tabernacolo
o dopo la scommessa col Signore che perdevo regolarmente
ma con altra voce e schiena di serpente
con voce roca dolce suadente e schiena di serpente
di quando chiedo soldi, soldi in prestito
e tiro avanti un pasto—confesso che so di morire
ma adesso lasciami stare, o quante cose ti firmo che scade
    domani
ma adesso lasciami stare, ho mangiato, e mi pento di tutti i
    peccati.

Humbly I Confess That I Am Mortal

Humbly I confess that I am mortal
placed like a baby before the tabernacle
or after the wager with the Lord I regularly lost
but with another voice and serpent's back
with hoarse sweet persuasive voice and serpent's back
when I ask for money, money as a loan
and I get myself a meal—I confess that I know about dying
but let me stay for now, oh I sign so many things over to you which are forfeited
    tomorrow
but let me stay for now, I have eaten, and I repent all my
    sins.

Canto d'amore

Avevi gambe da cavalla pregna
e capelli di stoppa, le tue forme
fatte da un falegname ho combattuto
sicuro di rifare, immaginando
se tiravo coi denti i tuoi capezzoli
una turgida ricchezza. Stavi bene
vestita da marinaio, bianco e blu.

Sulla sabbia ho lottato per aprirti
e scioglierti d'un dubbio, sottoveste
da treni popolari.
                        Sa Dio cosa
credevo di vedere, nei suoi mobili
occhi.
            Se questa fosse colpa!, andiamo,
illusione d'età, che lascia il segno
è la menzogna: dichiarata grande
la vita, eccomi a torcere la schiena
a dire: è strano è strano, come un'oca.

Riconosco che invece di affogare
ti ho adoperata come un salvagente.

Qui, dove il mare ha rotto, non rimane
memoria, e se mi coglie tradimento
dal profondo, è la notte la chiarezza
connubio mare luna in queste terre
basse, è Villa Serena cosí spoglia,
silenzio, smarrimento alle minacce
dell'alba.

Love Song

You had the legs of a pregnant mare
and stringy hair, your forms
made by a carpenter I struggled
sure of remaking them, imagining
a turgid richness if I took your nipples
in my teeth. You looked good
dressed like a sailor, white and blue.

I wrestled on the sand to open you up
and resolve a doubt for you, underwear
with popular flounces.
                      Lord knows what
I thought I'd see, in her restless
eyes.
      If this were sin!, come on,
illusion of age, what leaves its mark
is the lie: life having been declared
grand, here I am to bend my back
and say: it's strange it's strange, as a goose.

I realize that instead of drowning
I used you as a life-preserver.

Here where there's a break in the sea, no memory
remains, and if treachery seizes me
from the depths, it's the night the clearness
marriage sea moon in these low
lands, it's Villa Serena so empty,
silence, dismay at the threats
of the dawn.

Narcissus pseudonarcissus

È un po' come dire che c'è poco da bruciare, oramai
lo zeppelin è sgonfiato, il fusto è nudo
che fa spavento
              io ho avuto tutti i numeri per finir male
l'amore vizioso, l'ingegno e piú l'ambizione pudica
e al momento opportuno un buco nei pantaloni
che ci passano due dita
                    allora bruceremo pali di ferro
il nostro paese aggiornato, la draga la gru l'idroscalo.

Ma se:
    ho lottato con vigliaccheria e tenacia
    pasto per pasto, e non intendo mollare

    non so come risponde la corteccia
    ma intendo seguitare

    il mio bagaglio non è pesante
    la mia schiena non è ingombrante
    tengo un tessuto connettivo che permette
    alcune metamorfosi

    dopo la pioggia con i rospi in mezzo alle strade
    ho fede che mi potrai trovare.

Oh, la nostra razza è la piú tenace, sia lode al suo fattore
l'uomo è l'unico animale che sverna ai poli e all'equatore
signore di tutte le latitudini che s'accostuma a tutte le abitudini
cosí ho violenta fiducia
non importa come lo dico—ah l'infinita gamma dei toni
che uguaglia solo il numero delle anime sensibili delle
                    puzze della terra
ho violenta fiducia, non importa, che tu mi trovi in
                    mezzo alla furiana
e dopo, quando le rotaie dei tram stanno per aria.

Narcissus Pseudonarcissus

It's a bit like saying there's little to burn, now that
the zeppelin is deflated, the fear-inspiring frame
is naked
         I have everything you need to end up badly
depraved love, genius and what's more modest ambition
and at the opportune moment a hole in my trousers
you can pass two fingers through
                         so we'll forge iron piles
our modernized country, the dredger crane loading dock.

But if:
     I wrestled with cowardice and tenacity
     meal after meal, and I don't intend to give up

     I don't know how the cortex responds
     but I intend to pursue

     my luggage isn't heavy
     my back isn't loaded down
     I have connective tissue which allows
     some metamorphoses

     after the rain with toads in the middle of the streets
     I have faith you'll be able to find me.

Oh, we have the most tenacious race, let his maker be praised
man is the only animal who winters at the poles and the equator
lord of all latitudes who adapts himself to all situations
thus I have a violent faith
it doesn't matter how I say it—ah the infinite gamut of tones
that equals only the number of sensitive spirits of the
                     earth's stenches
I have a violent faith, it doesn't matter, that you'll find me
                     in the middle of the storm
and after, when the tram-rails stand in the air.

No? È successo un caso, un incidente?, a te gloria, se a
te non ti tocca
io, tanto, ho consegnato un biglietto—c'è scritto che non
rinuncio:
a me amen, la volta che mi tocca.

No? Something happened, an accident?, good for you if you
                    don't get hurt
anyway, I delivered a note—it's written there that I won't
                    give up:
amen to me, the time when it's going to be my turn.

Poème antipoème

Io non prendo le cose come vengono, tu non eri
in programma, Mamsell, le mie figure
di donna portano altri segni distintivi:
nessuna mai, e baciata con piú ardore
che avesse una volta uno dei tanti
tuoi profumi di guerra e di vacanza.
                              È meglio
guardarti il profilo in lontananza
e non con gli occhi d'ora, ma a memoria
per esempio sullo scoglio, distesa in fronte al mare
morbida, palpitante. Ma lo sai
che mi viene in mente perfino Rita da Cascia, protettrice
degli impossibili? che il tuo riso allo squillo di un telefono
non mi si spegne piú? Oh, basta
sii lusingata e scrollane le spalle al tuo ritorno
da te, dove non sto, né so, né posso o voglio, dove non sarei
io se mi fossi.

Scappa Mamsell, che il mio amore non ti uguagli
          le mie pallide figure
Se io ti prendo anch'io ti sono vita
          certo, ma con mani pesanti
Scappa Mamsell, l'amore fa piú ricchi
solo i poveri:
              nemmeno io lo sono.

Quando scrivere è vizio. [Perché non sempre
scrivere è vizio: può costare all'Austria
piú di una battaglia perduta.] Perché
se c'è da spremere una verità
                      la Chiesa lo sa
                      che la verità
                      è trina
si tratta di righe inutili: | se veramente ci fosse volontà
che la giovane estranea se ne vada | o « scappi », che fa piú effetto

Poème Antipoème

I don't take things as they come, you weren't
in my plans, Mamsell, my female
figures had other distinguishing marks:
no woman had, or kissed with more passion
than any of your perfumes
of war and holiday.
                    It's better
to look at your profile from a distance
and not through golden eyes, but from memory
for example on the rock, stretched out in front of the sea
soft, throbbing. But did you know
that even Rita da Cascia, protectress of the impossible,
comes to my mind? that your laugh at the ringing of a telephone
is in my head all the time? Oh, let that be enough
flattery and shrug your shoulders when you come back
from your place, where I neither am, nor know about, nor can nor wish, where
                                                    I wouldn't be
if I were myself.

Run away Mamsell, so that I don't love as much as you do
        my pallid figures
If I take you I am also life to you
            certainly, but with heavy hands
Run away Mamsell, love enriches
only the poor:
            And I'm not one of those.

When writing is vice. [Because writing
is not always vice: it can cost more than
a lost battle in Austria.] Because
if there's a truth to wring out
                        the church knows
                        that truth
                        is lace
it's a matter of useless lines: | if you really wanted
the young foreign woman to go away | or "run away" which is more emphatic

l'unica è non parlarle | o urlarle dietro le notti
che sudi e diventi viscido.

(Oppure c'è un altro sistema « t'amo » | dille, insisti che l'ami molto
se proprio hai deciso di perderla | vedrai come se ne va placata.)
Se invece è una finta e si vuole | che pensi « come è generoso (o orgoglioso)
lui e il suo cuore, aspetta che in risposta | io lo sorprenda buttandogli
tutti i miei arti al collo » | si tratta di meschinità.
E anche piú dell'idea del raggiro | è meschina la scelta prepubere
del mezzo.
            Quindi si chieda impudicizia alla cronaca
dicendo da che mondo è mondo
massime sulle donne
e altre banalità.

(E lei, Mamsell, non ha da dire niente?
è data assente? non c'è una verità di lei?
Certo: risulta—ma s'è già detto, almeno nel commento—
che se ne è andata naturalmente.

O è già in secca nel banco del pallore?)

the only thing to do is not speak to her | or shout after her during the nights
when you sweat and become sticky.

(Or there's another way "I love you" | tell her, insist that you love her very much
if you've really decided to get rid of her | you will see how she leaves

if however she's a fraud and you want her to think "how generous (or proud)
he and his heart are, except that in reply | I would surprise him by throwing it
                                                                                                    away
throwing all my arts at his neck" | it's a matter of meanness.
And even meaner than the idea of trickery | is the prepubescent choice
of compromise.
                    Therefore one asks for modesty from history
saying that since the world is the world
especially for women
and other banalities.

(And you, Mamsell, you don't have anything to say?
do you agree? don't you believe in truth?
Certainly: it so happens—but it's already been said, at least in the comment—
that she went away naturally.

Or is she really left high and dry on the pallid bank?)

Oggetti e argomenti per una disperazione

ad Alfredo Giuliani

Che sappiamo noi oggi della morte
nostra, privata, poeta?
                  Poeta è una parola che non uso
di solito, ma occorre questa volta perché
respinti tutti i tipi di preti a consolarci non è ai poeti che
                          tocca dichiararsi
sulla nostra morte, ora, della morte illuminarci?
                                Tu
corrispondesti quando dissi con dei versi
che ho sofferto e avuto vertigine orgogliosa, temendo adolescente
di non poter morire. O credendo.
                        Faccio una pausa
rileggo questo inizio non è male mi frego le mani
dove c'è un po' di reumatismo stagionale, sollevo gli occhiali
mi guardo l'occhio allo specchio. Non lo capisco, non so giudicare
ma so che i medici spiano gli occhi, io non so se il mio
è torbido o dilatato o sporgente, che cosa può rivelare: so che mi tirano ora
le corde del collo che scrivere questa notte
mi terrà eccitato parecchio che direi ne vale la pena sapessi
che fra tre notti riprendo un ritmo di sonno.
                          Alfredo e chiedo
in giro agli amici com'è la mia faccia, il colore.
                              Anche tu
quello stesso pensiero adolescente, anche tu
sbianchi alle volte d'improvviso dopo un pasto.

Immortali per le strade non ce n'è
ci avevano detto che gli uomini, non un uomo, sopravvivono
che a noi tocca la stessa immortalità come alle belve
nell'amore che genera, e sapessi o no che era
il solo atto consentito oltre il limite di uno
l'ossequio necessario alle consuetudini della specie
anch'io mi sono sentito in gran ritmo naturale
sopra una donna e ci guardava un mare
come avessimo avuto un senso, o guardavamo un mare
come avesse avuto un senso.

Subjects and Arguments for an Act of Desperation

for Alfredo Giuliani

Poet, what do we know today of our
private death?
                    Poet is a word I don't often
use, but it's needed this time because
having thrown out all other types of consoling priests isn't
                              it for poets to discuss
our death, now, and from death to enlighten us?
                                        You
agreed with me when I said in a poem
that I suffered from the vertigo of pride, fearing as an adolescent
that I wouldn't be able to die. Or believing.
                                    I'm taking a break
I'm rereading this beginning it's not bad I'm rubbing my hands
where I get a bit of seasonal rheumatism, I'm raising my glasses
I look at my eye in the mirror. I don't understand it, I can't judge
but I know that doctors look in your eye, I don't know what it may mean
if mine is muddy or dilated or bugged out: I do know that my neck muscles
are strained right now that writing tonight
will keep me really excited that I would call it worthwhile if I knew
that after three nights I will regain a rhythm of sleep.
                                    Alfredo, and I'm asking
around at my friends how my face looks, my complexion.
                                              Even you
this same adolescent thought, even you
sometimes go suddenly pale after a meal.

There are no immortals in the streets
they have said that mankind, not one man, survives
that we have the same immortality as the beasts
in procreative love and whether I knew it or not that was
the only permissible act beyond the limit of one
the necessary homage to the habits of the species
I too felt part of a great natural rhythm
when I was on top of a woman and an ocean watched
as if we had a higher meaning, or we watched an ocean
as if it had a higher meaning.

Elio Pagliarani   191

Ma ciò che distingue l'uomo è la scommessa
ecco una frase inventata dalle élites, in ogni modo è vero che qualcuno
scommette di non morire.
                    Ci vuole orgoglio: credere
che il proprio lavoro la pena non se stessi ma il proprio modello sia utile
agli altri; fiducia: che la storia
paghi il sabato; eccetera: e il bello è che di questa scommessa
l'unico a non avere le prove se l'opera gli sopravviva
magari di una sola luna
è chi ha scommesso, che muore.
                    Le dissi: lo stesso anno
che conobbi gli stimoli del sesso tradussi un sonetto di
                    Shakespeare
male, « Shall I compare thee to a summer's day? »
tra il trentanove e il quaranta, col finale
« il mio verso vivrà finché gli uomini
sapranno respirare e tu con quello ».
                            E tu con quello
volto di donna, sei ormai finale?
                        È ora conchiudendosi
il respiro che la clausola s'adempia
risolutiva?
          Ho fumato duecento sigarette
per non amarla, in dodici ore accanto
il volto nel calore
le si apriva in dolcezza lievitata
ma da me è travasata soltanto
la malafede degli intestini
                    in bile e escremento
e il panico poi, e l'attrazione della clinica.

E il fisico con il cancro nel ginocchio, col ginocchio di vaccina
che urli, picchia lí avrebbe detto al fascista, picchialo nel
                        ginocchio che c'ha il cancro.
Quanto alibi ormai per non amare
                        e lei insiste al telefono
se è questo di me che ti interessa, ti aggiungo che è a Bologna
che ormai gli amputeranno la gamba.
                        Da tempo io non mi esalto
piú delle avventure dello spirito, da tempo ciò che brucia
mi devasta soltanto e non posso continuare
a far versi sulla mia pelle, a sublimare

But the thing which distinguishes man is the stakes of the game
there's a line invented by elitists, nevertheless it's true that someone
bet he wouldn't die.
                        That takes arrogance: to believe
that your work the effort, not in themselves, but your model might be useful
to others; faith: that history
pays you off in the end; etcetera: and the beauty of it is that in this bet
the only one who will never know whether his work will survive him
even one short month
is the one who made the bet, who dies.
                                    I told her: the same year
that I first felt sexual urges I did a bad translation of a
                    Shakespearian sonnet,
"Shall I compare thee to a summer's day?"
either '39 or '40, with the couplet
"So long as men can breathe or eyes can see,
So long lives this, and this gives life to thee."
                                    And you with
that woman's face, have you reached your end yet?
                                    Now that my breath
is running out, will the couplet
be fulfilled?
            I smoked two hundred cigarettes
to avoid making love to her, in the twelve hours next to
her face in the heat
she expanded to a leavened sweetness
but from me there only flowed
an intestinal bad faith
                    in bile and excrement
and then panic, and the attraction of the sanitarium.

And the body with the cancer in the knee, with the vaccinated knee
what howls, hit him there he would say to the Fascist, hit him
                    there in the knee with cancer.
So many alibis for not making love
                            and she keeps asking on the phone
if it is this about me which interests you, I should add that it is in Bologna
that they will finally amputate his leg.
                                It's been a long time since I've
gotten excited by adventures of the spirit, for a long time what burns
only destroys me and I can't continue
to write poetry on my skin, to sublimate

le mie sconfitte, a presumere significativi
me e lei e le penultime esplosioni
                              a trarre una morale
di morte universale a consolarci della nostra.

Ma se avessi soltanto bestemmiato
allora Brecht ai vostri figli ha già lasciato detto
perdonateci a noi per il nostro tempo.

my failures, to presume that he and I
and our last eruptions are significant enough

                                 to draw a moral
from universal death to console us for ours.

But if I had only babbled
Brecht has already left it said for your children
forgive us for our times.

The New Hermeticism

Andrea Zanzotto

Born in Pieve di Soligo (near Treviso) in 1921, where he still lives, Zanzotto teaches in a *scuola media*. Zanzotto started out his poetic career as a talented follower of the hermetic school, but he has been developing his work in experimental directions since that time. There is much of the classical Latin and Greek in his poems. He has written odes and eclogues which incorporate ancient languages and syntax, in addition to the classical literary forms.

His books of poetry are:

Dietro il paesaggio.
    Milano: Mondadori, 1951.
Elegia e altri versi.
    Milano: Edizioni della Meridiana, 1954.
Vocativo.
    Milano: Mondadori, 1957.
IX Ecloghe.
    Milano: Mondadori, 1962.
Sull'altopiano.
    Venezia: Neri Pozza, 1964.
La beltà.
    Milano: Mondadori, 1968.
Pasque.
    Milano: Mondadori, 1973.
Poesie (1938−1972).
    Edited by Stefano Agosti. Milano: Mondadori, 1973.

Declivio su Lorna

Mese di pochi giorni,
o tu dalla docile polpa,
chiaro collo curioso
seno caldo che nutre,
dolce uva nella gola,
teneri uccelli che si districano
dai vischi della lontananza
e che indugiano audacemente
tra gli equilibri delle dita
a illustrare le loro piume
e le loro gioie minute,
uccelli disingannati,
maiuscoli pavoni delle siepi,
aiole come mazzi improvvisati,
laghi dallo stupore di goccia:
ogni albero ha dietro di sé
l'ombra sua bene abbigliata,
paradisi di crisantemi
si addensano in climi azzurri.

Ho raccolto la foglia di colore
e la ciliegia dimenticata
sul colle meno visibile;
infanzia raccolta acino ad acino,
infanzia sapido racimolo,
la formica ha consumato il gusto
mutato della ciliegia,
l'acqua movenza timida
inizia radici.

Tra le folle ricciute delle vendemmie
la frescura guasta ed apre
l'innocuo lume del sole
alle rapine svagate dei bimbi.

Lorna Slope

Month of few days,
o you with the soft pulp,
bright intriguing neck
warm nursing breast,
sweet grapes in the throat,
delicate birds which extricate themselves
from bird-lime in the distance
and which linger audaciously
balancing on their claws
to show their feathers
and their tiny joys,
undeceived birds,
huge peacocks of the hedges,
flower beds like improvised bouquets,
lakes astonishing as a drop of water:
behind every tree there
stands a well-dressed shadow,
paradises of chrysanthemums
throng in azure climates.

I gather the colored leaf
and the cherry forgotten
on the even less visible hill;
infancy gathers grape by grape,
infancy delicious cluster of grapes,
the ant consumes the changed
taste of the cherry,
water's timid movements
start roots.

Among the curly multitudes of the vines
the coolness decays and opens
the harmless light of the sun
to the casual plunder of little boys.

Da un'altezza nuova

I

Ancora, madre, a te mi volgo,
non chiedermi del vero,
non di questo precluso
estremo verde ch'io ignorai
per tanti anni e che maggio mi tende
ora sfuggendo; alla mia inquinata
mente, alla mia disfatta pace.
Madre, donde il mio dirti,
perché mi taci come il verde altissimo
il ricchissimo nihil,
che incombe e esalta, dove
beatificanti fiori e venti gelidi
s'aprono dopo il terrore—e tu, azzurro,
a me stesso, allo specchio che evolve
nel domani, ancora mi conformi?
Ma donde, da quali tue viscere
il gorgoglio fosco dei fiumi,
da quale ossessione quelle erbe
che da secoli
a me misero imponi?
Amore a te, voce a te, o disciolto
come nevi silenzio, come raggi
rasi dal nulla: sorgo, e questo gemito
che stringe, questo fiore che irrora
di rosso i prati e le labbra, questa porta
che senza moto si disintegra
in canicole ed acque . . .

. . . .

E, come da un'altezza nuova,
l'anima mia non ti ricorda—
in scalinosi
sogni, in impervie astenie,
tra dolce fumo e orti approfonditi
là sotto il lago, là nelle rugiade
traboccanti, dall'occhio

From a New Height

Once more, Mother, I turn to you,
don't ask me about the truth,
not about this barred
intense green which I ignored
for so many years and which the now fleeing May
holds out to me; to my polluted
mind, my ruined peace.
Mother, why do I speak to you,
why do you refuse to speak to me like the highest green
the richest nihil,
that hangs over and exalts, where
beatifying flowers and frigid winds
open after terror—and you, azure,
do you adapt to me, to myself,
to the mirror which evolves in tomorrow?
But why, from what part of your womb
the dark bubbling of rivers,
from what obsession those herbs
which you forced
on miserable me for centuries?
Love for you, voice for you, o silence
melted like snows, like sunbeams
skimmed from nothing: I rise, and this moan
which wrings me, this flower that sprinkles
meadows and lips with red, this door
which disintegrates without moving
into dog-days and waters . . .

. . . .

And, as if from a new height,
my soul doesn't recall you—
in dreams filled
with stairs, in inaccessible asthenias,
between sweet smoke and deepened kitchen gardens
there under the lake, there in the brimming
dewdrops, inherited from

Andrea Zanzotto

ereditati ancora,
ancora al tocco triste
dell'alba lievitanti . . .

II

Un senso che non muove ad un'immagine,
un colore disgiunto da un'idea,
un'ansia senza testimoni
o una pace perfetta ma precaria:
questo è l'io che mi désti, madre e che ora
appena riconosco, né parola
né forma né ombra?
Al vero—al negro bollore dei monti—
con insaziate lacrime
ancora, ancora sottratto
per un giorno all'aculeo del drago,
ritorno e non so
non so tacere.

. . . .

Nulla dunque compresi
del brancicare avido di bestie
d'insetti e fiori e soli,
nulla m'apparve del lavoro
là sussurrato e sparso
nei campi, aggrinzito nel nido,
né il sudore m'apparve, l'altrui vigile
combustione, ed io solo
io trasceso
in un feroce colloquente vuoto
fronte a fronte m'attinsi?
Calda la mano accarezza ancora il frutto.
Nel vicolo il bambino e l'artigiano.
Vivo il lume degli occhi nel profondo.
Questo fu mio, né mai seppi, mai vidi?
Per voi non m'allietai né piansi ancora?
Madre ignorai il tuo volto ma non l'ansia
proliferante sempre
in ogni piega in ogni bene in ogni
tuo rivelarmi,
ma non l'amore senza riparo
che da te, mostro o spirito, m'avvolge
e aridamente m'accalora.

the eye once again,
once again rising to the sad
touch of dawn . . .

II

A sense that doesn't move to an image,
a color detached from an idea,
an anxiety without witnesses
or a perfect but precarious peace:
is this the I you gave me, Mother, and that now
I barely recognize, neither word
nor form nor shadow?
To the true—to the black boiling of mountains—
with insatiate tears
stolen again and again
for a day with the dragon's sting,
I come back and I don't know
I don't know how to keep quiet.

. . . .

So I understood nothing
of the greedy pawing of beasts
insects flowers and suns,
nothing to do with work murmured
there or lost in the fields, wrinkled
in the nest, appeared to me,
nor did sweat, the watchful burning of others,
appear to me, and did I,
I alone, having transcended
in a fierce talking emptiness
head to head, did I attain myself?
The hand that still caresses the fruit is warm.
The child and the craftsman in the alley.
The light of the eyes in the depths is bright.
Was this mine, and I never knew, never saw?
Did I not rejoice and cry for you again and again?
Mother, I ignored your face but not the anxiety
which kept proliferating
in every wrinkle in every blessing in every
one of your revelations to me,
but not the shelterless love
from you, monster or spirit, that wraps me
and arouses me aridly.

Andrea Zanzotto

Ecloga IV

Polifemo, Bolla fenomenica, Primavera

Animula vagula blandula
Imperatore Adriano

Persone: *a, Polifemo*

a—« Dolce » fiato che muovi
    le nascite dal guscio, il coma, il muto;
    « dolce » bruma che covi
    il ritorno del patto convenuto;
    uomo, termine vago,
    impropria luce, uomo a cui non rispondo,
    salto che il piede spezza sopra il mondo.

    Godono i prati acqua silenzio e viole;
    da fiale laghi, nevi si versano.
    Occhio, pullus nel guscio: ho veduto
    nell'errare del mondo errante il sole.

    Mondo, termine vago, primavera
    che mi chiami nel tuo psicoide fioco.
    Ancora un poco è giusto
    ch'io stia al gioco, stia al fiato,
    all'afflato,
    di lutea passibile cera,
    io, e mondo primavera.
    E vengo dritto, obliquo,
    vengo gibboso, liscio;
    come germe che abbonda
    di dente ammicco e striscio
    e premo alle lane onde ammanta
    il dí le sue fetali clorofille.
    M'adergo, prillo, come a musicale
    sferza la trottola. Poi che qui tutto è « musica. »
    Non uomo, dico, ma bolla fenomenica.
    Ah, domenica è sempre domenica.
    Le bolle fenomeniche alle mille
    stimolazioni variano s'incupano
    scintillano. Sferica
    è anche la speranza, anche la sete.
    Abiuro dalle lettere consuete.

Eclogue IV

Polyphemus, Phenomenological Bubble, Spring

Animula vagula blandula
Emperor Hadrian

Characters: *a, Polyphemus*

a—"Sweet" breath that you move
   births from the shell, the coma, the mute;
   "sweet" mist you brood over
   the return of the pact you agreed upon;
   man, ambiguous term,
   unseemly light, man to whom I don't respond
   jump which breaks the foot over the world.

The meadows enjoy water silence and violets;
lakes and snows spill out of phials.
Eye, pullus in its shell: I have seen
the sun wandering in the world's wandering.

World, ambiguous term, Spring
you call me with your faint psychoid.
It's still all right for me
to stay a bit longer in the game, in the breath,
in the afflatus,
of vulnerable yellow wax,
I, and world Spring.
And I come straight, slanting,
I come hunchbacked, smooth;
like an embryo with
many teeth I wink and crawl
and press on the wool with which the day
mantles its fetal chlorophyll.
I rise, I whirl like a top
to its musical lash. Since everything is "music" here.
Not man, I say, but phenomenological bubble.
Ah, Sunday is always Sunday.
With a thousand stimuli the phenomenological
bubbles vary darken
sparkle. Hope is
spherical too, as is thirst.
I swear off ordinary letters.

Andrea Zanzotto   207

O primavera di cocchi e di lendini,
primavera di líquor, dei, suspense,
« vorrei trovare
parole nuove » :
ma il petalo e la frangia, ma l'erba e il lembo muove,
muovono al gioco i giocatori. Monadi
radianti, folle, bolle a corimbi e tu
tondo comunque, a tutta volta, estremo
occhio di Polifemo.

Po.—No, qui non si dissoda, qui non si cambia testo,
qui si ricade, qui
frigge nel cavo fondo della vista
il renitente trapano, la trista
macchina, il giro viziosissimo.
E qui su questo,
assestandomi, giuro:
io Polifemo sferico monocolo
ebbro del vino d'Ismaro primavera,
io donde cola, crapula, la vita
(oh: vino d'Ismaro; oh: vita; oh: primavera!).

O Spring of eggies and nits,
Spring of liquor, gods, suspense,
"I want to find
new words":
but petal and fringe, but grass and its margin moves,
move the players to the game. Radiant
monads, multitudes, bubbles like corymbs and you
no matter how round, all the way around, intense
eye of Polyphemus.

Po.—No, here you don't till, don't change the text,
here you fall, here
the reluctant drill, the wicked
machine, the most vicious turning
sizzles in the deep cave of sight.
And here settling
on this, I swear:
I Polyphemus spherical one-eyed man
drunk with the Ismarine wine Spring,
I where it drips from, guzzling, life
(oh: Ismarine wine; oh: life; oh: Spring!).

13 settembre 1959 (variante)

Luna puella pallidula,
Luna flora eremitica,
Luna unica selenita,
distonia vita traviata,
atonia vita evitata,
mataia, matta morula,
vampirisma, paralisi,
glabro latte, polarizzato zucchero,
peste innocente, patrona inclemente,
protovergine, alfa privativo,
degravitante sughero,
pomo e potenza della polvere,
phiala e coscienza delle tenebre,
geyser, fase, cariocinesi,
Luna neve nevissima novissima,
Luna glacies-glaciei
Luna medulla cordis mei,
Vertigine
per secanti e tangenti fugitiva

La mole della mia fatica
già da me sgombri
la mia sostanza sgombri
a me cresci a me vieni a te vengo
. . . .
. . . .
(Luna puella pallidula)
. . . .

September 13, 1959 (Variation)

Luna puella pallidula,
Luna hermetic flora,
Luna unique moon girl,
distonia misled life,
atonia avoided life,
mataia, mad woman morula
vampirism, paralysis,
glabrous milk, polarized sugar,
innocent plague, merciless patroness,
protovirgin, alpha privative,
degravitating cork,
apple and power of dust,
vial and consciousness of shadows,
geyser, phase, withered Chinese,
Luna snow snowiest newest,
Luna glacies-glaciei
Luna medulla cordis mei,
Vertigo
fugitive by secants and tangents

The mass of my fatigue
you clear away from me
you clear away my substance
to me you grow to me you come to you I come
. . . .
. . . .
(Luna puella pallidula)
. . . .

Andrea Zanzotto   211

La perfezione della neve

Quante perfezioni, quante
quante totalità. Pungendo aggiunge.
E poi astrazioni astrificazioni formulazione d'astri
assideramento, attraverso sidera e coelos
assideramenti assimilazioni—
nel perfezionato procederei
piú in là del grande abbaglio, del pieno e del vuoto,
ricercherei procedimenti
risaltando, evitando
dubbiose tenebrose; saprei direi.
Ma come ci soffolce, quanta è l'ubertà nivale
come vale: a valle del mattino a valle
a monte della luce plurifonte.
Mi sono messo di mezzo a questo movimento-mancamento radiale
ahi il primo brivido del salire, del capire,
partono in ordine, sfidano: ecco tutto.
E la tua consolazione insolazione e la mia, frutto
di quest'inverno, allenate, alleate,
sui vertici vitrei del sempre, sui margini nevati
del mai-mai-non-lasciai-andare,
e la stella che brucia nel suo riccio
e la castagna tratta dal ghiaccio
e—tutto—e tutto-eros, tutto-lib. libertà nel laccio
nell'abbraccio mi sta: ci sta,
ci sta all'invito, sta nel programma, nella faccenda.
Un sorriso, vero? E la vi(ta) (id-vid)
quella di cui non si può nulla, non ipotizzare,
sulla soglia si fa (accarezzare?).
Evoè lungo i ghiacci e le colture dei colori
e i rassicurati lavori degli ori.
Pronto. A chi parlo? Riallacciare.
E sono pronto, in fase d'immortale,
per uno sketch-idea della neve, per un suo guizzo.
Pronto.
Alla, della perfetta.

« È tutto, potete andare. »

The Perfection of Snow

So many perfections, o so
many totalities. It adds, stinging.
And then abstractions starfactions the making of stars
frost-bite, across sidera and coelos
frost-bites assimilations—
in perfection I would go beyond
the huge dazzling, of the full and the empty,
I would look for processes
to catch the eye, avoiding
the dubious and obscure; I would know I would tell.
But we're so enriched, the snow is so abundant
so valuable: downhill from the morning downhill
uphill from the light with many sources.
I put myself in the midst of this radial movement-swoon
ah the first shiver of rising, of understanding,
they leave in ranks, they defy: that's the whole thing.
And your consolation solar radiation and mine, fruit
of this winter, you train, you ally yourself,
on the glassy summits of forever, on the snow-covered borders
of I-never-never-let-it-go,
and the star which burns in its husk
and the chestnut taken out of the ice
and—everything—and all-eros, all-free. freedom in the trap
it's there for me in the embrace: it's there
it's there for the asking, there in the program, the business.
A smile, huh? And vi(ta) (id-vid)
you can't do anything about, not hypothesize,
in the doorway it becomes (caress?)
Evoè along the ice floes and the breeding of colors
and the encouraging works in gold.
Hello. Who am I talking to? To proceed.
And I'm ready, in immortal phase,
for a sketch-idea of snow, for one of its flashes.
Hello.
To the, of the perfect.

"That's all, you can go now."

Andrea Zanzotto   213

Al mondo

Mondo, sii, e buono;
esisti buonamente,
fa' che, cerca di, tendi a, dimmi tutto,
ed ecco che io ribaltavo eludevo
e ogni inclusione era fattiva
non meno che ogni esclusione;
su bravo, esisti,
non accartocciarti in te stesso in me stesso

Io pensavo che il mondo cosí concepito
con questo super-cadere super-morire
il mondo cosí fatturato
fosse soltanto un io male sbozzolato
fossi io indigesto male fantasticante
male fantasticato mal pagato
e non tu, bello, non tu « santo » e « santificato »
un po' piú in là, da lato, da lato

Fa' di (ex-de-ob etc.)-sistere
e oltre tutte le preposizioni note e ignote,
abbi qualche chance,
fa' buonamente un po';
il congegno abbia gioco.
Su, bello, su.
                Su, münchhausen.

To the World

World, let it be, and good;
exist in a goodly way,
make sure, try to, try for, tell me everything,
and here I was overthrowing dodging
and the inclusions were just as effective
as the exclusions;
keep going, old man, exist,
don't curl up into yourself into myself

I thought that a world so conceived
with this super-falling super-dying
a world so debased
it was only a badly-hatched I
I was indigestible daydreaming horrors
daydreamed horrors lousy pay
but not you, old buddy, not you "saint" and "sanctified"
a bit more that way, sideways, sideways

keep on (ex-des-obs etc.)-isting
and beyond all known and unknown prepositions,
take a chance,
keep it goodly for a bit;
let the gears have full play.
Keep going, old buddy, keep going.
                              Keep going, münchhausen.

Andrea Zanzotto   215

Subnarcosi

Uccelli
crudo infinito cinguettio
su un albero invernale
qualche cosa di crudo
forse non vero ma solo
scintillio di un possibile
infantilmente aumano
ma certo da noi che ascoltiamo
     —allarmati—lontano
     —o anche placati—lontano
uccelli tutta una città
pregna   chiusa
           glorie di glottidi
           acumi e vischi di dottrine
un chiuso si-si-significare
nemmeno infantile ma
adulto occulto nella sua minimità
               [disperse specie del mio sonno
               che mai ritornerà].

Subnarcosis

Birds
cruel neverending chirping
on a winter tree
something cruel
perhaps not true but only
twinkling of a possible
childishly non-human
but certainly for those of us who listen
      —terrified—far away
      —or also soothed—far away
birds a whole city
pregnant   closed
          glories of glottises
          insights and traps of doctrines
a closed s-s-significance
not even childish but
adult occult in its minimality
              [lost species of my sleep
              which will never return].

Luciano Erba

Born in Milan in 1922, Erba continues to live
there and is Professor of French Literature at
Catholic University. He has been involved
with several magazines, Italian and American: *Officina*, *Botteghe Oscure*, and *Poetry*.
His quiet, ironic tone and anecdotal style are
unique in contemporary Italian literature.
One measure of his success, more than the
volume of his work, is the immediate recog-
nizability of his voice. With Piero Chiara he
edited *Quarta generazione* in 1954. It was the
first major attempt to anthologize the postwar
generation of Italian poets.

His books of poetry are:

Linea K.
    Modena: Guanda, 1951.
Il bel paese.
    Milano: Edizioni della Meridiana, 1955.
Il prete di Ratana.
    Milano: Scheiwiller, 1959.
Il male minore.
    Milano: Mondadori, 1960.

La Grande Jeanne

La Grande Jeanne non faceva distinzioni
tra inglesi e francesi
purché avessero le mani fatte
come diceva lei
abitava il porto, suo fratello
lavorava con me
nel 1943.
Quando mi vide a Losanna
dove passavo in abito estivo
disse che io potevo salvarla
e che il suo mondo era lí, nelle mie mani
e nei miei denti che avevano mangiato lepre in alta montagna.
In fondo
avrebbe voluto la Grande Jeanne
diventare una signora per bene
aveva già un cappello
blu, largo, e con tre giri di tulle.

La Grande Jeanne

La Grande Jeanne didn't distinguish
between English and French
as long as their hands were groomed
the way she wanted them
she hung around the harbor, her brother
worked with me
in 1943.
When she saw me in Lausanne
where I was passing by in a summer suit
she said I could save her
and that her world was there, in my hands
and in my teeth that had eaten jackrabbit up in the mountains.
Deep down
la Grande Jeanne had always wanted
to be a respectable lady
she already had a blue
hat, a wide one, and with three turns of tulle.

Un'equazione di primo grado

La tua camicetta nuova, Mercedes
di cotone mercerizzato
ha il respiro dei grandi magazzini
dove ci equipaggiavano di bianchi
larghissimi cappelli per il mare
cara provvista di ombra! per attendervi
in stazioni fiorite di petunie
padri biancovestiti! per amarvi
sulle strade ferrate fiori affranti
dolcemente dai merci decollati!
E domani, Mercedes
sfogliare pagine del tempo perduto
tra meringhe e sorbetti al Biffi Scala.

A First-Rate Equation

Your new blouse, Mercedes
of mercerized cotton
has the air of grand department stores
where you get outfitted with big
white hats for the beach
(expensive way to buy shade!) for waiting
in railroad stations full of petunias
(for white-suited fathers!) for admiring
flowers along the tracks
(gently decapitated by the freight trains!)
And tomorrow, Mercedes
to leaf through the pages of time lost
between meringues and sherbets at the Biffi Scala.

Terra e mare

Goletta, gentilissimo legno, svelto
prodigio! se il cuore
sapesse veleggiare come sai
tra gli azzurri arcipelaghi!

ma tornerò alla casa sulla rada
verso le sei, quando la Lenormant
avanza una poltrona sul terrazzo
e si accinge ai lavori di ricamo
per le mense d'altare.

Navigazione blu, estivi giorni
sere dietro una tenda a larghe maglie
come una rete! bottiglie
vascelli tra rocchi di conchiglie
e la lettura di Giordano Bruno
nel salotto di giunco, nominatim
De la Causa Principio e Uno!

Land and Sea

Schooner, noblest wood, nimble
prodigy! if the heart
only knew how to sail like you
through azure archipelagoes!

but I'll return home through the harbor
around six, when Lenormant
pushes an armchair onto the terrace
and sets about the task of embroidering
for the communion services.

Blue navigation, summer days
evening behind a curtain as loosely knit
as a net! bottles
vessels among piles of conches
and reading Giordano Bruno
in the salon of rushes, *nominatim*
On Cause, Principle, and Unity!

Incompatibilità

Sin tanto che don Oldani
e i venticinque esploratori
si rincorrono su queste lastre di piombo
io mi immagino il popolo di donne
della cerchia piú antica della città.
Addormentate agli ultimi piani
in un letto di ferro
quante sognano la mia sciarpa di seta?
Guardo la città grigiorossa
domenicale, dal terrazzo del duomo
ma potessi volare
ai bei gerani sulle lunghe ringhiere
varcare porte, a piedi nudi
camminare sugli esagoni rossi
poi vedermi alle vostre specchiere
brune ninette, che abitate il verziere!
Partono adesso i crociati
io rimango quassú
con una spia albanese
che fotografa torri e ciminiere.

Incompatibility

As long as Don Oldani
and the twenty-five explorers
are running on these lead slabs again
I picture the population of women
in the city's oldest circle.
Having slept on the top floors
in an iron bed
how many dream of my silk scarf?
I look at the gray-red Sunday
city, from the terrace of the cathedral
but if I could fly
to the beautiful geraniums on the long railings
pass through doors, walk
barefoot on the red hexagons
then see myself in your mirrors
brown Ninettas who live in the marketplace!
The crusaders are now departing
I remain up here
with an Albanian spy
who photographs towers and smokestacks.

Lombardo-veneto

Le donne
al capoluogo scese a servire
in locande di lungofiume
(è un fiume verde scorre tra i sassi
sotto lunghi balconi di legno)
le donne un tempo brave come i preti
nell'andare in cerca di funghi
con passi segreti sulla montagna
ora spolverano i vetri viola e gialli
sulla veranda, le teste di capriolo e
un tavolino da gioco nel vestibolo
sapevano del cielo stellato
stanotte a un abbaiare di cani
all'alba già preparavano il bagno
a un viaggiatore, di legno di castagno
era il fumo entrato nel soppalco
ridevano e che odore di bosco!
Ricordo che ho letto su un giornale
che le donne quaggiú sono le vittime
della rivoluzione industriale.

Lombard-Venetian

The women
in the district capital went down to work
at inns along the river
(it's a green river it runs through rocks
under long wooden balconies)
at one time the women were as clever as priests
in tracking down mushrooms
with secretive steps on the mountainside
now they dust the violet and yellow windowpanes
on the veranda, the stag heads and
a gaming table in the vestibule
they knew there'd be a starry sky
last night from the barking of dogs
at dawn they were already preparing a bath
for a traveler, it was smoke from chestnut
wood that went into the loft
they were laughing and what a woodsy odor!
I recall having read in a newspaper
that the women down here are victims
of the industrial revolution.

Tabula rasa?

È sera qualunque
traversata da tram semivuoti
in corsa a dissetarsi di vento.
Mi vedi avanzare come sai
nei quartieri senza ricordo?
Ho una cravatta crema, un vecchio peso
di desideri
attendo solo la morte
di ogni cosa che doveva toccarmi.

Tabula Rasa?

It's an ordinary evening
criss-crossed by half-empty trams
moving to be dissected by wind.
Do you see me going along as usual
in the districts without memory?
I have a cream tie, an old burden
of desires
I await only the death
of everything that had to touch me.

The New Experimentalism

Born in Milan in 1920, Risi currently lives in Rome. He has a degree in medicine, but has never practiced that profession. After receiving his degree, he became interested first in journalism and then in documentary film-making. His poetry most often has a satirical edge to it, but like most satire, there is also an underlying sense of compassion and humanity. He won the Premio Cittadella in 1958 and the Premio Libera Stampa in 1962.

His books of poetry are:

Le opere e i giorni.
> Milano: Scheiwiller, 1941.
Polso teso.
> Milano: Mondadori, 1956.
Il contromemoriale.
> Milano: Scheiwiller, 1957.
Civilissimo.
> Milano: Scheiwiller, 1958.
Pensieri elementari.
> Milano: Mondadori, 1961.
Minime massime.
> Milano: Scheiwiller, 1962.
Dentro la sostanza.
> Milano: Mondadori, 1965.
Di certe cose.
> Milano: Mondadori, 1970.
Amica mia nemica.
> Milano: Mondadori, 1976.

I meli i meli i meli

Quell'albero che mi sorprese
con i suoi rami gonfi
quanti corvi sul ramo piú alto.

Quel toro che si accese
per una macchia scura al mercato
quanto sangue versato alle frontiere.

Quella ragazza in tuta che si intese
prima con francesi e polacchi
quanti viaggi il suo corpo tra le braccia.

Quel soldato che mi chiese
la via breve oltre Sempione
quanta ansia in uno sguardo.

Apple Trees Apple Trees Apple Trees

This tree which surprised me
with its swollen limbs
so many crows on the highest branch.

That bull which flew into a fury
because of a dark stain at the market
so much blood spilled at the borders.

That girl in overalls who got along so well
first with Frenchmen then with Poles
so many voyages, her body in their arms.

That soldier who asked me
the short cut over Sempione
so much fear in one glance.

L'altra faccia

Tutt'intorno, fuori porta
la città non ha niente di un villaggio
il moderno stinge presto
la campagna è sporca
che l'operaio attraversa con un ultimo sforzo.
Le motorette prolungano l'industria.
Lembi di nebbia radono un canale
qua i detriti, là dei mucchi di letame. La giuntura
tra la Città che vomita e la Bassa che rumina
si fa nell'iride delle vacche
o sul ciglio della strada ora che il cielo
è tutto in una macchia d'olio.
C'è ancora qualche uccello senza nido
o forme che seguono un richiamo lontano
ma il tono generale non è allegro. Eppure l'amo.
Un po' d'oro era nei campi, tra la paglia delle foglie
o in quelle mosche verdi traccianti teoremi nell'aria;
Finché di nebbia in nebbia la campagna
guadagna la città dove i delitti
si sanno l'indomani dai giornali.

The Other Side

All the way around, outside its gates
the city has no suburbs
the modern fades quickly
the countryside the worker crosses
with an ultimate effort is filthy.
Motorscooters extend the industries.
Strips of fog skim a canal
rubbish here, heaps of manure there. The link
between the City which vomits and Bassa which chews the cud
is found in the irises of the cows
or on the edge of the road now that the sky
is enclosed in a slick of oil.
There are still some birds without nest
or form which follow a distant call
but the general tone isn't happy. I love it anyway.
There was a bit of gold in the fields, in the leafy straw
or in those green flies tracing theorems in the air;
Until the countryside from fog to fog
turns into the city where crimes
will be known in the newspapers the next day.

Trinità dei Monti

Su queste scale
tarmate nei marmi
usate come suole
dove è appena spiovuto
e ancora deserte, stamane
al primo sole sto così bene
che respiro a fondo con la mente—
anche il giornale
parla di distensione.

Trinità dei Monti

On these moth-eaten
marble stairs
worn out like soles
where the rain's just stopped
and still deserted, this morning
at first sun I feel so fine
that I take a deep breath in my mind—
even the newspaper
speaks of relaxing tensions.

Tautologia

Su
   e giú
      sull'altalena
a ripagarci d'ogni pena
ogni sera ci auguriamo
un mattino migliore.
Ma i nostri sforzi sono frivoli
ma non si può che
          peggiorare in meglio.

Tautology

Back
    and forth
        on the swing
and to compensate for every pain
every evening we hope for
a better morning.
But our efforts are useless
and you can't do anything but
        get worse better.

Manovre

nel Nevada osservate da un bambino di 5 anni

Al quasi dolce autunno velato di malva
in un alito d'aria oscillano
le prime salve. Il cielo
ha una ghirlanda di fiocchetti buffi
tanti palloni scappati di mano
a un gigante buono, e tutti
chi piú su chi meno
crepano con un tonfo lungo
in un fungo da non toccare!

I bravi boys
fanno la nanna
in caverna
o scrivono a mamma
schiacciando sotto l'unghia gli isotopi attivi
pronti all'urto
come un sol morto.

Una luce natalizia
dentro un pino di calore
che mio padre generale
aveva già visto prima
alla sagra di Hiroshima
sbianca la città cavia
e il paese in malora
frigge e sbrodola
come un getto di coca-cola.

God! un centro cosí urbano
con tanto di edifici federali
e un poco di ideale americano
un vero centro con bella vista
anabattista, asettico
dotato di orizzonte
ma che lo spostamento ha decentrato.

Maneuvers

in Nevada as observed by a 5-year-old boy

In the almost sweet autumn veiled by mallow
in a breath of air the first
salvoes flash. The sky
has a garland of odd tufts
so many balloons escaped from the hands
of a good-natured giant, and all
of them burst at a lower level
with a long boom
into a mushroom you shouldn't touch!

The good little boys
are taking their naps
in the cavern
or they write to Mommy
crushing active isotopes under their fingernails
ready for the impact
just one dead.

A Christmas light
inside a pine tree of heat
which my father the General
had already seen before
at the Hiroshima festival
bleaches the guinea pig city
and the countryside in ruin
fries and stains
like a spout of Coca-Cola.

God! such a sophisticated city
with so many federal buildings
and a little of the American Dream
a true city with a beautiful view
Anabaptist, ascetic
gifted with a horizon
but which the shock has decentralized.

Nelo Risi   245

L'effetto è massiccio
una primizia
del resto prevista,
un'opera di scavo
un colpo d'occhio sul mondo nuovo
un superdeserto
senza miraggio
un po' malconcio al mezzo
simile a un marrone sgranato dal riccio.

Ma dall'alto
dall'alto e d'un sol balzo va visto il paese
nero palato velato di malva
fino alle case
e al fu pezzato scozzese
con vene dure di strade che si torcono silenziose
in un vesuvio di ceneri anche

dove una merla sola rimasta
liscia le poche penne tutte bianche
al quasi dolce autunno velenoso.

The effect is massive
a first taste
of the predicted conclusion,
a work of excavation
a glance at the new world
a superdesert
without mirage
a bit ragged at the center
like a chestnut taken out of its husk.

But from above
from above and with just one jump the countryside is seen
as a black palate veiled with mallow
up to the houses
and to the spotted Scot
with hard veins of streets which twist silently
in a Vesuvius of ashes too

where a lone blackbird remains
it preens its few all white feathers
in the almost sweet poisonous autumn.

Il teatro privato

Che bellezza scaricare tutto sull'inconscio!
purché l'inconscio lo si lavi in famiglia
si può uccidere il padre fottere la madre

La psicoanalisi è una indagine borghese
un processo simbolico tanto rispettabile
(conta il denaro la cura è interminabile)

Fughe e censure sono piaceri da narciso
un murarsi dentro la scena familiare
che l'uomo di fabbrica l'uomo della terra

neanche sospettano—per i subalterni
vale ancora la vecchia coscienza

The Private Theater

What a beautiful thing to dump everything on the unconscious!
if the unconscious would cleanse the whole family
you could kill your father fuck your mother

Psychoanalysis is a bourgeois inquiry
such a respectable symbolic process
(only money matters the cure never ends)

Escapes and censures are narcissistic pleasures
a self-enclosure in the familial scene
which the factory worker the man of the earth

don't even suspect—for the lower ranks
it's still the old conscience that counts

Nelo Risi   249

DA Variazioni sul bianco

Il prigioniero
dalle percosse reso cieco
muto e offeso nell'udito
costretto a scavarsi la fossa
prima che gli passino sopra
una mano di calce trova ancora
la forza di migrare in un qualcosa
che gli appartiene mentre assiste
fisicamente alla sua fine

FROM Variations on White

The prisoner
rendered blind mute
and deaf by the beatings
forced to dig his own grave
before they put a coat
of lime over him still finds
the strength to wander off into
something of his own while he
physically witnesses his end

Bartolo Cattafi

Born in Barcellona, Sicily (near Messina) in 1922, Cattafi moved to Milan, working in industry and pursuing his literary career at night. Although he made a point of demystifying poetry and debunking literary cliques, Cattafi was acknowledged by all as an important contemporary writer. He said that poetry is "beyond intellectual schemes, foolish ambitions, frigid acts of will and scholarly masturbations . . . poetry is born under the sign of the unexpected." Cattafi died of cancer in March, 1979.

His books of poetry are:

Nel centro della mano.
    Milano: Edizioni della Meridiana, 1951.
Partenza da Greenwich.
    Milano: Edizioni della Meridiana, 1955.
Le mosche del meriggio.
    Milano: Mondadori, 1958.
Qualcosa di preciso.
    Milano: Scheiwiller, 1961.
L'osso, l'anima.
    Milano: Mondadori, 1964.
L'aria secca del fuoco.
    Milano: Mondadori, 1972.
Il buio.
    Milano: All'insegna del Pesce d'Oro, 1973.
La discesa al trono, 1972–1975.
    Milano: Mondadori, 1975.

Antracite

Fabbriche e treni perdono lucore,
invecchiano, sbiadiscono col tempo,
sconfinano nel bigio della nebbia.
L'antracite perdura, abbasso, nera,
fragile, dura, riflessi di metallo,
terra chiusa e remota
a lumi spenti.
Ne intendo i segni, i cippi calcinati del confine,
l'ala del fossile confitta sulla costa
le mani rattrappite dei compagni
naufraghi morti nel golfo senza mare.
Può darsi avvenga domani un altro rogo
non l'aperta l'allegra combustione
che macchia l'aria di fumo e d'amaranto,
la soffocante perdita dell'anima
noi incastrati nell'ombra.

Penso alla pioggia, alla cenere, al silenzio
che l'uragano lascia amalgamati
nella vergine lapide di melma
dove drappelli d'uomini e di bestie
verranno ancora a imprimere
un transito nel mondo,
all'alba ignari sul nero
cuore del mondo.

Anthracite

Factories and trains lose luster,
they get old, fade with time,
cross over into the gray of the fog.
Anthracite lasts, down there, black,
brittle, hard, metallic reflections,
remote and enclosed land
of extinguished lights.
I understand its signs, the calcified boundary stones,
the fossil's wing fixed to the shore
the numb hands of its shipwrecked
comrades who have died in the gulf without sea.
Tomorrow there may be another pyre
not the open joyous burning
that stains the air with smoke and amaranth,
but the suffocating loss of spirit
as we remain embedded in shadow.

I think of the rain, dust, silence
which the hurricane leaves mixed
into the virgin rock of slime
where squads of men and beasts
still will come to mark
a passing in the world,
ignorant in the dawn on the black
heart of the world.

Apertura d'ali

E l'apertura d'ali?
Essa varia; ve n'è
di micron, di centimetri, di metri.
Dipende dal modello, dalla materia, dalla
forza motrice; il motivo, la quota da raggiungere.
Ripiegate, richiuse, accantonate
sotto un serto verdissimo, nell'Eden
pasto a tarme felici;
oppure sottoghiaccio coi relitti, ossa
regali, mammut, mosche spente
in fondo all'ombra del tempo.
Camminammo piú a lungo che potemmo,
spesso vedemmo, alto nella memoria, doloroso,
un bianco stormo di brandelli . . . (appena
un gioco, un aiuto, una finzione
se sulla scena del deserto il fuoco
s'apprende alla pelle delle prede
se il gelo aggruma nomi disumani).
Un battito d'ali su per le vaste
pareti della memoria non ci sottrae
all'ombre che ci seguono; la iena,
il lupo, gli angeli
abietti dall'obliquo incedere.

Wingspan

And the wingspan?
It varies; it can be
in microns, in centimeters, in meters.
It depends on the model, the material, the
driving force; the purpose, the height to be reached.
Folded, closed up, sheltered
beneath a wreath of bright green, in Eden
feeding on happy moths;
or under ice with the detritus, majestic
bones, mammoths, flies extinguished
in the depths of the shadow of time.
We traveled longer than we were able,
we often saw, high in the memory, painful,
a white bundle of rags . . . (hardly
a game, a relief, a fiction
if on the desert stage fire
clings to the victim's skin
if ice curdles inhuman names).
A beating of wings up the vast
walls of memory doesn't free us
from the shadows who pursue us; the hyena,
the wolf, the angels
abject from their creeping pace.

Bartolo Cattafi   257

Qualcosa di preciso

Con un forte profilo,
secco, bello, scattante,
qualcosa di preciso
fatto d'acciaio o d'altro
che abbia fredde luci.
E là, sul filo della macchina, l'oltraggio
d'una minima stella rugginosa
che piú corrode e corrompe piú s'oscura.
Un punto da chiarire, sangue
d'uomo, briciola
vile oppure grumo
perenne, blocco di coraggio.

Something Precise

With a bold profile,
lean, handsome, taut,
something precise
made of steel or something else
with a cold gleam.
And there, on the machine's edge, the outrage
of the tiniest rusty star
which dims the more it corrodes and decays.
A point of clarification, human
blood, cowardly
splotch or perpetual
clot, hunk of courage.

Tabula rasa

D'accordo, amore. Espungiamo
dal testo perle d'acqua
su petali,
le frange estese,
le bolle della schiuma.
Le cose lietamente necessarie.
Togliamo anche
l'acqua l'aria il pane.
Giunti all'osso buttiamo
fuori della vita
l'osso, l'anima,
per credere alla tua
tabula che mai
avrà l'icona, l'idolo, la cara calamita?

Tabula Rasa

OK, love. Let's take
"pearls of water on the
petals" out of the text,
the fancy frills,
the bubbles of froth.
Those delightfully necessary things.
Let's also take out
water air bread.
Having gotten down to the bone shall we toss
both bones and soul
out of life,
in order to believe in your
tabula which will never
contain icon, idol, sweet disaster?

Al quinto piano

Era marmo per poveri
né costoso né candido
a lastre sovrapposte, rampe, gradini.
Poi la casa, celle
sospese ad un ultimo piano.
Nome, numero, strada, città,
l'ascensore portò giorno per giorno
notizie di nera consistenza,
carta-garza, rinforzo di catrame,
sigillate di rosso, ceralacca
sulle cose dell'anima, silenzio.
« È ciò che amo, ne stivo finché posso
con orgoglio e saggezza,
con follia, con tenera fiducia. »
A volte cambia il giro delle cose,
l'attesa contempla anche un nonnulla
lungamente chiamato, costruito
pezzo per pezzo, atomo
perfetto che sconvolga
stemperi scolori
il catrame impietrito dell'inferno.
Intanto Sedici e Venti
—verdi tranvai—
stipavano a bordo il bene e il male
sferragliando al traghetto d'una parte
del mondo o dell'inferno.

On the Sixth Floor

It was a poor man's marble
neither expensive nor bright
one slab on another, flights, steps.
Then the house, cells
stacked up to the top floor.
Name, number, street, city,
day after day the elevator brought
news with a dark consistency,
thin paper, reinforced with tar,
sealed in red, sealing wax
on matters of the soul, silence.
"It's what I love, and I won't stow it until I can
with pride and wisdom,
with madness, with tender faith."
Sometimes the usual pattern changes,
expectation contemplates even
a long desired trifle, constructed
piece by piece, perfect
atom which could disturb
melt discolor
the hardened tar of hell.
Meanwhile Sixteen and Twenty
—green trams—
packed good and evil on board
ferrying them from some part
of the world or from hell.

Filo nero

Erano loro che ti chiamavano
nascosti dietro i muri
filo nero che segue
la punta degli aghi
nella cruna
e tu rispondevi con parole
gemiti gesti
firmando interminabili missive
mimetica bestia in questa terra
pronto a lasciare i vivi
per giungere a quel niente a quel nessuno.

Black Thread

It was they who called you
hidden behind the walls
black thread which follows
the point of the needle
through the eye
and you replied with words
groans gestures
signing endless letters
imitative beast in this land
ready to leave the living
in order to reach that nothing that no one.

Il buio

In un'ora di grande luce
in una grande piazza lastricata
di pietra biancastra
il buio nasce come una fonte
una bestia un volatile una pianta
sparnazzante in silenzio
cessa allora ogni alito di vento
e puoi cadere in quei fili tesi
là in mezzo impigliarti
crollando in avanti
ad occhi spalancati verso il buio
sbattere la fronte.

Darkness

In an hour of great light
in a large piazza paved
with whitish stone
darkness is born like a fountain
an animal a bird a plant
scattering in silence
then every breath of wind ceases
and you can fall into those taut wires
get tangled there in the middle
tumbling forward
toward the darkness with bulging eyes
to smash your forehead.

Vulnerabilità

Evita i grandi recipienti
posti in piazze viali
vasche fontane dove
talvolta tumultuano acque stigie
e fafnir si svuota del suo sangue
sfuggi agli spruzzi all'orrenda vernice
furbo e saggio amante di viaggi
in alto mare
sii foglia tremante
asciutta accartocciata autunnale.

Vulnerability

It avoids the large receptacles
placed in piazzas boulevards
basins fountains where
Stygian waters sometimes riot
and fafnir spills out his blood
you escape from the spray of the horrible paint
cunning and wise lover of voyages
on the high seas
you might be a trembling leaf
dry crumpled autumnal.

Born in Bologna in 1923, where he still lives, Roversi was a partisan in World War II. After the war he became a rare book dealer in Bologna. In 1955 he began a magazine, *Officina*, in his bookstore. Some of the most notable Italian writers of the time were among his collaborators. Roversi's poems are full of the profuse details of all periods of history. He chooses history not so much for ideological reasons as for the richness of imagery it affords.

His books of poetry are:

Ai tempi di re Gioacchino.
    Bologna: Palmaverde, 1952.
Poesie per l'amatore di stampe.
    Bologna: Officina, 1954.
Il margino bianco della città.
    Bologna: Officina, 1955.
La raccolta del fieno.
    Torino: Einaudi: "Il Menabò," 1960.
Dopo Campoformio.
    Torino: Einaudi, 1965.
Registrazione d'eventi.
    Milano: Rizzoli, 1974.

Roberto Roversi

Giorno di mercato

I contadini scendono dalle corriere.
Nei vecchi dagli occhi sereni
vivono età di odi più guerrieri,
di lotte a viso aperto
come si addice a uomini.
Vanno con passo diritto,
arsi come la bambagia delle nuvole
dal tramonto, nei capelli di ghiaccio
nascondono la paglia.
Dentro le case, tra i filari
e i canali bianchi di vele,
le donne accendono il fuoco,
le figlie ancora calde d'amore
gridano ai vitelli,
immergono i mastelli dentro i pozzi.
Mentre la città carica
di notte, di noia,
appena si risente a un sole
sfuocato dalla nebbia,
i campi vivono con voce di tuono.
Questi vecchi indugiano
sul marmo della piazza,
parlano in un dialetto
che dice parole meravigliose.
L'Italia è scesa con essi dalla corriera
e la razza dei buoi dalle lunate corna che strappano
l'aratro dal cuore della pianura.
La terra custodisce anfore, tazze,
tombe, città, scheletri di guerrieri
con elmo verderame sulle ossa
e la paura dei secoli;
tazze sfiorate da un segno che indugia
sul viso di una donna adagiata
o sul collo di un ragazzo in lotta.
Gli uomini affondano la mano
nell'onda della terra,

Market Day

The peasants get off the mail trains.
In the tranquil eyes of the old ones
live the ages of more warlike odes,
of battles face to face,
as are fitting for men.
They walk with a straight step,
burnt like the cotton-wool of the sunset
clouds, in their hair of ice
they hide straw.
Inside the houses, between rows
and canals white with sails,
women light fires,
daughters still hot from love
shout at the calves,
they dip buckets in the wells.
While the city burdened
with night, with boredom,
hardly feels the effects of a sun
cooled by fog,
the fields live with a voice of thunder.
These old people linger
on the marble of the piazza,
they use a dialect
which speaks marvelous words.
Italy has gotten off the mail train with them
and the race of oxen with moon-shaped horns which rip
the plough through the heart of the plain.
The earth guards amphorae, cups,
tombs, cities, skeletons of warriors
with helmet verdigris on the bones
and the fear of centuries;
faded cups with a sign which lingers
on the face of a reclining lady
or on the neck of a boy in battle.
Men plunge a hand
into the waves of the earth,

Roberto Roversi   273

alzano i misteriosi vasi
che risplendono ancora.

Oggi, appena scesi dalle corriere.
Gli abiti odorano
di legno, resina.
Dicono che il grano darà
buona resa, che è annata da fieno:
raccontano guardandosi gli occhi.

they bring up mysterious vases
that still shine.

Today, having just gotten off the mail trains.
Their clothes smell
of wood, resin.
They say that there'll be a good
harvest of grain, that it's a good year for hay:
they look each other in the eye as they speak.

La bomba di Hiroshima

[I. Le ossa calcinate   II. La notte non finisce a Hiroshima]

La bomba di Hiroshima
bruciò troncando le ultime parole.
L'ossa calcinate
riverberano il cielo senza fiato.
L'erba per sempre ha il verde rovesciato,
l'albero ha il suo tronco congelato
per sempre, la natura scompare
per sempre, nell'orrore dell'uomo
dentro a un fuoco di morte.
File di carri cercano le frontiere,
appena cadute le barriere
di filo spinato
la gente beve nelle mani screpolate
e corre forte sperando lontano
per la pianura, macerie a frugare
macchie nere di lava paura;
nel sole la guerra è seppellita
con gli ultimi soldati in pietra dura.
Nel Giappone una città nuova
cresce adesso funebre violenta
sopra uomini esanimi che al sole
si scuoiano nei fossi.
E qua è l'Italia, non intende, tace,
si compiace di marmi, di pace
avventurosa, di orazioni ufficiali,
di preghiere che esorcizzano i mali.
Ma nel mondo le occasioni perdute
sono i sassi buttati dentro il mare;
nei luoghi devastati dalla lebbra
o accucciati nell'ombra a imprecare
non un granello di polvere nel fondo
dell'occhio incantato che li domina.
Tutti i morti oramai dimenticati.
Il ventre della speranza è schiacciato
nella polvere da una spada antica;
anni interminabili, senza amore,
inchiodano col fuoco alla fatica.

The Hiroshima Bomb

[I. The bleached bones   II. The night never ends in Hiroshima]

The Hiroshima bomb
burned cutting off the last words.
The bleached bones
re-echo the breathless sky.
The green of the grass has been destroyed forever,
the trunk of the tree has been frozen
forever, nature disappears
forever, in the horror of the man
inside a death fire.
Lines of carts seek out the borders,
the barbed-wire barriers
having just fallen
people drink from their cracked hands
and run hard for the plain with a distant
hope, debris to search
black spots of lava fear;
the war is buried in the sun
with the last soldiers in hard stone.
In Japan a new city now
grows, funereal, violent
on top of lifeless men who peel
in the trenches in the sun.
And here is Italy, it doesn't hear, it keeps quiet,
it delights in marbles, in adventurous
peace, in official orations,
in prayers which exorcise evils.
But in the world lost opportunities
are stones thrown into the sea;
in places devastated by leprosy
or curled in shadow to curse
not a grain of dust in the depths
of the enchanted eye which rules them.
All the dead by this time forgotten.
The belly of hope is crushed
into the dust by an ancient sword;
with fire they nail interminable years,
without love, to weariness.

Roberto Roversi

Regala la sua vita un aviatore:
fatto legno, con sdegno
ammonisce con la bocca ferita
che quanto è accaduto può ancora accadere,
che la vita di tutti si consuma
in un bieco silenzio e in cenere.
Gli altri usurpano e straziano,
non affondano i denti nel bicchiere
acre della verità che fa morire.
Macerati dagli anni, legati
con la canapa al giorno travolgente,
ascoltano crescere l'erba
stenta, con la mente il passare del tempo,
odiano la voce che dà gelo all'inverno,
che conduce al fondo dell'inferno,
che monotona assale
i seduti nelle sale addobbate,
poi percuote e subito affonda
nella pietra tombale . . .
sempre contando i caduti d'Europa,
i trafitti dal cielo a Nagasaki.
Esule nella patria la voce conduce
a un amore dimenticato, a un dolore
irto, indifeso, spina da patire;
al mondo che lo ignora
offre l'orrore
della sua morte e di una gloria vile.
Dietro il muro del pianto si è difeso;
ma ritorneranno l'ora derelitta
le giornate con l'anima confitta
nel fango, se un orgoglio conteso
da questo acerbo cuore
che non s'arresta di fronte a pena alcuna
girerà nel dolore la fortuna.
L'hanno preso, legato, è prigione
in cima a una collina di carbone.
I naufraghi che vanno alla deriva
troveranno da lui che è sulla croce
nuove parole, il ricordo, ragione?
La notte non finisce a Hiroshima.

A flyer makes a gift of his life:
made into wood, in rage
he admonishes with wounded mouth
that what has happened can happen again,
that everyone's life burns up
in ashes and a sinister silence.
The others usurp and torture,
they do not plunge their teeth into the acrid
glass of truth that kills.
Ruined by the years, tied
by rope to the overwhelming day,
they listen to the stunted grass
grow, the passing of time in their minds,
they hate the monotonous voice that gives ice
to winter, that leads to the depths
of hell, that seizes
those seated in the decorated rooms,
then strikes and suddenly plunges
into the tombstone . . .
forever counting the fallen of Europe,
those wounded by the sky at Nagasaki.
Exile in your own country the voice leads
to a forgotten love, to a thorny
pain, defenseless, thorn to be suffered;
to the world which ignores him
he offers the horror
of his death and a vile glory.
He defended himself behind a wall of tears;
but the days with the spirit stuck
in the mud will return the abandoned
hour, if the contested pride
of this bitter heart
which doesn't stop at any pain
will accept suffering as its fortune.
They took him tied up, he's a prisoner
at the top of a carbon hill.
The shipwreck victims who drift
will they find new words, memory, reason
from the one on the cross?
The night never ends in Hiroshima.

Roberto Roversi   279

Le costumanze politiche

I

Che età avevi quando irruppe il Medo?

II

Il giuramento al lume di candela
nella cattedrale di Brunswick
davanti alla tomba
di Enrico l'Uccellatore (vedere a pagina ottanta)
con gli occhi azzurri e i capelli biondi, essi
e il pelo sul cuore . . .

III

Una strada non c'è. C'è una strada (un fiume), c'è un fiume
—credo che ci sia, è cosí—un profondo
fosso, una siepe, un fiore d'albero
sotto il garbino spappolato, c'è il pianto
di una bambina nuda col tracoma c'è
il sangue di un uomo per terra decapitato
la milza di un animale sul bancone di legno;
c'è il filo bianco (un rosso filo) che stende
dal labbro di chi parla fino a una casa laggiú,
una carta su cui il dito striscia con raccapriccio,
l'orgasmo della donna fra l'erba affumicata
da un vecchio incendio, un bombardiere che non si vede.
Vilipendio di istituzioni (di gravi legittime colpe).
Non c'è piú l'eco, il suono non c'è, il percuotere
dell'ultimo dissenso, le voci
placate (finalmente?), i refusi scomposti,
ribolle un altro piombo per piú degne canzoni
—la caratteristica del tempo è una misurata indifferenza,
tutto interessa un poco per brevissimo tempo,
ogni cosa muore, deperisce, sé consuma e sfoltisce
nel forno della memoria.

IV

Dice Kant la disciplina del genio
(ossia l'educazione) è il gusto: gli ritaglia

Political Customs

I

How old were you when the Medes broke through?

II

The oath by candlelight
in Brunswick Cathedral
before the tomb
of Henry the Fowler (see page 80)
with blue eyes and blond hair, that
and hair on his heart

III

There's no road. There is a road (a river), there's a river
—I believe there is, it's so—a deep
ditch, a hedge, a tree blossom
under the soggy sou'wester, there are the tears
of a naked baby with trachoma there is
the blood of a decapitated man on the ground
the milt of an animal on the wooden pen;
there is the white thread (a red thread) which extends
from the lips of the one who speaks to a house over there,
a map on which the finger creeps in terror,
the woman's orgasm in the grass burned
by an old fire, a bombardier you don't see.
Scorn of institutions (of grave but lawful crimes).
There is no longer an echo, there is no sound, the punches
of the last dispute, the placated
voices (finally?), the unseemly misprints,
another pot of lead boils for more worthy poems
—the characteristic of the times is a cautious indifference,
everything is a little bit interesting for a little while,
everything dies, decays, burns itself out and scatters
in the furnace of memory.

IV

Kant says that the discipline of genius
(i.e. education) is taste: it notches

Roberto Roversi   281

le ali e lo rende pulito e costumato.
Il grande Kant, savio nella sua stanzuccia
di legno, con l'onda delle idee
che si scioglie in un silenzio ordinato
e sulle vie (deserte) lo zoccolo di un cavallo.
Ma questo, che siede anch'egli, è un uomo, nella casa
con moderati calori, in un quarto piano
di paese italiano, che è, che sarà? cosí lontano
dai rumori. Ah, non è costumato e polito. Non costumato,
è tutto dentro sbrecciato, pendente,
insolente, tenero e terso, muscolo
macellato in una sordida ignominia,
ingorgo meschino, è gramigna spersa secca
raccolta da una vecchiaccia che insacca.
Questo non sarà polito, eh no, costumato non è (le circostanze
non lo permettono), non è pulito—tutti sentono
sulla via lo zoccolo di una morte
passare alternando il suono con quello dello spazzino
(e la sua tromba). L'alba, all'alba, l'alba
—disegnare contro i vetri col fiato—
è, nello strizzarsi delle vene,
cosí distesa distante, la mano aperta, occhiaia
di questa giornata incerta nella scelta, stramazzerà
fra noi farneticando (presto, fra noi) di dolori antichi
e dei nuovi congegni. Ammonisce cosí riservata superba
a non perdere le occasioni (la vita è un fulmine nel tempo)
intanto—una ragazza sulla gamba perfetta
nell'ambito di una stanza indossa la vestaglia
spenna se stessa nello scirocco ferito da una calza
irride alla varietà degli umori
agitata da una innocua speranza.

V

Accendere una sigaretta (fumata dopo sei anni).
Il potere agli operai e ai contadini
—si elidono a vicenda sopraffatti
da queste contraddizioni che non distinguono
fra la necessità e il bisogno, fra chi
(si può dire) di una corda che si sfilaccia
trattiene il bandolo e colui che esautorato esausto
si lascia colpire dal canapo alla faccia.
L'affare è grave e merita considerazione.
Oggetto di ogni disputa, *nel caldo della stanza*
mentre fuori si apre il mondo

its wings and makes it clean and well-mannered.
The great Kant, wise in his wooden
garret, with the wave of ideas
which dissolve into an ordered silence
and on the streets (deserted) the horse's hoof.
But he, sitting on his bottom too, is a man, in the house
with moderate heat, on the fifth floor
of an Italian village, what is, what will be? thus distant
from noises. Ah, it isn't fashionable and polished. Not fashionable,
it's all chipped inside, hanging,
insolent, tender and clear, muscle
butchered in a filthy act of infamy,
miserable obstruction, it is scattered dry weed
gathered by an old hag who sacks it.
This will not be polished, oh no, fashionable it is not (the circumstances
don't permit it), it is not polished—on the street everyone
hears the hoof of the Angel of Death
passing, alternating his sound with that of the street sweeper
(and his trumpet). The dawn, at dawn, the dawn
—to sketch on the windows with your breath—
it is, in the squeezing of the veins,
so stretched out distant, the open hand, this day's
eye socket uncertain in its choice, it will collapse
among us raving (right away, among us) of ancient woes
and of new devices. It warns us thus reserved proud
not to lose opportunities (life is a thunderbolt in time)
in the meantime—a girl on perfect legs
within the limits of a room puts on the nightgown
plucks herself in the scirocco wounded by a stocking
she laughs at the variety of moods
stirred up by an innocuous hope.

V

To light a cigarette (smoked after six years).
Power to the workers and the peasants
—they annul one another overwhelmed
by these contradictions which don't distinguish
between necessity and need, between the guy who
(one might say) has a rope which unravels
and hangs on to the end and the one who, deprived of authority, exhausted,
allows the rope to hit him in the face.
The matter is serious and merits consideration.
Subject of every dispute, *in the heat of the room*
while outside the world opens up

Roberto Roversi   283

distrutto dall'acquazzone
e rigurgita una cloaca con la gola di vacca
e si fa notte fra i lampi
e una pietà di noi si distende spora le forme immobili
(con noi) nell'attesa perfida dello spettacolo
—la consumata mente, l'usura, il sillogismo,
il calembour sul titolo di chi si compiace al caffè—
è
la fine del mondo, un'arca ribaltata,
sulle pianure le ossa della città
—allora tu dici che il momento del contrasto
si invera in una nuova necessità (questo è il punto),
ognuno di noi che sediamo
sillogizza ma non opera, la disputa si fa arcaica
e tutti noi (il giro del dito è ampio)
degradiamo nella mistificazione.
Accendere una sigaretta.
Sono anni bui o sono anni nuovi?
Per la verità credo che il buio
sia il buio arcigno tetro gelido perfetto
che sia una luce nuova.

VI

Ieri in via Andegari scura e stretta, raffinata via che conduce a
una foresta di simboli scalcagnati la moglie incontro incontrai ho
incontrato di un compagno fucilato.
Stormiscono le foglie della memoria.
Con una testa di capelli rossi, in quelle case sporche di fango o
dell'ottusa avidità borghese la spalla modulata dolcemente suonava.
La sua giovinezza (incantava) ancora.
L'ora del giorno, incerta un poco colma
o piuttosto il luogo distaccato dai rimorsi, in una incerta
ombra, distaccato dalla buriana ossessiva,
la giuliva felice voce di addio ciao
o R. che (un attimo) . . . dimenticato, al mio cuore . . .
Si possono dimenticare i morti per sempre.
Leggeri andavamo a braccio
i suoi capelli di fiamma disse sono sposata ho due figli
neppure un ritratto piú, mi puoi capire
una gran voglia di vivere
questa città fa impazzire.
La provincia fa morire.
A notte ancora nella sua casa, fra i figli e il marito
nella casa a mezz'aria

destroyed by the cloudburst
and a sewer regurgitates with a cow's throat
and night falls in the midst of the lightning
and our piety spreads out over the immobile forms
(including us) in the spectacle's perfidious suspense
—the perfect mind, usury, the syllogism,
the pun on the title of the guy who takes his pleasure at the café—
it's
the end of the world, a capsized ark,
the bones of the city on the plains
—then you say that the moment of contrast
justifies itself in a new necessity (this is the point),
every one of us who sits
syllogizes but doesn't work, argument becomes archaic
and all of us (the circling motion of the finger is wide)
lower ourselves in mystification.
Lighting a cigarette.
Are they dark years or new years?
For in truth I believe that the darkness
is the sullen, dismal, icy, perfect darkness
which is a new light.

VI

Yesterday in Via Andegari dark and narrow, classy street which leads to
a forest of shabby symbols I meet I met I have met
the wife of an executed comrade.
The leaves of memory rustle.
With a head of red hair, in those houses filthy with mud or
with dull bourgeois greed the modulated shoulder played sweetly.
Her youth (enchanted) still.
The time of day, uncertain a bit overflowing
or rather the place detached from remorse, in an uncertain
shadow, detached from the obsessive thunderstorm,
the cheerful happy voice of goodbye so long
or R. who (just a second) . . . forgotten, in my heart . . .
One can forget the dead forever.
With light hearts we went arm in arm
her flaming hair said I am married I have two sons
not even a snapshot anymore, you can understand
my great desire to live
this city drives you crazy.
The country bores you to death.
At night still in her house, among the sons and the husband
in the house suspended in mid-air

sui rami di un albero fortunato di cristallo, verde.
Baciò me sulla bocca
perfida, e dolcemente, vicino alla porta.
Tutto scomparso, assopito, scancellato, annegato,
visi di uomini trapassati sbiancavano in polvere
non era vero piú niente.

on the branches of a happy crystal tree, green.
She kissed me on my perfidious
mouth, and sweetly, at the door.
Everything vanished, drowsy, obliterated, drowned,
faces of dead men who have passed away whiten in the dust
nothing was true anymore.

Roberto Roversi

Iconografia ufficiale

La diga del Vaiont è in Val Cellina
a dodici chilometri da Belluno
la diga del Vaiont è la piú grande diga ad arco del mondo
alta 265 metri consente di invasare sino a un massimo
di 168 milioni di metri cubi d'acqua del fiume Piave
per alimentare la centrale idroelettrica di Soverzene.
190 metri di coronamento carrozzabile
spessore al coronamento di 3 metri e 40 centimetri
spessore alla base 22 metri e 11 centimetri,
per costruirla sono stati impiegati
350 000 metri cubi di calcestruzzo
e mezzo milione di quintali di boiaca.
Crolla la diga del Vaiont
travolgendo interi paesi immersi nel sonno.
Era la piú alta d'Europa.
Si cercano le vittime nel fango
il fango ha sommerso cinque borgate
fra i superstiti rassegnazione e
fatalismo: i superstiti non piangono.
Il dolore del paese, messaggio del Papa.
Le prime telefoto dal mare di sangue sopra Belluno.
A Pirago il paese si è frantumato
su questa piana c'era Longarone
ora è un mare di fango pavimenti di case.
La morte è scesa dall'occhio azzurro del Vaiont.
Gli uomini vivevano sereni ai piedi della diga,
il fianco della montagna che si specchiava nel lago,
era da migliaia d'anni che si ergeva compatta e possente.
Quell'immenso ghiaieto dove una volta erano case
ha oggi un aspetto allucinante.
Il paesaggio è lo stesso di quella città giapponese
dove era scoppiata una bomba,
alla luce del cielo terso
il paesaggio è di un biancore insopportabile,
televisione programmi sospesi,
dolore e mistero, catastrofe biblica.
Prime polemiche. Si poteva evitare?

Official Iconography

The Vaiont dam is in Val Cellina
twelve kilometers from Belluno
the Vaiont dam is the largest arch dam in the world
265 meters high it holds up to a maximum
of 168 million cubic meters of water from the Piave River
to feed the hydroelectric power plant of Soverzene.
190 meters of driveable top
width at the top 3 meters and 40 centimeters
width at the base 22 meters and 11 centimeters,
to build it they used
350,000 cubic meters of concrete
and 75,000 tons of cement.
The Vaiont dam collapses
carrying away entire towns immersed in sleep.
It's the highest in Europe.
They search for victims in the mud
the mud has buried five villages
among the survivors resignation and
fatalism: the survivors don't cry.
The country's grief, message from the Pope.
The first telephotos from the sea of blood over Belluno.
At Pirago the town was smashed
Longarone was on this level ground
now it's a sea of mud the floors of houses.
Death descended from the blue eye of Vaiont.
Men lived quietly at the foot of the dam,
for thousands of years the mountainside
reflected in the lake rose solid and powerful.
This huge gravel pit where at one time there were houses
today has the look of an hallucination.
The countryside is the same as that Japanese city
where a bomb exploded,
in the light of the clear sky
the countryside is unbearably white,
television programs suspended,
grief and mystery, biblical catastrophe.
First polemics. Could it have been avoided?

Roberto Roversi   289

Il presidente della repubblica
ha erogato una cospicua somma
per i primi soccorsi.
Il testo del telegramma
—la notizia del gravissimo disastro
—le laboriose popolazioni della valle del Piave
—l'unanime sentimento di cordoglio del paese
—animo profondamente commosso
—reverente pensiero agli scomparsi
—le famiglie cosí tragicamente provate
—piú affettuosi sentimenti di solidarietà.
Oggi Leone si recherà nel Cadore
—sentimenti vivo dolore
    et profonda solidarietà
—pregola recare popolazioni colpite tanto flagello
    sensi affettuosa solidarietà.
Un processo si deve fare
i responsabili si debbono trovare e debbono pagare.
Longarone Pirago Rivalta Villanova Faè
Codissago San Martino Spessa.
Calcolata perfettamente la diga
si è trascurata la parte geologica;
un sistema di centoquarantatre equazioni
con altrettante incognite
risolto per controllare
le caratteristiche costruttive; approssimative
le prove sulla struttura delle rocce.
Non è rimasto nulla.
Non nulla per dire poca roba: proprio nulla.
Quattro chilometri quadrati precipitati nel
fondo delle ere geologiche
in un tempo preumano
« l'Ava la stava qua?
magari la stesse qua. La stava a Rivalta
e a Rivalta non ghe piú niente ».
Diga perfetta ma roccia pericolosa.
L'anima nostra si raccoglie in preghiera
invocando eterna pace agli scomparsi
—per far rifiorire in quelle terre cosí laboriose
la speranza di un avvenire
piú sereno e sicuro.
Certo è che, per citare un caso,
il paese di Valesella
un certo giorno cominciò ad andare in briciole
molte case dovettero essere abbandonate.

The President of the Republic
has raised a considerable sum
for the first relief missions.
The text of the telegram
—the news of the very grave disaster
—the hard-working people of the Piave valley
—the country's unanimous sentiment of deep sorrow
—spirit deeply affected
—respectful thoughts for those missing
—the families so tragically tested
—fondest sentiments of solidarity
Today Leone is going to the Cadore
—sentiments of vivid grief
    and deep solidarity
—I beg of you to bring the stricken people on whom such
    calamity has fallen feelings of fond solidarity
There has to be a trial
those responsible must be found and they must pay.
Longarone Pirago Rivalta Villanova Faè
Codissago San Martino Spessa.
The dam having been perfectly calculated
the geological side had been neglected;
a system of one hundred forty-three equations
with so many unknowns
resolved in order to verify
the characteristics of construction; the tests
on the structure of the rocks were approximate.
Nothing remained.
Not a thing to tell us even a little: absolutely nothing.
Four square kilometers having fallen to
the bottom of the geological ages
in a prehuman time
"was Ava living here?
I wish she had been. She lived in Rivalta
and Rivalta is no more."
Perfect dam but dangerous rock.
Our spirits gather in prayer
invoking eternal peace for those missing
—to make the hope for a more
peaceful and secure future
reblossom in these hard-working lands.
It is certain that, to cite one case,
the town of Valesella
on a certain day started to break to pieces
many houses had to be abandoned.

Roberto Roversi   291

Ecco la valle della sciagura
nel crepuscolo del mattino
fango silenzio solitudine
e capire subito che tutto ciò è definitivo
piú niente da fare e da dire.
In tempi atomici si potrebbe affermare
che questa è una sciagura « pulita »
tutto è stato fatto dalla natura
che non è buona e non è cattiva ma indifferente.
Mi ricordo che mentre la facevano
l'ingegnere Gildo Sperti della Sade
mi portò alla vicina centrale di Soverzene
dove c'era un grande modello in ottone
dello sbarramento in costruzione
ed era una scultura stupenda
Arp e Brancusi ne sarebbero stati orgogliosi.
Piú arrivano bare piú arriva gente
in questo grande mercato della morte.
Il presidente Segni è a Longarone
circondato dalle autorità
le autorità impettite e vestite a puntino
facevano gruppo isolato
attorno premeva la gente della montagna
« vieni qui, da noi, ad ascoltarci ».
Il consiglio dei ministri ha rivolto un riverente pensiero
ha espresso la commossa solidarietà
ha rinnovato l'assicurazione
—i provvedimenti intesi a dare pronta assistenza.
Un giovane piange la sua casa distrutta.
Nei magazzini degli aiuti ufficiali
vi sono soltanto quintali
di latte in polvere.

I discorsi de' miei concittadini.

Here is the valley of misfortune
in the twilight of the day
mud silence solitude
and knowing suddenly that all that is definitive
nothing more to do or say.
In the atomic age one should affirm
that this is a "clean" disaster
everything was done by nature
which isn't good and isn't bad just indifferent.
I remember that while they were building it
the engineer Gildo Sperti of Sade
took me to the nearby power plant of Soverzene
where there was a huge model in brass
of the dam under construction
and it was a stupendous sculpture
Arp and Brancusi would have been proud.
More coffins arrive and more people arrive
in this tremendous market of death.
President Segni is at Longarone
surrounded by the authorities
the authorities stiff and properly dressed
made up an isolated group
the mountain people pressed around
"come here, over to us, and listen to us."
The cabinet voiced a respectful sentiment
it expressed its deep-felt solidarity
it renewed its assurance
—the measures undertaken to give immediate assistance.
A young man weeps over his destroyed house.
In the storehouses of official aid
there are only bags
of powdered milk.

The speeches of my compatriots.

Born in Milan in 1928, Majorino still lives and works there. He is the editor of *Il Corpo* and is one of the poetry editors of *Il Paragone*. Majorino's poetry probes topics of social and cultural significance, but he is also interested in experimentation with style and technique.

His books of poetry are:

La capitale del Nord.
    Milano: Schwarz, 1959.
Lotte secondarie.
    Milano: Mondadori, 1967.
Equilibrio in pezzi.
    Milano: Mondadori, 1971.
Sirena.
    Milano: Guanda, 1976.

Giancarlo Majorino

Strappo

L'unico 3 gennaio 1962
e l'unica notte del 4 gennaio che hai
se Enrica telefona ch'io vada da lei a me piace
anche prendere in bocca Freud masticarlo piano
ore di tennis ricominci Goethe?
devi ficcarti nel corpo (carne ossa pensieri) che sei
l'eroe di niente
      quanti brutti film guardati
      quante brutte canzoni incise
      nel cuore ragazzo
      cresceva intanto il futuro
      costruttore d'aereoporti Togni
alla parola *Fine* tu non ritorni a casa
diecimila giorni—se non si rompe prima.

Rip

The only January 3, 1962
and the only night of January 4 that you have
if Enrica phones to ask me over I also
like to put Freud in my mouth and chew him slowly
will you take up Goethe again at the tennis hour?
you must conceal in your body (flesh bones thoughts) the fact that you're
the hero of nothing
       so many lousy films watched
       so many lousy poems inscribed
       in the boyish heart
       meanwhile the future builder
       of Togni airports was growing up
at the words *The End* you don't go home
for ten thousand days—if it doesn't fall apart first.

La miopia

Paragonato all'albero, all'uomo morto,
paragonato alle bestie sei fortunato;
onesto per necessità
via dal giardino armonioso
nell'universo che non ha piú guide
e un buco nero sotto.
Baudelaire bisogna,
tu che insegni l'onestà
(vita e morte da vivere-morire), ridurre
ma oltre il tuo libro,
libero in una stanza e per un uomo, le nostre
« poesie caratteristiche » nel migliore dei casi
(sei miope; hai gli occhiali?)
o di uno spazio dato in un tempo dato.
Non ingannarsi, che Dante non è piú
(lui e la sua poesia che era il tuorlo di un uovo);
certo è seccante—e non basta la mano ferma, leggera—
questa considerazione di miopia personale, di fuochi fissi.

Myopia

Compared to a tree, compared to a dead man,
compared to the beasts you're lucky;
honest by necessity
away from the harmonious garden
in the universe which no longer has guides
and a black pit below.
Baudelaire is necessary,
you who teach honesty
(life and death from living-dying), to reduce
your book even more,
free in a room and for a man, our
"characteristic poems" in the best of cases
(you're nearsighted; do you have glasses?)
or of a given space in a given time.
Don't fool yourself that Dante no longer exists
(he and his poetry that was the yolk of an egg);
sure it's frustrating—and a firm hand isn't enough, neither is a light one—
this matter of personal nearsightedness, of fixed focus.

Anniversario

Freddo vento mia moglie è morta che m'importa però che freddo. È il vento
Se mia moglie morisse scriverei cosí? Non ho moglie.
Lumumba è morto e non ho niente da scrivere.
Sono passati tanti mesi.
Pochi; ma sono passate tante notizie su quella notizia, tante indignazioni dopo
quella; gli faremo un monumento a Bologna.
Però è freddo anche qui (con questa frase allusiva non te la caverai;
meglio descrivere allora il modo d'impigrire che hai, la falsa maturità che
è assopimento, questa pancia che s'intonda davvero allusiva).
È che guardiamo chi ha la stringa piú nuova.
Di questo però sono certo: i poeti della sua terra canteranno Lumumba.

E noi cosa facciamo?
gli eredi della cultura classica,
l'orgoglio della razza, gli eredi del nazismo,
cosa diciamo?
parole che scritte sembrano discorsi benedicenti le armate che conquistarono,
stermineranno, sfruttano.

Anniversary

Cold wind, my wife is dead, what really matters though . . . boy, it's cold. It's
the wind
If my wife died would I write this way? I don't have a wife.
Lumumba is dead and I have nothing to write.
So many months have passed.
Few; but so many stories on that news, so much indignation after
that; we're putting up a monument for him in Bologna.
But even here it's cold (you won't get away with this allusive line;
better to describe the lazy ways you have, the false maturity which
is complacency, this allusive paunch which is really bulging).
It's just that we watch whoever has the latest thing.
Of this, however, I'm sure: the poets of his land will sing of Lumumba.

And what do we do?
the heirs of classical culture,
racial pride, the heirs of Nazism,
what do we say?
words which, when written, seem like speeches blessing the armies which
conquered,
shall destroy, and now are plundering.

Bisoccupato

Questa carta da mille
sotto il piede del vento
sul lago sono io?
fuori orario lontana
dall'ufficio farina
di carne non adatta
all'alimentazione
legno in tronco o in liste scortecciato
o sgrossato con l'ascia o dimezzato
questo rotto biglietto sono io?

    carte geografiche marine celesti
    senza asterischi né segni di pesci
    semplicemente salati, secchi, affumicati,
    la casa del Poeta era nascosta
    da ciuffi di negozi scintillanti
    gas spettralmente puri
    e volatili macellati (lardo)
    dormivano sul tavolo di marmo
    scriveva "treni di laminazione
    continua, a nastro,
    in tiepido, in calore"
    il Poeta piazzista di colle
    di origine animale
    orecchie trapassate da sirene
    di trattenuti transatlantici mani
    da guanti nascoste e protette
sotto quelle sirene tra negozi
io camminavo come un magro importo
su lunghi assegni poco regolari
di firma con girata sconosciuta
sprovvisti anche di data maltratti
da cassieri perché con pochi zeri
    olii essenziali di mirto, timo,
    menta, salvia, sclarea, rosmarino
    frenavano il Poeta rilanciavano
    "treni di laminazione continua,
    a nastro, a caldo, a freddo, a semifreddo"

Doubly Employed

This 1,000 lira bill
under the foot of the wind
on the lake is it me?
off schedule far
from the office powdered
meat not suitable
for eating
wood in the trunk or debarked in stacks
or roughed out with an ax or split
this torn bill is it me?
        maps sky-blue seas
        without asterisks or signs of fish
        simply salted, dried, smoked,
        the Poet's house was hidden
        from clusters of sparkling stores
        gases spectrally pure
        and slaughtered birds (lard)
        slept on the marble table
        he was writing "continuous sheets of laminated
        steel, in strips,
        lukewarm, red-hot"
        the Poet hawker of glues
        of animal origin
        ears pierced by sirens
        of detained transatlantic ships hands
        hidden and protected by gloves
under those sirens I walked
among stores like a paltry amount
on long checks with irregular
signatures with endorsement unknown
and lacking a date abused
by the tellers because there aren't enough zeros
        essential oils of myrrh, thyme,
        mint, sage, clary, rosemary
        slowed the Poet down they started again
        "continuous sheets of laminated steel,
        in strips, hot-rolled, cold-rolled, semi-cold-rolled"

Giancarlo Majorino

con le colle di origine animale
pennellavo geografiche marine
carte celesti su fabbriche e muri
di file d'operai "scusi le spalle"
e là dove ostentate noncuranze
tradivano tradiscono (e domani?)
esenzioni dall'oro e privilegi
io guardavo col muso tra guanciali
di doppie file di negozi colmi
la dipinta cravatta a belle strisce
lo scrittoio col mogano e col cuoio
le tende gonfie al vento dolce e al lago
sembravo un uomo avevo un rispettabile
feltro sul capo un golf sopra il torace
il dente bianco per il dentifricio
doppio mestiere aumenta guerra e pace.

with glues of animal origin
I brushed sky-blue maps
seas on factories and walls
of lined-up workers "excuse my back"
and there where ostentatious neglect
betrayed betrays (and tomorrow?)
exemptions from gold and privileges
I watched the face between pillows
of double lines of loaded stores
the painted tie with beautiful stripes
the writing desk with mahogany and leather
the curtains swollen by a soft breeze and at the lake
I appeared to be a man of importance I had a respectable
felt hat on my head a sweater on my chest
my teeth whitened by toothpaste
double profession increases war and peace.

Paesaggio industriale

Siedono con le nuche sotto le lampade
con le ginocchia avanti come a Mauthausen
sulle carrozze tranviarie o ritti sentono
nove metri di tubo intestinale
gorgogliare nell'interno
domani ricominciano risalgono
verso stanzoni dove chinano il collo
sotto gli occhi a mannaia
di piccoli gerarchi che così mangiano
alcuni ruotano chiusi nell'auto
urtandosi schivandosi augurando morte a chi supera.
Stupisci dell'assalto dei giovani a Torino?
Stupisci che resista ancora! un mondo con tali crepe
nelle piante dei piedi; e dentro il cranio volteggiano
fiabe lettesognate d'amore, di lusso, di gioia.

Industrial Landscape

They sit with necks under the lights
with knees straight ahead as in Mauthausen
on tram-cars or standing they feel
nine meters of intestinal canal
rumbling inside
tomorrow they begin again head back
toward large rooms where they bend their necks
under the meat-ax eyes
of kapos who eat this way
some drive along closed up in cars
getting mad swerving wishing death on anyone who passes.
Are you surprised by the young people's assault at Turin?
Surprised that it's still holding out! a world with such cracks
in the soles of its feet; and inside its skull read-dreamed
tales of love, splendor, joy are whirling.

The New Avant-Garde

Born in Pesaro in 1924, Giuliani now lives in Rome. Giuliani is the editor of "Grammatica," and he was the poetry editor of "Il Verri" at its inception in 1961. He has collaborated with the painters Nonni, Novelli, Scialoja, and others in producing collages which have been shown throughout Italy. Giuliani was one of the leading figures of the "Gruppo '63," and with Nanni Balestrini he edited the anthology of the same name. He also edited an anthology of five "Gruppo '63" writers entitled *I novissimi*.

His books of poetry are:

Il cuore zoppo.
    Varese: Magenta, 1955.
Pelle d'asino.
    Milano: Scheiwiller, 1964.
Povera Juliet e altre poesie.
    Milano: Feltrinelli, 1965.
Il tautofono.
    Milano: Scheiwiller, 1969.
Chi l'avrebbe detto.
    Torino: Einaudi, 1973.

Resurrezione dopo la pioggia

Fu nella calma resurrezione dopo la pioggia
l'asfalto rifletteva tutte le nostre macchie
un lungo addio volò come un acrobata
dalla piazza al monte
e l'attimo sparí di volto in volto
s'accesero i fanali e si levò la buia torre
contro la nostra debolezza
i secoli non ci hanno disfatti

Resurrection after the Rain

It was in the calm resurrection after the rain
the asphalt reflected all our stains
a long farewell flew like an acrobat
from the piazza to the mountain
and the moment flew from face to face
the street lamps lit up and the dark tower rose
against our weakness
the centuries have not destroyed us

I giorni aggrappati alla città

I giorni aggrappati alla città e diseredati,
la vuota fornace ribrucia scorie morte.
Tortuoso di scatti e abbandoni, il polso feroce
misura l'orologio di sabbia, il sangue le orme ineguali
dell'ansia. Lo scrimolo del mare, oltre di me
nel mio canto si sporge.

Segreto è il lavoro che a farmi l'occhio sereno
nomina il mare distante. Nessun amico può dirmi
menzogne che io non conosca, nessuna donna
oltrepassare il suo messaggio di lode o di resa.

                          Io vedo le mie parole,
le mie terre brucate dal silenzio mortale, schierarsi
lungo l'ultima ora del giorno tormentato di vele,
e rievocarmi.

The Days Clinging to the City

The days clinging to the city and disinherited,
the empty furnace reburns dead cinders.
Tortuous from leaps and skips, the wild pulse
measures the hour glass, the blood the irregular marks
of anxiety. The edge of the sea, beyond me
leans out into my song.

Secret is the work which names the distant sea
to calm me. No friend can tell me
lies that I don't know, no woman
surpass its message of praise and surrender.

                              I see my words,
my lands burned by the deadly silence, drawing up
alongside the day's final hour tormented by sails,
and recalling me.

Alfredo Giuliani   315

Predilezioni

I

Accordo è la passione della mia ignoranza,
questo mondo lambito dai canili, sesso d'un sogno,
veramente s'umilia in periferie ricciute e rosa,
puerilmente si macchia per capire l'ospitalità.

I torti sono tortosi, ma il nudo movimento
tenta di vivere la sua esistenza, il mimato dolore
è il sollievo che parla. Pure, il cuore si ghiaccia,
súbito è tempo per la rivoluzione delle pene.

L'anno licantropo ha dodici lune soltanto. La mia viltà
per la bellezza è incredibile, ho bisogno dell'ansia.
Perché fortuna e danno rapiscono la fiamma e
nella grigia ossea dignità non c'è che eleganza.

II

Non c'è rimedio al disordine d'aprile,
scossa di paradiso dei cieli che spurgano
e rovesciano l'inverno nei fossi, dei venti
che s'irradiano asciutti di colpo.

Non c'è rimedio a quei nostri disguidi,
al lezzo delle rose, notturne per la mente
e per l'aria gelose. Amore sempre fiorisce
prima del conoscere, in un buio tremore.

E il rammarico non apre questa porta chiusa,
fa misera la lotta, tradisce solitudine.
L'odore disfatto in scirocco soffoca le sere;
e non c'è onore, né calma, né tregua.

III

Prendi il nero del silenzio, tanto parlare
disinvoglia la nuca, in sé pupilla, palato
di cane, oppure pensa le notti che risbuca
nel gelo il firmamento dei gatti, amore.

Predilections

I

Harmony is the passion of my ignorance,
this world licked by kennels, sex in a dream,
really humbles itself in frills and pink,
childishly gets dirty to understand hospitality.

Crookedness is crooked, but naked movement
tries to live its own existence, mimed pain
is the relief that counts. Yet the heart freezes,
suddenly it's time for the revolution of suffering.

The lycanthrope year has only twelve moons. My cowardice
for beauty is incredible, I need anxiety.
Because fortune and losses ravish the flame and
in gray bony dignity there's nothing but elegance.

II

There's no cure for April's disorder,
jolt of paradise of skies which purge
and overthrow winter in the trenches, of spreading
winds which suddenly blow dry.

There's no cure for these miscarriages of ours,
for the stench of roses, nocturnal for the mind
and jealous for the air. Love always blossoms
before you're aware, in a dark tremor.

And regret won't open this closed door,
it makes the struggle miserable, it betrays solitude.
The scirocco's rotten smell suffocates the evenings;
and there's neither honor, nor peace, nor truce.

III

Take the black of silence, talking so much
makes the skin on your neck crawl, pupil in itself, dog's
palate, or think about nights when
the firmament of cats punctures the ice, love.

Alfredo Giuliani   317

Prendi l'alito dell'ansimo nero, cosí dolce
in punta di lingua, fumo di mosto s'arrotola
sulla fronte, mescola l'osceno e l'assurdo,
cambia di posto, e sia come non detto, amore.

Prendi il volo nero, valica l'altra tua vita,
voltano il fianco i terrori, non gridano piú.
Un sorso d'alba, che nausea, è splendido ora
questo barbaglio stanco, mucosa fiorita, amore.

Take the breath of black panting, so sweet
on the tip of your tongue, musty smoke rolls
against your forehead, mixes obscene and absurd,
changes places, and let's leave it unsaid, love.

Take the black flight, cross your other life,
terrors turn aside, they no longer cry out.
A sip of sunrise, what nausea, this weary glitter
is splendid now, mucous blossoming, love.

Alfredo Giuliani   319

Il vecchio

a Leo

Spenta l'imminenza, l'ombra che sale riconosce.
Il piú terribile fuoco è adolescenza sui vetri,
caldo getto dei rami nella stanza sognata di fresco.
Il farnetico sciala di queste minuzie invase.

Barcolla nella ruota che invecchia l'aria,
velocemente, i polsi lenti incespicano
nel passo della gru, lo scampanio scivola
sulla volta dei carpini in fondo al parco.

I nani intagliati nella pietra non sono
piú bizzarri del cane buono figlio dell'uomo.
Il padrone è triste, tira al bersaglio, stecca,
rigano le biglie invisibili il prato che abbaia.

Frenesia degli usignoli! Nessuno sa compatire,
e tu vaneggi, minacci, la misura súbito colma.
Siamo davvero pazzi di paura. Se il cielo esagera,
sottrai la gabbia alla plumbea alleanza.

Cicli s'annientano contro una ragione ostile.
Evadi, pensa la luna che si strofina il dorso
ai ruscelli primaverili. In Cina, sai, i cani,
è quasi l'ora di cena, sí, li frollano vivi.

The Old Man

to Leo

Snuffed out imminence, the rising shadow recognizes it.
The most terrible fire is adolescence on glass,
warm sprouting of branches in the dreamed room of coolness.
The madman thrives on these invading trifles.

He staggers in the wheel which ages the air,
quickly, the slow pulsebeats stumble
in the crane's footstep, the pealing of bells glides
along the vault of hornbeams at the bottom of the park.

The dwarfs carved in stone are no
more bizarre than the good dog child of man.
The owner's sad, he shoots at the target, he puts up a fence,
the invisible marbles furrow the barking field.

Frenzy of nightingales! No one understands compassion,
and you rave, you threaten, the measure suddenly brimming.
We're actually crazy with fear. If the sky exaggerates,
you save the crow's-nest from the leaden alliance.

Cycles annul themselves against a hostile reason.
You escape, the moon thinks it might rub its back
on the brooks of springtime. In China, you know, dogs,
it's almost dinnertime, yes, they cure them alive.

Azzurro pari venerdí

Come devo comportarmi, domandai per sapere (per avere,
invece, si chiede) se l'ala nera sarebbe infine abbattuta.

L'astrologo disse: (il destino): generalmente buono,
sarà accaduto e non dovrà rimpiangere, di fianco la luna
falcata radiosa, considerando l'epoca, una piccola soddisfazione
(*in pieno giorno galleggiare nel prato*), la posizione
potrebbe indurla, di Urano o l'inverno che viene dagli spazi
coincide con qualche amica o parente, non esiti a farlo,
procurandole notorietà (*rumore di cesoie dal giardino*),
allo scopo di screditarla, tenga sempre con sé il talismano,
sarà un mese piuttosto monotono.

E lo psichiatra disse: (a proposito del sogno): l'immagine
del bambino con la merda in mano è il mondo
largo luminoso vuoto stretto oscuro colmo elevato profondo
mobile impuro immobile sudicio contagioso disgustante
accogliente minaccioso illimitato doloroso
velenoso vischioso decomposto penetrante
fisiognomico ignominioso numinoso è il mondo
sanguinoso tagliente spermatico molle terrificante
dissipante vertiginoso appropriante metamorfico
vendicativo scaltro ostinato innamorato (sia chiaro)

finché non (finisci di penetrare nella penetrazione) ritorni
alla contemplazione (*il cancello ha una leggiadra gualdrappa di edera*) e
io risposi: che bella pace qui, dove gli oggetti scavano
la loro superficie: volevo voltarmi, ma è fuggita piangendo.

Friday, You Look Blue

How should I act, I demanded to know (to get something,
however, one asks) if the black wing would finally be struck down.

The astrologer said: (your future): generally good,
it will come and you should have no regrets, oblique rays
from the crescent moon, due to the season, a small pleasure
(*to float in the fields in broad daylight*), the position
of Uranus or the invernal influence can resolve the matter,
in conjunction with some friend or relative, don't hesitate to do it,
gaining her notoriety (*sound of clippers from the garden*),
in order to discredit her, always carry a charm,
it will be for the most part a monotonous month.

And the psychiatrist said: (in reference to my dream): the image
of the baby with shit in his hand is the world
vast luminous empty narrow dark overflowing elevated profound
mobile impure immobile filthy contagious disgusting
accommodating menacing boundless painful
venomous viscous rotten penetrating
the world is physiognomical ignominious numinous
bloody sharp spermatic soft terrifying
dissipating vertiginous adaptive metamorphic
vindictive shrewd obstinate enamored (let it be clear)

until you (finish penetrating into the penetration) return
to contemplation (*the gate has a graceful harness of ivy*) and
I replied: there's such a lovely peace here, where objects dig beneath
their surfaces: I wanted to turn around, but she ran away crying.

Lettera della terapia montana

caro padre ho dormito da leone e poi quando il sole innocente mi ha scrutato
con un lampo avevi ragione di colpo tutto solo mi sono affollato col naso e
le braccia spalando dietro i vetri che ho voglia di spezzare i cadaveri frizzanti
perché le boccate di fumo fanno voltare il sole e ho deciso di far crescere i baffi

ne risalta l'intensità dell'intaglio intorno alla mascella atletica e sono
veramente utili al ricercatore di essenze dato che i bambini possono ferirmi
                                                                        mentre
attraverso l'atrio dell'albergo allontanandomi per le cieche distese finalmente
disabitate da quelli orribili embrioni con la coda urlanti e picchi di vigore

le mie punture interne devo agire con calma posarle sul cielo della punta dei
                                                                          peli
farle colare dalla schiuma delle palpebre è troppo pericoloso le conche si
                                                                      spengono
a una a una le vie di scampo il cuore non può essere il cuore non duole
                                                                     sgocciola
sarebbe opportuno dire piú infastidito che feroce sono molto gentile con tutti

per celare la mia indipendenza anche la cugina di Marienbad è qui le sue
                                                                     ginocchia
a punta potrei servirmene lei che mi crede allibito dalla sua indecenza
                                                                    sprezzante
al Mandrillo Bianco in una gita del '61 una vera mangiagalli col suo falsetto
di cucchiaino agitato in un bicchier d'acqua ci sono per fortuna i
                                                              tappa-orecchie

cosí umide o secche le punte ingannano il sottile strato d'aria elettrizzato
dallo strofinio impalpabile e annoiato dei simboli e dello spazio di tre buchi
quadrati elevati ridicolmente nel vuoto spaventato di finestre e carbone l'aria
è piena di croci che scavano la neve e già sento la notte che trottano ispide

Letter from the Mountain Sanitarium

dear father I slept like a lion and then when the innocent sun had searched me
with a flash you were right suddenly all alone I huddled up with my nose and
my arms sweeping behind the windows I want to break the pungent cadavers
because the mouthfuls of smoke make the sun turn and I decided to grow a
moustache

the intensity of the carving stands out next to the athletic jaw and they're
really useful to the researcher of essences given the fact that the children can
hurt me when
I cross the entrance hall of the hotel leaving through the blind spaces
finally
deserted by those horrible screaming embryos with tails and strong picks

I want to act calmly to put my internal pains on the sky of the points of the hair
to make them drip from the eyelid foam is too dangerous the conches go out
one by one the escape routes the heart can't be the heart doesn't ache it trickles
it would be appropriate to say more weary than ferocious I am very kind to
everyone

in order to hide my independence even the cousin from Marienbad is here her
knees
pointed I could use them she who believes me dismayed by her scornful
indecency
to the White Mandrill in an excursion in '61 a real chicken eater with her
falsetto
of teaspoon stirred in a glass of water luckily there are ear plugs

so moist or dry the points deceive the thin layer of air electrified
by the continuous rubbing impalpable and weary of the symbols and the space
of the three holes
squared elevated absurdly in the frightened emptiness of windows and carbon
the air
is full of crosses which dig in the snow and I already feel the night they run
bristly

Alfredo Giuliani

325

Il canto animale

ho rivisto il nostro cantante a me piaceva lo stesso i lunedí mattina come sono
belli i lunedí io gli toglievo il fiato esplodendo le vocali dal naso
                                                              completamente
libero di labiali e dittonghi genuini insomma quando non canta è uno
                                                              spettacolo
e appena non canta piú è una creatura forse soltanto le gengive piú erotiche e
                                                              minerali

la nostra piccola atmosfera soffre di un accumulo di onde disritmiche e ci
                                                              perturba
piú del barrito degli elefanti e poi c'è la grande lezione silenziosa dei gatti dio
com'era bello con la ventosa della gola godere le strisce d'aria e sputare sul
                                                              sole
quanto mi piace il muso ottuso dell'amore che respira muto tra la vegetazione
                                                              nasale

Animal Song

I saw our singer again I liked him as much as ever Monday mornings how
beautiful the Mondays are I took his breath away the vowels exploding from his
nose completely
free of labials and genuine diphthongs that is when he doesn't sing it's a real
performance
and as soon as he stops singing he's a creature perhaps only the most erotic
gums and minerals

our small atmosphere suffers from a build-up of arrhythmical waves and it
bothers us
more than the trumpeting of elephants and then there's the great silent lesson of
cats goodness
how beautiful it was with the suction cup throat to enjoy the layers of air and
spit on the sun
how I do like love's blunt snout which breathes silently in the nasal vegetation

Alfredo Giuliani

Chi l'avrebbe detto

Chi l'avrebbe detto, invitato a pranzo scherzavo,
impedimento accecante, mordevo il cappello, non dicevo
niente: ho il naso finto, si spengono le luci, finché
scoprono che distruggevo rispettosamente un mondo;
ragazzi! invece era davvero lo spolpamento del sangue.

È detto, la chiamo col suo nome ma la costrizione
resta, allungo le gambe ma son corte, mi riassetto,
mi trasferisco da una natica sull'altra, ma la fitta
è qui, nel mezzo; ragazzi! che cosa avrebbe dato quest'uomo
al suo paese se non fosse stato costretto a morire?

Enumero a precipizio, fingo di dormire, emergo dal lago
solo per ridere, metto in guardia l'uccello mortale,
mi riconcilio, volo all'appuntamento, ho bisogno;
mentre decado le brillano gli occhi, rive spopolate dove
vado in punta di piedi, spettri che non sono altro.

Un'ora dopo, grandi sciarpe dai tetti e per le strade,
da vero cristiano che deplora l'Italia, la Cina, il mercato,
toccando la borsa, non avevo nemici, mi tuffo tra i brividi
interni, approvo il tipo freneticamente medio, sono fuori
pericolo, sul piano « Povero cor, che pensi? » cerco l'aria.

Who Would Have Said It

Who would have said it, invited for dinner I joked,
blinding obstacle, I chewed my hat, I didn't say
a thing: I wear a false nose, out go the lights, until
they find that I was respectfully tearing a world apart;
boy, instead they bloody skinned me alive!

It is said, I called out her name but the tightness
remains, I stretch my legs but they're short, I shift,
I move from one buttock to the other, but the pain
is still here, in the middle; boy, what might this man
have done for his country if he hadn't been forced to die?

I count straight down, I pretend to sleep, I emerge from the lake
only to laugh, I put the mortal bird on guard,
I am reconciled, I fly to the appointment, I must;
her eyes flash as I come down, deserted shores where
I walk on tiptoe, ghosts which are nothing more.

One hour later, huge banners on the roofs and in the streets,
like the true Christian who hates Italy, China, the market,
while clutching a moneybag, I had no enemies, I dive into
internal shivers, I endorse the frenetically mediocre man, I am out
of danger, on the piano "Dear Heart, What Do You Think?" I search for the air.

Giancarlo Marmori

Born in La Spezia in 1926, Marmori is the
Paris correspondent for *Il Giorno*. Marmori's
use of irrationality and his arbitrary creation
of a new reality for each poem have been
likened to Kafka. However, in spite of these
experimental qualities, there is also a strong
sense of human personality and emotion in
his poems. Marmori has written several experimental novels, but only one collection of
poems.

His book of poetry is:

Poesie.
    Paris: Editions Caracteres, 1957.

Il tuo totem è la serpe opulenta

Il tuo totem è la serpe opulenta,
grigia di terra, corsiera di calda ombra,
palpito primo del cuore invisibile.
La forza appena creata è in meraviglia
di ascolto, gioiosa d'essere in luce.
E' l'impulso famelico impossibile
a uccidere. Ma tuo costrutto è una forma
accessibile, è violazione amorosa.
Ne parli l'anima a terra. E sia preghiera,
sia ordine e grazia, qui dove solo il giudizio
delimita e il coraggio può assumere.

Your Totem Is the Opulent Serpent

Your totem is the opulent serpent,
gray from the dust, hot shadow charger,
first beat of the invisible heart.
Just after birth the force is astonished
to be hearing, joyous to be in the light.
It's the impulse of greed, impossible
to kill. But your creation is an accessible
form, it is passionate violation.
You speak of it, spirit to earth. Let it be prayer,
let it be order and grace, here where only judgment
limits and only courage can assume.

Stava sempre medicando qualche sua umana ferita

Stava sempre medicando qualche sua umana ferita.
Contava i pochi denari nell'animo chiuso.
Senza serrare mordeva in crudeltà voluttuosa.
Era caldo e nolente nei dolci solchi del corpo.
Da sempre la coscienza germinava sull'azione.
La saggezza non fu che strumento del suo delirare.
Muta la disfatta compariva all'orgoglio alchimico.
Era commedia il suo accadere di pianta già morta.
Egli fu anima e terra composte in un povero mucchio.

He Was Always Nursing Some Human Wound of His

He was always nursing some human wound of his.
He counted his small change in a locked soul.
He bit, not hard, but with voluptuous cruelty.
It was hot and unwilling in the soft furrows of his body.
His conscience had always sprouted in the act.
Wisdom was nothing but a tool of his madness.
Mute, defeat revealed itself to alchemical pride.
It was comedy, his felling of a tree already dead.
He was spirit and earth mixed in a poor heap.

Ancora la tua traccia fine d'animale

Ancora la tua traccia fine d'animale
in allarme ed il suo batticuore,
alla memoria di te solitaria,
o la tua mano bambina che m'urta
e vanifica. Ancora tu, mia furtiva.
Ma ti so libera almeno, tu m'avventuri
la vita, graffio di favola. Le impronte
della volpe traversano la neve di domani.

Still Your Footprint Delicate as an Animal's

Still your footprint delicate as a frightened
animal's and its heartbeat,
at the solitary memory of you,
or your little girl's hand which slaps me
and vanishes. Still you, my furtive one.
But at least I know you're free, you make
my life exciting, fabled scratch. The footprints
of the fox cross tomorrow's snow.

Nulla conosco del sonno che t'ammansisce

Nulla conosco del sonno che t'ammansisce
sul corpo e lo incammina alla terra.
Nulla dei sogni dove un avvampo solleva
la tua figura in orgasmo. So appena importi
la servitú d'una forma, perché tu possa subire
il demonio. Posala qui, contestata. Le civiltà
della fronte restano a guardia. Tu dormi.

I Know Nothing of the Sleep Which Tames You

I know nothing of the sleep which tames
your body and leads it to earth.
Nothing of the dreams where a flame lifts
your body in orgasm. I know slavery to form
means nothing to you, because you can stand
the devil. Place it here, contested. The civilities
on your face remain on guard. You sleep.

Born in Florence in 1926, Pignotti still lives there. He was among the founding editors of *Quartiere*, *Protocolli*, and *Dopotutto*. He was a member of the "Gruppo '63" and the "Gruppo '70." Pignotti has done many exhibitions of *poesia visiva*, also editing the *Antologia della poesia visiva* (Bologna: Sampietro, 1965). He contributes to the Florence daily newspaper *La Nazione* and to the literary supplement of *Paese Sera* in Rome. Pignotti is also a frequent contributor to the cultural programs of RAI-TV. He won the City of Florence Prize in 1958 and the Cino del Duca in 1961, both for his collections of poetry.

His books of poetry are:

Significare.
    Bologna: Leonardi, 1957.
Elegia.
    Firenze: Quartiere, 1958.
Come stanno le cose.
    Lecce: Il Critone, 1959.
L'uomo di qualità.
    Torino: Einaudi, "Il Menabò," 1961.
Nozione di uomo.
    Milano: Mondadori, 1964.
Le nudità provocanti.
    Bologna: Sampietro, 1965.
I postdiluviani.
    Milano: D'Ars, 1967.
Una forma di lotta.
    Milano: Mondadori, 1967.

DA Vita zero

3

Mettere in evidenza
che tutti o quasi salgono di dietro e scendono davanti
mettere in evidenza
ciò che è di marmo
se c'è una corrente d'aria
e il numero di volte in cui prendono il caffè.
Nei casi in cui si giunge a cose avvenute
guardando il piú vicino possibile
inventare.

6

Si riconosce subito chi vive e viceversa.
Se qui si pone
la rappresentazione grafica dell'età e della professione
risulta che le modalità della natura morta
sono quelle stabilite.
Sussiste pure
l'importante proprietà pressoché evidente
che non c'è via d'uscita.

8

Si vede qualcosa
ma non si sa con esattezza che cosa:
apparentemente oggetti
che sfuggono alle leggi di gravità
e al concetto di peso:
la natura non oppone piú resistenza:
anche gli alberi
sono diventati schemi ideologici:
il tema centrale passa in seconda linea:
riassumiamone intanto la trama.

11

In modo tale
che le sole cose a risultare concrete
sono gli ambienti e gli oggetti
gli arredamenti e le fasi della luce

FROM Zero Life

3

Place in evidence
the fact that everyone comes up the back way and leaves out front
place in evidence
things done in marble
if there is a breath of air
and the number of times they drink coffee.
In cases where you come upon things which have already happened
catch the nearest way
to invent.

6

One realizes immediately who is alive and vice versa.
If one places here
a pictorial representation of the age and the profession
it turns out that it is the formality of a still life
which is established.
That important propriety
persists even when it is nearly evident
that there is no exit.

8

One sees something
but one doesn't know exactly what:
apparently objects
that defy the laws of gravity
and the concept of weight:
nature no longer resists:
even the trees
have become ideological schemes:
the central theme becomes secondary:
meanwhile we summarize the plot.

11

In a way such that
the only concrete things to result
are objects and background
the furnishings and phases of light waves,

insomma tutto ciò che può essere visto
e fissato in immagini in quanto tale
fornendo al tempo stesso
la massima illusione di verità
e la piú completa sensazione di astrattezza.
Poi quelle presenze contrapposte
che si distruggono a vicenda e disorientano.

15

Se la commissione
avesse la cortesia di ricordare con me
taluni fatti caratteristici
sui quali desidererei portare la sua attenzione
tenendo anche presente che sono a dieta
e ho quadri astratti alle pareti.

17

Era ancora troppo presto
e allora seduti a finestra aperta
parlammo
e forse sarebbe stato opportuno
tentare di riassumere
sia pure in termini succinti e schematici
le principali conclusioni cui pervenimmo
nell'intervallo di tempo trascorso
prima che come sempre in questi casi
fosse troppo tardi.

22

In altri termini
si tratta di una cronaca intercambiabile
che mira piú a fornire una certa materia
che a raccontare una storia.
Si rompono perciò i contatti con la realtà concreta
e il matematico
si ritira a tu per tu col suo modello
per analizzarlo
studiarlo
semplificarlo
e per risolvere poi
i problemi analitici che esso implica.
È questo il momento piú emozionante
piú poetico.

in other words everything that can be seen
and fixed into images
and simultaneously provide through quanta
the maximum illusion of reality
and the most total sense of abstraction.
Then those contraposed appearances
destroy each other and scatter.

15

If the commission
would have the kindness to remember with me
certain characteristic facts
to which I would like to draw its attention,
always keeping in mind that I'm on a diet
and that I have abstract paintings on my walls.

17

It was still too early
so we sat and talked
by the open window
and perhaps it would have been opportune
to try to go over again
even though in brief and schematic terms
the principal conclusions at which we arrived
in the interval of time which had transpired
before, as always in these cases,
it was too late.

22

In other words
what we're dealing with is an interchangeable chronicle
which aims more at providing a certain material
than telling a story.
And so contacts with concrete reality are broken
and the mathematician
retires to you (and for you) with his model
for analyzing it
studying it
simplifying it
and in order then to resolve
the analytical problems it implies.
This is the most touching moment
the most poetic.

DA Riduzioni

IV

QUI ALLARMI ALLA RINFUSA
E LA FEDE NEPPURE UNA MERCE DI TRANSITO
QUI LO SPESSORE DELLA NAUSEA
E LA BONTÀ UN LUSSO

VII

STANCHEZZA DEGLI AVVENIMENTI
MECCANIZZAZIONE DELLA NOIA
ANCHE L'AMORE A VARIAZIONE DELLA NOIA
LA NOIA UN DIVERTIMENTO
LA NOIA IL COSTO DELLA VITA
VITA SENZA ISTRUZIONI PER L'USO
VITA SOTTOCOSTO

VIII

SESSO E PUBBLICITÀ
SESSO ALL'INGROSSO
FASCINO IN SERIE
APPUNTAMENTI DI MASSA
INCONTRI CON NESSUNO
DI SCENA IL PEGGIO

IX

ASSUEFAZIONE ALL'INSUCCESSO
PRATICA DELLA SOTTOMISSIONE
VIA L'ALTEZZA
VIA LA PROFONDITÀ
VIA TUTTO
SEMPRE IL BISOGNO DEL DOPPIO

FROM Reductions

IV

HERE YOU GET ALARMED AT THE CONFUSION
AND FAITH NOT EVEN A TRANSIT COMMODITY
HERE THE THICKNESS OF NAUSEA
AND KINDNESS A LUXURY

VII

WEARINESS FROM EVENTS
MECHANIZATION OF BOREDOM
ALSO LOVE AS A VARIATION OF BOREDOM
BOREDOM AN ENTERTAINMENT
BOREDOM THE COST OF LIVING
LIFE WITHOUT INSTRUCTIONS FOR OPERATION
LIFE AT LESS THAN COST

VIII

SEX AND PUBLICITY
WHOLESALE SEX
MASS-PRODUCED CHARM
MASS-RENDEZVOUS
MEETINGS WITH NO ONE
THE WORST OF SCENES

IX

GETTING USED TO FAILURE
EXPERIENCE IN SUBMISSION
VIA THE HEIGHTS
VIA THE DEPTHS
VIA EVERYTHING
ALWAYS IN NEED OF TWICE AS MUCH

Poesia e politica

I sentimenti rasi al suolo,
lavorando in comune,
confrontando
verità con verità
errore con errore,
li abbiamo ricostruiti, fatti piú alti,
ma una foglia esita a darsi totalmente.
Anche il sole e il cielo,
questo sole e questo cielo, sono recenti.
Oggi si inventa un colore, domani si colma un sogno
e ciò assume un valore politico,
un significato di poesia.
Le parole come i fatti si bagnano alla pioggia,
si arroventano al sole.
Non è fatica
questa di estrarre la vita,
di depurarla dalle scorie,
è vivere, vivere piú forte.
Con cosa viene incontro il vento?

Poetry and Politics

Feelings razed to the ground,
working together,
confronting
truth with truth
error with error,
we have reconstructed them, made them higher,
but a leaf hesitates to give itself totally.
Even the sun and sky,
this sun and this sky, are recently built.
Today one invents a color, tomorrow one fills a dream
and that takes on a political value,
a poetic meaning.
Words as deeds get wet in the rain,
get red-hot in the sun.
It isn't tiring
this business of extracting life,
of purifying it from dross,
it is to live, live more strongly.
What does the wind bring?

Amelia Rosselli

Born in Paris in 1930, Rosselli has lived in Switzerland, England, and the United States; she now lives in Rome. Rosselli studied music throughout Europe and has composed for theater and film. She has also done experimental compositions of *musica concreta*. Her poems have appeared frequently in Italian, American, and international magazines.

Her books of poetry are:

24 poesie.
    Torino: Einaudi: "Il Menabò," 1963.
Variazioni belliche.
    Milano: Garzanti, 1964.
Serie ospedaliera.
    Milano: Garzanti, 1969.
Documento (1966–1973).
    Milano: Garzanti, 1976.

DA Variazioni belliche

Nel letargo che seguiva l'ingranaggio dei
pochi, io giacevo, felice e disordinata, disordinata
all'estremo; e le lingue dei serpi s'avventavano
come fuoco vicino al capezzale. Vicino al capezzale
moriva un drago, salumiere con i suoi salumi, le
sue code che pendevano molto puzzolenti, ma delicate
nel loro odorare insieme.

E se l'antigone che vegliava silenziosa, molto silenziosa
ai miei poderi i miei prodotti disordinati, disadorni
di gloria, se essa fosse venuta col suo gradito grido
d'allarme, io morivo, molto silenziosa allarme.

FROM Martial Variations

In the lethargy which follows the machinations of the
few, I was lying down, happy and disheveled, disheveled
in the extreme: and the tongues of snakes flickered
like fire near my pillow. Near my pillow
a dragon was dying, a deli butcher with his sausages,
his tails hung there stinking, but delicate
in their aroma when taken together.

And if the silent, very silent Antigone who at
my farm watched over my messy produce, stripped of its
glory, if she had come with her welcome shriek
of alarm, I was dying, very silent alarm.

Affascinata dalla praticità osservai un
uomo usuale senza curve portare lievemente un materasso
rosa sulle spalle, mentre ridendo come pulcinella ricordavo
che v'eri. E non finí male la serata, se non che tu esistevi
oltre ogni riflessione, e fuori d'ogni previsione. Tornata
a casa dopo tante e tante insegne luminose v'eri ancora
e ancora e ancora. Ancorata a te la tua immagine in me
non si disfa, tu la proteggi: l'immagine che disfaceva
giornate e giornate e giornate ritornava con te, senza di
te per te nella solitudine di questa primavera che gal-
leggia in pieno inverno, la mia anima!

Fascinated by practicality I watched an
ordinary unmuscular man easily carry a pink mattress
on his shoulders, while smiling like Pulcinella I remembered
that you were there. And the evening wouldn't have ended badly, except that
you existed
beyond every reflection, and outside every expectation. Having returned
to my house after so many neon signs you were there again
and again and again. Anchored to you your image in me
doesn't melt, you protect it: the image which melted
days and days and days returned with you, without
you, through you in the solitude of this Spring which floats
in the middle of Winter, my soul!

Per una impossibile gagliarda esperienza
rompevamo isolamenti faticosamente, ma
i carri che ci portavano come frutta al
mercato erano lugubri automobili bianche
se nevicava, infernali nella pioggia. Corrompendo
guardie e guardie la mente si decise per
un sopraluogo faticoso perché ingannava
anche se stessa: la festa fu un incontro
tra diavoli alla moda, ogn'amore fuggí
quando tu slacciasti la finestra del tuo
potere avvelenato alle braccia del mio
incanto versione povera dell'invidia, ma
lo spirito vinceva ancora con decisioni
povere prese in cantina.
        Dopo miserie e
nascoste disperazioni la Domenica fu un
perdono e una disperazione, il mare in
moto soffocò querele dello spirito mentre
ingranaggi portarono sollievo e la colpa
fu la colpa accettata se disperazioni sono
moto alla felicità.

seventy beggars and a shirt which was ripping
to nothing, on a whim I stretched myself out in
the nothing and everything was laurel and beneficence, the king
of the poor people benefitted, camel which crawled. A hard,
fine rain penetrated, because I needed help
I penetrated into rooms furnished with a true life
which with capital letters moved away from mine, those who
were condemned to death were kindly obliging. Invitations
slid over the foundations of a permeable
city: no hidden beast dusted off
the goats which marched enraptured through the mountains of
the Trinità: a camel, two Indians and people who were masters
of all the arts, music and mathematics, the fury
of achievable dreams. Lost in the basin of shadow
the white cobwebs and the dust on the eyelashes,
particles and small pearls under a terrible rain
resolved for the better on a closed life.

settanta pezzenti e una camicia che si rompeva
nel nulla, per un capriccio io mi stendevo nel
nulla e tutto era alloro e beneficenza, benefatto
il re dei poveri, cammello che strisci. Una pioggia
dura, sottile, penetrava, per un bisogno d'assistenza
io penetravo in camere arredate ad una vera vita
che con le maiuscole si scostava dalla mia, gentilmente
servizievoli erano i condannati a morte. Inviti
strisciavano per i cardini piovosi d'una città
permeabile: nessuna bestia nascosta spolverava
le capre che marciavano estasiate per i monti della
Trinità: un cammello, due indiani e la gente maestra
di tutte le arti, musica e matematica, il furore
di sogni realizzabili. Perduta nella vasca d'ombre
le ragnatele bianche e la polvere per le ciglia,
granelli e piccole perle sotto una pioggia miserissima
decidevano per il meglio una vita chiusa.

Through a vigorous and impossible experience
we broke our isolation laboriously, but
the carts which carried us like fruit to
market were funereal automobiles white
if it was snowing, hellish in the rain. Corrupting
guards and guards the mind settles on
exhaustive on the spot investigation because it deceived
even itself: the festival was an encounter
of fashionable devils, every lover ran away
when you undid the window of your
poisonous power on the arms of my
enchantment poor version of envy, but
the spirit still conquered with poor
decisions made in the cellar.
                              After miseries and
hidden desperation Sunday was
pardon and desperation, the sea in
motion stifled complaint of the spirit while
mechanisms will bring relief and guilt
was accepted guilt if desperation is
a means to happiness.

Neve

Sembrano minuscoli insetti festeggianti
uno sciame di motori squillanti, una
pena discissa in faticose attenzioni
e una radunata di bravate.

Nevica fuori; e tutto questo rassomiglia
ad una crisi giovanile di pianto se
non fosse che ora le lacrime sono asciutte
come la neve.

Un esperto di questioni meteorologiche
direbbe che si tratta di un innamoramento
ma io che sono un esperto in queste
cose direi forse che si tratta di una

imboscata!

Snow

They seem to be tiny insects celebrating
a swarm of shrill motors, a
pain split into difficult attentions
and a gathering of daring actions.

Snow outside; and all this resembles
a youthful crisis of tears if
it weren't for the fact that now the tears are dry
as the snow.

An expert on meteorological questions
would say that this had to do with an infatuation
but I who am expert in these
things would say that it has to do with an

ambush!

Amelia Rosselli

Nessuno

Nessuno
ammise d'esser stato tradito
finsi calma frenavo il pianto
poi riportando il dato in
cronaca.

Stanando periodici dal loro
comodo cassetto,
il pavimento costretto a
spianarsi.

Sminuito impero,
non era sicuro di poter tentare il tragitto
passato il tempo in cui nello *slip*
ti guardavi contenta, accontentata
d'un umore qualsiasi
follie-bergères dietro ogni
mobile, spostabile definitivamente
ogni mattina.

Gli si chiedeva l'artifizio
la nona sinfonia, l'estratto
coniugale stretto tra due pugni:
un nervosismo
forse una angolazione
sbadata:

come la promiscuità.

No One

No one
admitted to having been betrayed
pretending calm I held back my tears
then reported the fact in
the chronicle.

Ferreting periodicals out of their
comfortable drawer,
the floor forced to
smooth itself out.

Diminished empire,
he wasn't sure he could make the trip
time past when you looked at yourself
happily in the slip, satisfied
by just any old whim
folies-bergères behind every
piece of furniture, definitively moveable
every morning.

One asked him what artifice it was
the ninth symphony, the conjugal
extract tight between two fists:
a nervousness
perhaps a careless
angle shot:

like promiscuity.

Dialogo con i morti

scendete voi, abbracciate questa vostra
figlia che annaspa tra tomboloni e
mussulmani che giocano con le sue braccia
che invece, bianche, vorrebbero abbracciare
o strozzare ma mai fallire questi colpi
che diurnamente ricevono, pieni di
lividi e lividamente promuovete una
sete di dolcezza e aspra giustizia
oppure non lasciate più ch'io tormenti
(ed essi mi tormentano) questa mente
che muore ad ogni istante piena di
stretti nodi che ingombrano la sua
piana marcia ad un paese più bello introvabile
mentre muore lividamente anche la voglia
di essere più belli di quello che si è.

Scendete, e scendete ancòra—e infilate
nella vostra banale gioia il significare
d'una vita che ballonzola rattristata
dalla piena potenza del male degli
altri e del mio—il non sapere difendermi
da ottusa voglia.

Vivere un istante o mezz'ora e poi
ritrovarsi per una svista del pensiero
ancora più ingombra di inessenziali
rabbie!

Voce in capitolo non ebbero le sagge
mani: vi incontrai per poi farmi ostinatamente
massacrare da voi.

E il massacro volge in lussuria: e
la lussuria in estasi contemplata nel
grano sifilitico che s'attorciglia al
mio collo, stremato dai troppi abbandoni.

Dialogue with the Dead

descend, embrace this daughter
of yours who gropes among ruins and
Moslems who play with her arms
which instead, white, they'd like to embrace
or flay but never missing these beatings
they receive daily, covered with
bruises and lividly you promote a
thirst for sweetness and hard justice
or you won't leave off until I torment
(and they torment me) this mind
that dies every moment full of
tight knots which obstruct its
slow march to a more beautiful undiscoverable country
while even the wish to be
more beautiful than you are dies lividly.

Descend, and keep descending—and thread
through your banal joy the meaning
of a life which trips along saddened
by the full power of others' evil
and my own—not knowing how to defend myself
from dull desire.

To live for an instant or a half an hour and then
find yourself through an oversight
still more encumbered by inessential
angers!

Wise hands had no say in the
matter: I met you to let you slaughter
me again and again.

And slaughter turns into luxury: and
luxury into ecstasy contemplated in the
syphilitic grain which coils itself
around my neck, exhausted by too many betrayals.

Amelia Rosselli   365

Abbandonarsi al vuoto sesso e poi ritenersi
anche insudiciati dalla nera pece del
fare così angusto dei poveri.

Sesso e violenza s'abbandonarono e
si ritrovarono infradiciati quel mattino
glorioso ove tutto cadde a pezzi, e
se saggezza con le sue microscopiche
usanze non ritira truppe dal votarsi
all'angoscia, e se una piccola fierezza
o svista può provocare angosce ritardate
allora cade a pezzi la giornata triste
per la tua feconda grettezza.

Ed è inerme che io battaglio per una
chiarezza che non ha permesso d'esistere
sinché tu giochi con questa providenza
che ci stampò in faccia quell'ansia
di esistere fuori d'un commerciale
attenersi alle più basse voglie; ma
vidi anche nella tua faccia il sigillo
della noncuranza e del vuoto armarsi
alla morte senza pensare alla vita!

Abandoning yourself to empty sex and then holding back
still sweaty from the black pitch of
the low doings of the poor.

Sex and violence are indulged and
rediscovered soaked that glorious
morning when everything falls to pieces, and
if wisdom with its microscopic
customs doesn't call troops back from spilling themselves
into anguish, and if a small boldness
or oversight can provoke it distresses you delay
then the sad day falls to pieces
because of your fertile shabbiness.

And I battle unarmed for a
clarity that has no right to live
as long as you play with this providence
which printed on our faces that fear
of existing outside a commercial
clinging to the basest desires; but
I also saw in your face the seal
of indifference and emptiness arming itself
for death without thinking of life!

Sciopero generale 1969

lampade accesissime e nell'urlo
d'una quieta folla rocambolesca
trovarsi lì a far sul serio: cioè
rischiare! che nell'infantilismo
apparente schianti anche il mio
potere d'infischiarmene.

Un Dio molto interno poteva bastare
non bastò a me il mio egoismo

non bastò a queste genti il sapore
d'una ricchezza nella rivincita

del resto strozzata. Dovevamo
esprimere il meglio: regalarsi

ad una retorica che era urlo
di protesta ad una distruzione

impavida nelle nostre impaurite
case. (Persi da me quell'amore
al verticale, a solitario dio
rivoluzionandomi nella gente
asportandomi dal cielo.)

Rosa ripulita
solitudine dimenticabile
contadino meticoloso
migliore del mondo
riconoscersi serbatoio
di nullità recondita
sfinita sopraffazione
morte-solitudine
tanto più pregevole
se sottile m'armo.

General Strike 1969

lamps all lit up and in the shouting
of a peaceful but rumbling crowd
to find yourself there to do something serious: in
other words, to run a risk! even my ability
not to care snapped in that obvious
infantilism.

A God deep inside might have been enough
my egoism was not enough for me

the smell of a strangled wealth
which came from winning back the rest wasn't

enough for these people. We had to
express a better way: allowing ourselves

a rhetoric which was a shout
of protest for a fearless

destruction in our frightened
houses. (I lost that vertical
love, to solitary God
revolutionizing myself in the people
removing myself from heaven.)

Tidied rose
forgettable solitude
meticulous peasant
best in the world
recognizing your reservoir
of hidden nothingness
exhausted abuse
death-solitude
so much more valuable
if, slender, I arm myself.

Amelia Rosselli   369

Edoardo Sanguineti

Born in Genoa in 1930, Sanguineti now lives
in Salerno, teaching Italian literature at the
University. Dante is his specialty and he has
written several books on the subject. Sanguineti has written fiction and opera libretti,
as well as poetry. He was a member of the
"Gruppo '63" and "i novissimi." Perhaps
more than any other member of the Italian
avant-garde, he has close connections with
contemporary French experimental writers.
His poetry is often a cross between *nouveau
roman* techniques and poetic surrealism.
And through it all shines his peculiarly Italian
political consciousness.

His books of poetry are:

Laborintus.
     Milano: Magenta, 1956.
Opus metricum.
     Milano: Rusconi e Paolazzi, 1960.
K e altre cose.
     Milano: Scheiwiller, 1962.
Triperuno.
     Milano: Feltrinelli, 1964.
Wirrwarr.
     Milano: Feltrinelli, 1972.
Catamerone, (1951–1971).
     Milano: Feltrinelli, 1974.

DA Laborintus

Titulus est
Loborintus
quasi laborem
habens intus

1

composte terre in strutturali complessioni sono Palus Putredinis
riposa tenue Ellie e tu mio corpo tu infatti tenue Ellie eri il mio corpo
immaginoso quasi conclusione di una estatica dialettica spirituale
noi che riceviamo la qualità dai tempi
                          tu e tu mio spazioso corpo
di flogisto che ti alzi e ti materializzi nell'idea del nuoto
sistematica costruzione in ferro filamentoso lamentoso
lacuna lievitata in compagnia di una tenace tematica
composta terra delle distensioni dialogiche insistenze intemperanti
le condizioni esterne è evidente esistono realmente queste condizioni
esistevano prima di noi ed esisteranno dopo di noi qui è il dibattimento
liberazioni frequenza e forza e agitazione potenziata e altro
aliquot lineae desiderantur
                   dove dormi cuore ritagliato
e incollato e illustrato con documentazioni viscerali dove soprattutto
vedete igienicamente nell'acqua antifermentativa ma fissati adesso
quelli i nani extratemporali i nani insomma o Ellie
nell'aria inquinata
             in un costante cratere anatomico ellittico
perché ulteriormente diremo che non possono crescere

tu sempre la mia natura e rasserenata tu canzone metodologica
periferica introspezione dell'introversione forza centrifuga delimitata
Ellie tenue corpo di peccaminose escrescenze
                      che possiamo roteare
e rivolgere e odorare e adorare nel tempo
                desiderantur (essi)
analizzatori e analizzatrici desiderantur (essi) personaggi anche
ed erotici e sofisticati
          desiderantur desiderantur

FROM Laborintus

Titulus est
Loborintus
quasi laborem
habens intus

1

compound earths in structural compositions are Palus Putredinis
slender Ellie rests and you my body you slender Ellie were really my
imaginative body quasi-conclusion of an ecstatic spiritual dialectic
we who take the quality from the times
                                you and you my roomy body
of phlogiston which you raise and you materialize in the idea of swimming
systematic construction in filamentary sorrowful iron
leavened lacuna together with a tenacious thematic
compound earth of the dialogical extensions intemperate insistences
the external conditions it is clear really exist these conditions
existed before us and they will exist after us here is the debate
liberations frequency and power and potentialized agitation and other
aliquot lineae desiderantur
                       where you sleep heart cut out
and glued and illustrated with visceral documentation where above all
you see hygenically in the anti-fermentative water but those now
fixed the extratemporal dwarfs the dwarfs in other words or Ellie
in the polluted air
                  in a constant anatomical elliptical crater
because further on we will say they can't grow

you always my nature and cleared up you methodological canzone
peripheral introspection of the introversion defined centrifugal force
slender Ellie body of sinful excrescences
                         that we can swing
and turn and smell and adore in time
                       desiderantur (them)
analyzer and analyzeresses desiderantur (them) also characters
and erotic and sophisticated
                     desiderantur desiderantur

2

e una volta Mare Humorum guardami bene (la rottura di una personalità)
e dilatami (tutto suscettibile di assentimento) e combinami in un'epoca
indirizzando i sensi (il tempo dell'occhio che risuona nel quieto addome) e
toccami
            perché io sono al piú giusto confine organico sepolcro
complicato per godere e riuscirò dopo la fluida intromissione
una moltitudine riuscirò nella grammatica speculativa e simbolizzato in cifre
terribilmente armoniose di fronte all'eruzione di carbonizzanti passioni
infatti e alle distorsioni relative di fronte a lunghi funghi fumosi
che si gonfiano e indico l'ustione linguistica frammenti che costellano
il notturno giardino dei succubi sopra l'atollo delle labbra coralline
si impone e oscilla lo spettro maschile con voce telefonica
(sed non omnis emissio dice) dalla casa di giuoco
il compasso scottante io che colloco in calde comunicazioni prenotabili
gli opprimenti (humoris carnalis) ed enfiati fantocci continuatamente
Lacus Somniorum emuntori (al punto dell'inevitabile invocazione è carnalis)
dell'orinazione dell'encefalo in tutta la sua massa precipitabile
è finita è finita la perspicacia passiva primitiva è finita eppure
in uno stadio enunciatamente ricostruttivo di responsabile ricomposizione
è finita infine è atomizzata e io sono io sono una moltitudine
attraverso ritentate esperienze Mare Lacus accoglimi (est proprie pollutio)

il tenero mattino conduce la mastite a visitare il triste cervelletto
sensibile al vento per incantamento est duplex intellectus
e tu ascoltami bene amore Mare Lacus
                            non c'è piú divertimento
ridurremo forse la testa umana a secco luogo geometrico ma
comparata con l'ideale esigenza questa rivolta
non avrà fine

2

at one time Mare Humorum look at me carefully (the breakdown of a
personality)
and expand me (everything susceptible to approval) and combine me in an
epoch
addressing the senses (the eye's time that echoes in the peaceful abdomen) and
touch me
because I am at the most just organic outpost elaborate
sepulcher to enjoy and I will succeed after the fluid intrusion
a multitude I will succeed in speculative grammar and symbolized in ciphers
terribly harmonious before the eruption of burnt actual
passions and to the relative distortions before the long smoky mushrooms
which swell and I point to the linguistic scalding fragments which spangle
the nocturnal garden of evil spirits on top of the atoll of coraline lips
becomes necessary and the masculine spectre wavers with a telephone voice
(sed non omnis emissio he says) from the gambling house
the scorching compass I who place in hot reservable communications
the oppressive (humoris carnalis) and swollen puppets continuously
Lacus Somniorum emuntori (at the point of the inevitable invocation it is
carnalis)
of the encephalitic's urination in all his precipitable mass
it's finished it's finished the passive primitive perspicacity is finished and yet
in a stadium enunciatively reconstructed by responsible recomposition
it's finished it's finished it's atomized and I am I am a multitude
across retried experiences Mare Lacus receive me (est proprie pollutio)

the tender morning leads the mastitis to visit the sad little brain
sensitive to the wind because of enchantment est duplex intellectus
and listen to me well love Mare Lacus
there's no more enjoyment
perhaps we should reduce the human head to a dry geometric place but
comparative with the ideal exigency this revolt
will have no end

DA Erotopaegnia

3

afferra questo mercurio, questa fredda gengiva, questo miele, questa sfera
di vetro arido; misura attentamente la testa del nostro
bambino e non torcere adesso il suo piede
impercettibile:
                    nel tuo capezzolo devi ormai convertire
un prolungato continente di lampade, il fiato ossessivo dei giardini
critici, le pigre balene del ventre, le ortiche
e il vino, e la nausea e la ruggine;
                                        perché ogni strada subito
vorrà corrergli incontro, un'ernia ombelicale incidere
il suo profilo di fumo, qualche ippopotamo donargli
i suoi denti di forfora e di fosforo nero:
                                        evita il vento,
i luoghi affollati, i giocolieri, gli insetti;
e a sei mesi egli potrà raddoppiare il suo peso, vedere l'oca,
stringere la vestaglia, assistere alla caduta dei gravi;
strappalo dunque alla sua vita di alghe e di globuli, di piccoli nodi,
di indecisi lobi:
                    il suo gemito conquisterà le tue liquide ferite
e i suoi occhi di obliquo burro correggeranno questi secoli senza nome!

4

in te dormiva come un fibroma asciutto, come una magra tenia, un sogno;
ora pesta la ghiaia, ora scuote la propria ombra; ora stride,
deglutisce, orina, avendo atteso da sempre il gusto
della camomilla, la temperatura della lepre, il rumore della grandine,
la forma del tetto, il colore della paglia:
                                        senza rimedio il tempo
si è rivolto verso i suoi giorni; la terra offre immagini confuse;
saprà riconoscere la capra, il contadino, il cannone?
non queste forbici veramente sperava, non questa pera,
quando tremava in quel tuo sacco di membrane opache.

FROM Erotopaegnia

3

grab this mercury, this cold gum, this honey, this sphere
of arid glass; carefully measure our baby's
head and not twisting his imperceptible
foot now;
        in your nipple you must now change
an extended continent of lamps, the obsessive breathing of critical
gardens, the belly's lazy whales, nettles
and wine, and nausea and rust;
                because every street will
suddenly want to run to him, an umbilical hernia cutting
its profile of smoke, some hippopotamus presenting his teeth
of dandruff and black phosphorus to him:
                  avoid the wind,
crowded places, jugglers, insects;
and at six months he will have doubled his weight, looking at the goose,
wringing the dressing-gown, to watch the fall of the heavy ones;
tear him then from his life of algae and globules, of small lumps,
of wavering lobes:
          his groaning will conquer your liquid wounds
and slanting butter eyes will rectify these nameless centuries!

4

it slept in you like a dry fibroma, like a thin tapeworm, a dream,
now it crushes the gravel, now it shakes its own shadow; now it screeches,
swallows, urinates, having always waited for the taste
of camomile, the rabbit's temperature, the noise of the hail,
the shape of the roof, the color of straw;
              without remedy time
turns back on its days: the earth offers confused images;
will it know how to recognize the goat, farmer, cannon?
not these forceps it truly hoped, not this pear,
when it trembled in your sack of opaque membranes.

Edoardo Sanguineti

5

e lugubri incidono; vegetali (dell'utero) veneres; le caverne,
umidi; raschiano vel obscoenissimas, fermentano; ambigui fischiano
(e dunque ascoltali!) e notturni se optare exclamant; e a tratti (incubi!)
cantano: imprecisi injurii; mostruosi palpitando (i figli! impliciti)
petulantes inquieti; con deformi sogni schiume caldi spremono;
cotti! senza sesso et lascivientes; tra croste (et luxuriantes!) eterni.

6

ora consuma nel suo pollice il reggicalze e l'armadio:
il suo naso è il piccione;
                                        la sua pupilla è il dado;
morde già nel tuo piede la carrozza e il sedano:
non resiste il vetro, non il nastro;
                                        il cielo è la sua pelle tenera;
ma nella durezza delle sue ossa lo sorprendiamo esistere,
e vediamo pelle sue unghie crescere la nostra morte.

7

la cosa come la passa; (la porta appunto); (la coscia); (la finestretta): il pugnale!
(la passa!); e tremando! (proporzioni terribili!); ingigantito! premendo (. . .);
e la bottiglia appunto:
                                        nelle latrine; e cosí appunto; in quell'aria
infetta; lei paziente, bianchissima: e come la passa questo pugnale! tremando!

5

and mournful they cut; vegetables (of the uterus) veneres; the caverns,
damp; they scrape vel obscoenissimas, they ferment; they hiss ambiguous
(and then listen to them!) and nights se optare exclamant; and at intervals
(incubuses!)

they sing; imprecise injurii; monstrous palpitating (the children! implicit)
petulantes inquieti; with deformed dreams hot foams they squeeze;
cooked! without sex et lascivientes; between crusts (et luxuriantes!) eternal.

6

now it consumes its thumb the stocking-rack the armoire:
its nose is a dove;
its pupil is a die;

it already bites the carriage and sedan in your feet;
it doesn't resist the glass, nor the ribbon;
the sky is his tender skin;

but we surprise its existing in the hardness of its bones,
and we see our death growing in its fingernails.

7

how the thing passes by; (the door precisely); (the thigh); (the little window):
the dagger!

(it passes!); and trembling! (terrible proportions!); enormous! pressing (. . .);
and the bottle precisely:
in the latrines; and thus precisely; in that polluted

air: she patient, very white: and how this dagger passes! trembling!

DA Purgatorio de l'inferno

1
ti attende il filo spinato, la vespa, la vipera, il nichel
bianco e lucente che non si ossida all'aria
                                        ti attende Pitagora
che disse che delle cose è sostanza il numero
                                        e tu prendi del polipo
gli otto tentacoli guerniti di ventose e *An die Hoffnung* (op. 94)
perché questo, questo lo prendono (essi)
                              lo prendono perché lo trovano

osserva Iside e i costumi abruzzesi, le medaglie per la campagna di Cina
del 1901, la maschera di Peppe Nappa
                              la città di Cannstadt
che fu incorporata nella città di Stuttgart nel 1905
e conoscerai la confindustria e la svastica, il 13 maggio e il 24 gennaio
lo spillo di sicurezza che non sa pungere, il lecco lecco e lo Spirito
Santo
      e tu prendi il gliconio e la glicerina, e Hans Pfeiffer
che nacque a Kassel nel 1907, perché questo, questo lo prendono
(essi), lo prendono perché lo trovano
                              perché lo trovano a lavorare

perché questa è, Federico, la DESCRITTIONE DEL GRAN PAESE: è la targa
automobilistica della provincia di Foggia (FG)
                              è la nave di linea a vapore
1870, è il babbuino, è il bisonte
                        e tu prendi gli urodeli e il ministro
Pella, la méthode des tractions rythmées de la langue (due à
Laborde), il Petrus amat multum dominam Bertam
                                        perché questo,
questo lo prendono (essi), lo prendono perché lo trovano, perché
lo trovano a lavorare (. . .)
                        et anderà in pregione.

FROM Purgatory of Hell

1

the barbed wire awaits you, the wasp, the viper, the bright
and shining nickel that doesn't rust in the air
                                        Pythagoras awaits you
who said that number is the essence of things
                                        and you take from the polyp
the eight tentacles fitted out with suction cups and *An die Hoffnung* (op. 94)
because this, this they take (they)
                        they take it because they find it

he watched Iside and the Abruzzese costumes, the medals for the China
                                                        campaign
of 1901, the mask of Peppe Nappa
                        the city of Cannstadt
which was incorporated into the city of Stuttgart in 1905
and you will know the confindustria and the swastika, May 13 and January 24
the safety-pin which doesn't know how to prick, the little tidbit and the Holy
Spirit
        and you take the glyconic and the glycerine, and Hans Pfeiffer
who was born in Kassel in 1907, because this, this they take
(they), they take it because they find it
                        because they find it to work

because this is, Federico, the DESCRIPTION OF THE GREAT TOWN: it's the automobile
license plate for the province of Foggia (FG)
                                        it's the steamship of the line
1870, it's the baboon, the buffalo
                                and you take the urodeles and Minister
Pella, la méthode des tractions rythmées de la langue (two à
Laborde), the Petrus amat multum dominam Bertram
                                        because this,
this they take (they), they take it because they find it, because
they find it to work (. . .)
                        et he will go to prison.

Edoardo Sanguineti   381

2

ma le "compiaciute descrizioni"; e allora: oggi (disse); (e allora,
anche, *onze, rue Payenne*); ("complete di indirizzo"); oggi siamo,
lo siamo (disse, anche);
                                    —perché quello di Resnais (dissi)
è un film (inconsciamente) fascista—:
                                    ma oggi (disse Octavio Paz) tutti
lo siamo (marxisti); e intanto intendeva 'tutti' (e intanto soltanto
'nosotros'): ma il 12 luglio, allora: e qualcuno (io
dissi) aveva appena tentato (ma come aveva risposto a Weber?);
di decidere ("je suis un homme");
                                    —ricordi come oscillava
Weber, sotto la pioggia? come il tergicristallo—:
                                    la questione; poi
disse che dovevo ("de gauche") dunque spiegare (spiegarmi); (quello che
intendevo); (e intendeva, allora: quello che intendevo
per fascismo):
                  e io le dissi ("de gauche"): ah, non posso,
non posso; (amarti); ma il 5 luglio, allora; in questo (dissi),
ah in questo piccolo caffè; ah come, allora, mi pensava!
diverso! ah come diversa, allora! come la pensavo!
                                    —non amo
(disse poi); (le azioni simboliche, intendeva); ma Fautrier disse:
ora ci penso io (in tutti i sensi)—
                  poi Calvino mi disse
(al Norman) che Pavese diceva; allora dissi (a me stesso): spiegherò;
proprio le medesime cose (di Paz); anche questo (spiegherò); (anche
questo non poter[ti] amare); di altro si deve, dunque, parlare (io dissi):
di altro (ormai) dire (dirò): spiegherò; una poesia (dissi) scriverò: sul
fascismo:
                  parlerò a mio figlio; dirò: ma di tali insistiti segni
l'ostinata, figlio, riconosci dissimulazione (. . .); ma spiegherò
come la borghesia (alta) italiana; come non posso amarla; come sogna
(ancora); quel fascismo (spiegherò); (questo); come il figlio deve,
adesso; (di cui ha salvato); essere la figura; (la struttura); (. . .);
della speranza:
                  e al giornalista cattolico (P.R.I., forse?) scrissi,
infatti; come era; ah, io devo (dissi); (il Filius); doveva essere, ah;
io devo (a me stesso, dissi); la figura essere; una giustificazione;
(illustrazione); della disperazione; una spiegazione devo; della storica
impartecipazione (patita) alla storia:

but the "satisfied descriptions"; and then: today (he said): (and then,
as well, *onze, rue Payenne*); ("complete with address"): today we are,
we are that (he said, as well);
                              —because that Resnais film (I said)
is (unconsciously) Fascist—:
                         but today (said Octavio Paz) we're
all that (Marxists); and meanwhile I understood "all" (and meanwhile only
"nosotros"): but July 12, then: and someone (I
said) had just tried (but how had he answered Weber?);
to decide ("je suis un homme");
                              —do you remember how Weber
went back and forth, in the rain? like a windshield wiper—:
                                                       the question; then
he said that I had to ("de gauche") then explain (explain myself); (what I
understood); (and he understood, then: what I understood
as Fascism):
            and I said to them ("de gauche"): ah, I can't,
I can't; (love you); but July 5, then; in this (I said),
ah in this little café; ah what, then, he thought of me!
different! ah how different, then! what I thought about it!:
                                                       —I don't love
(I then said); (symbolic actions, he meant); but Fautrier said:
now I'll take care of it (in every sense)—
                                    then Calvino said to me
(to Norman) what Pavese said; then I said (to myself): I will explain;
even the very same things (as Paz); even this (I will explain); (even
this I can't love [you]); then one must speak of others (I said):
(now) to speak (I will speak) of others: I will explain; I will write (I said) a poem:
on Fascism:
            I will speak to my son; I will say: but you recognize dissimulation,
son, as the most stubborn of such insistent signs (. . .); but I will explain
how the Italian middle class (upper); why I can't love it; how it dreams
(still); that Fascism (I will explain); (this); as the son must,
now; (from which he has saved); to be the figure; (the structure); (. . .);
of hope:
         and to the Catholic journalist (P.R.I., perhaps?) I wrote,
in fact; how it was; ah, I must (I said); (the Filius); he had to be, ah;
I must (I said, to myself); be the figure; a justification;
(illustration); of desperation; an explanation I must; of the historic
imparting (sickly) to history:

Edoardo Sanguineti   383

della sofferta alienazione;
ma Calvino—perché avevo detto: 1848—: sei ben "lukacsciato," tu!
(disse); ma da te (dissi) è delusa (la storia): come natura; e dissi: non puoi
afferrare (oggi) quell'oggetto; (in tanta presente tenebra, intendevo: in tanto
fascismo); perché questa mano non è una mano (se non afferra); questa mano
che ancora è storia, che ancora non è natura;
                                                e forse la mano di mio figlio (dissi)
sarà natura; e quell'oggetto sarà quell'oggetto; quello che era; nel sogno;
perché adesso cerca un mondo, il figlio;
                                        ah, disse Calvino, perché
non scrivi una poesia sul coitus interruptus? (era un paradiso, l'America);
(da questo punto di vista); e io dissi—poiché era tornato, infine—
un paradisus interruptus:

3

cosí spiegammo:
                cosí (tetri, noi) del sogno spiegammo la duplice
dimensione: del ripiegato, dell'inerte, dell'importuno, deluso sogno; e
del radiante, mordente fantasma (in Europa):
                                            dell'invocato spettro;
spettro che invoco sopra le rovine:
                                    ora devo (il est indépassable, veramente)
(a mia moglie, anche) spiegare (le rovine, anche, dell'abbazia di Hambye), devo
les circonstances spiegare (il 4 luglio): spiegare devo che lo concepisco
come il costituirsi (nel giardino pubblico di Coutances, anche), le marxisme,
indépassable, il matrimonio concepisco (mordente, tra i misteriosi alberi),
pas encore depassées (les circonstances); (con monsieur de Gandillac, anche,
il 7 luglio), il costituirsi di una cellula (il matrimonio): una cellula (dissi)
di resistenza (e il 9 luglio, anche, con il generale Bouvard, sulla spiaggia);
et tamquam poeta (sulla spiaggia di Hauteville, anche, nella tempesta) e
in questo piccolo caffè, et tamquam homo, invoco:
                                                ma si toccheranno, adesso
(in questa selva), le nostre fronti; e a me stesso, ancora (invocando): oh non
sarebbe, questo (dissi), un amore? oh non sarebbe (dissi), questo, un amore
(in questa selva) fascista?
                        ah, cosí, invocando, mi definisco: tamquam
homme relatif:
                in questo PURGATORIO DE L'INFERNO; perché in questo (noi)
siamo redenti (a mia moglie dissi): in questo matrimonio; ah
in questa (dissi), (noi) siamo redenti, ah questa dovevamo (anche)
coscienza (questa coscienza politica) ritrovare: mordente, questa
(indépassable, questo: le marxisme);

of suffered alienation;
but Calvino—because I had said: 1848—: you are well "Lukacsized!"
(he said); but for you (I said) it's deceived (history): like nature; and I said: you

                                                                  can't

grasp (today) that object; (in such present darkness, I meant: in such
Fascism); because this hand is not a hand (if it doesn't grasp); this hand
which is still history, which is still not nature;

                           and perhaps my son's hand (I said)
will be nature; and that object will be that object: that which was; in the

                                                     dream;

because now he searches for a world, my son;

                                    ah, said Calvino, why
don't you write a poem about coitus interruptus? (it was a paradise, America);
(from this point of view); and I said—since it had returned, finally— :
a paradisus interruptus:

3

thus we explained:
                         thus (gloomy, us) we explained the double dimension of the
dream: of the folded, inert, boring, deluded dream; and
of the radiant, biting phantasm (in Europe):

                                 of the invoked spectre;
spectre which I invoke over the ruins:

                              now I must (il est indépassable, truly)
(to my wife, also) explain (the ruins, also, of Hambye Abbey), I must
explain les circonstances (July 4): I must explain that I conceive it
to be like self-creation (in the public garden of Coutances, as well) le marxisme,
indépassable, marriage I conceive as (biting, among the mysterious trees),
pas encore depassées (les circonstances); (with monsieur de Gandillac, as well,
July 7), the creation of a cell (marriage): a cell (I said)
of resistance (and July 9, as well, with General Bouvard, on the beach);
et tamquam poeta (on the Hauteville beach, also, in the storm) and
in this small café, et tamquam homo, I invoke:

                                 but they will touch, now
(in this forest), our foreheads; and to myself, now (invoking):
couldn't, this (I said), be love? oh couldn't it be (I said), this, a Fascist
(in this forest) love?

                    ah, thus, invoking, I define myself: tamquam
homme *relatif*:

                    in this PURGATORY OF HELL; because in this (we)
are redeemed (I said to my wife): in this marriage; ah
in this (I said), (we) are redeemed, ah we needed this (also)
to find consciousness (this political consciousness) again: biting, this
(indépassable, this: le marxisme);

Edoardo Sanguineti   385

e a Roberto dissi (al Norman,
ancora) come il prefigurante, lo spettrale sogno la forma assuma (talvolta)
della nostalgia;

        e dissi: il sogno (talvolta) è ripiegamento (ma
nell'apparenza); è (dissi) nostalgia, ma delusa nostalgia
di un futuro;

        ma poi (dai giornali): siamo classe dirigente
(qualcuno disse); e come tali (disse) siamo responsabili;
ma nei limiti (disse) del potere; perché non abbiamo poteri
adeguati (e si apre, intanto, un decennio decisivo) alle nostre
responsabilità:

        così (nella soffitta di via Pietro Micca) io e mia moglie
scrivemmo: W PCI (in ogni angolo); e io lo scrissi tre volte (sopra
il caminetto); e mia moglie disse: ma questo
è un covo di missini

        —e scrivevamo W PCI, rabbiosamente, sui muri
(e io incidevo la scritta con una chiave):

14

e parlavano, nel buio (e io, nel letto, leggendo un romanzo di Sollers); e
                            parlavano,
nel corridoio, e dicevano, forse (cioè qualcosa come:): ma sarà, lui,
tutto contento (perché entriamo così, di sorpresa, nella notte, nella sua stanza,
nel buio); e parlavano:

        poi Anne stava nella poltrona; e Françoise (la seconda),
e Odile (e Edith), sopra il mio letto; e Anne era in pigiama; e lui si svegliò
(nel suo letto); (e disse: che cosa vogliono?);

        poi portarono su la lavagna,
con le idiozie dei nomi deformi (e leggevano, tutte insieme,
a voce alta);

      poi io dissi a Ollier
che sembrava, lui, uno dei due preti del *Chien andalou*; e lui
fece una faccia triste (e disse, dunque: ma sono tanto démodé, dunque?); (e
il *Chien andalou* è del '29, mi pare); (e Thibaudeau
gridava: ma tutto è come nel romanzo; cioè nel mio); (e Roche diceva: ma
                             bisogna
spegnere la luce, qui);

        e spegnevo la luce, e la riaccendevo, e ancora la
                           spegnevo,
di nuovo; e dicevo, nel buio, ma immobile:

        ma non succede niente.

and I said to Robert (to Norman,
as well) as the prefiguring, the spectral dream the form of nostalgia it might
(sometimes) assume;
and I said: the dream is (sometimes) regrouping (but
in appearance); it's (I said) nostalgia, but deluded nostalgia
of a future;
but then (from the newspapers): we are ruling class
(someone said); and as such (he said) we are responsible;
but within the limits (he said) of power; because we don't have adequate
power (and, meanwhile, a decisive decade is opening) for our
responsibility:
thus (in the garret on Via Pietro Micca) my wife and I
wrote: W PCI (in every corner); and I wrote it three times (on
the fireplace); and my wife said: but this
is a den of neo-Fascists
—and we wrote W PCI, furiously, on the walls
(and I engraved the inscription with a key):

14

and they were talking, in the dark (and I, in bed, reading a Sollers novel); and
they were talking,
in the hall, and they said, maybe (that is, something like): but he'll be
delighted (because we're coming in this way, by surprise, in the night, in his
room,
in the dark); and they were talking:
then Anne sat on the easy chair; and Françoise (the second),
and Odile (and Edith), on my bed; and Anne was in her pyjamas; and he woke up
(in his bed); (and said: what do they want?);
then they will bring up the blackboard,
with the idiocies of twisted names (and they read, all together,
aloud);
then I said to Ollier
that he looked like one of the two priests in *Chien Andalou*; and he
pulled a long face (and said, then: but am I so démodé, then?); (and
Chien Andalou is from '29, it seems to me); (and Thibaudeau
shouted: but everything sounds like it's from the novel; mine, that is); (and
Roche said: but we've
got to turn out the lights now);
and I turned out the lights, and I turned them
back on, and then I turned them out again,
one more time; and I said, in the dark, but without moving:
but nothing's happening.

Edoardo Sanguineti   387

15

al di là di quel purgatorio di giardini (e la luce bianca, e le sedie
di ferro); e (ancora) al di là degli uccelli moribondi
nel verde:
        c'è la Galerie Vivienne;
al di là di noi, così, esiste quel vero cimitero (come ho detto): tre lunghe
scatole di cartoline illustrate, tutte scritte, con i francobolli:
                                        tutte da leggere.

16

proprio mentre dicevano: ma guardatela; (quella luna); ma proprio allora
io pensavo (ma tranquillo) alle parole già scritte a mia moglie: "ma
tranquillo"; (avendo spiegato): "ma tranquillo" (piú tardi); "per
sempre" (quel minaccioso significato):
                        i piedi
nell'erba bagnata, nel sentiero, dopo la pioggia, incerto, in mezzo alle mucche
normanne (. . .); e poi l'alba, appunto; e poi Madame Heurgon, che ci vede
da una finestra del castello (nell'alba);
                      e poi non importa, appunto, niente;
(dopo la colazione, la buonanotte, il buongiorno, nella cucina, nell'alba);
e poi: stanco di spiegare, poi, di giustificare (di giustificarmi); (e volevo
dire, appunto: di giustificarmi—come ho spiegato—"per sempre");
                                    e poi:
stanco di così insistente ricorso; (a fantasmi); (dicendo: perché avrai
notato come mi sono affrettato, insistente, a ricorrere . . . ;
e così via); (a fantasmi);
                ma tranquillo, Luciana, davvero (il 30
settembre), piú tardi; ma voglio poi dire, adesso: "per sempre" (. . .):

17

così, qui (a Cerisy); (così dicevano): abbiamo, noi, un cinese;
(e il cinese ero io, naturalmente);
                      e sull'autostrada spiegavo, anche,
il contraccolpo sopra l'operazione letteraria, radicalmente, immediato (e
così via); e si diceva dell'opportunismo trionfante, anche (e quando dissi, poi,
riformismo, infatti, volevo proprio dire opportunismo, invece);
                            perché
la posizione cinese (dissi) giustifica ogni speranza (e che non sia questione
di élite operaia, insomma, ma della fine della preistoria, davvero,
e così via);

15

beyond that purgatory of gardens (and the white light, and the wrought-
iron chairs); and (what's more) beyond the moribund birds
in the greenery:
                    there's the Galerie Vivienne;
beyond us, therefore, exists that real graveyard (as I have said): three long
boxes of picture postcards, all covered with writing, stamped:
                                        all to read.

16

just when they were talking: but look at it; (that moon); but just then
I was thinking (but tranquil) of the words already written to my wife: "but
tranquil"; (having explained): "but tranquil" (later); "forever" (that threatening meaning):
                    my feet
in the soaking grass, on the path, after the rain, uncertain, in the midst of Norman
cows (. . .); and then the dawn, precisely; and then Madame Heurgon, who
                                    sees us
from a window of the castle (in the dawn);
                      and then it doesn't matter at all, precisely;
(after breakfast, the goodnight, the good morning, in the kitchen, in the dawn);
and then: tired of explaining, then, of justifying (of justifying myself); (and I
wanted to say, precisely: of justifying myself—as I explained—"forever");
                                  and then:
tired of such insistent returning; (to ghosts); (saying: because you will
have noticed how hasty, insistent, I am to go back . . . ;
and so forth); (to ghosts);
                  but tranquil, Luciana, really (the 30th
of September), later; but I wish then to say, now: "forever" (. . .):

17

so, here (in Cerisy); (so they were saying): we have a Chinese;
(and the Chinese was me, naturally);
                        and on the expressway I also explained
the reaction against the literary operation, radically immediate (and
so forth); and one spoke of triumphant opportunism, even (and when I said,
                                  later on,
revisionism, in fact, what I really wanted to say instead was opportunism);
                                  because
the Chinese position (I said) justifies every hope (and that it might not be a
                                  question
of a worker elite, after all, but the end of prehistory, in fact,
and so forth);

e a mia moglie dicevo della quantità di infelicità, intanto (della
qualità; e cosí via);
e volevo dire: giustifica anche noi; e anche i figli;
e volevo dire: giustifica il momento dell'utopia (ma davvero, ma per noi, anche,
ma qui, adesso): questo momento (giustifica);
e volevo dire: per sempre;
(ma nel night, a Palermo, li ho sentiti davvero, io, che dicevano: perché
vivi, tu? e dicevano: come ti giustifichi?
dicevano: ma ti giustifichi, tu?);
ma adesso, vedi: ma adesso, quale stanchezza? e quale (in questa nostra
preistoria), quale tranquillità?
ma vedi il fango che ci sta alle spalle,
e il sole in mezzo agli alberi, e i bambini che dormono:
i bambini
che sognano (che parlano, sognando); (ma i bambini, li vedi, cosí inquieti);
(dormendo, i bambini); (sognando, adesso):

and I spoke to my wife about the quantity of unhappiness,
meanwhile (about the
quality; and so forth);
and I wanted to say: it justifies even us; and also our children;
and I wanted to say: it justifies the moment of utopia (but really, for us, even,
here, now): this moment (it justifies);
and I wanted to say: forever;
(but in the night, in Palermo, I really heard them, the ones who said: why
do you go on living? and they said: how do you justify yourself?
they said: but do you justify yourself?)
but now, you see: but now, what weariness? and what (in this our
prehistory), what tranquility?
but you see the mud which sticks to our backs,
and the sun in the trees, and the children who sleep:
the children
who dream (who speak, dreaming); (but the children, you see them, so restless);
(sleeping, the children); (dreaming, now):

Nanni Balestrini

Born in Milan in 1935, Balestrini currently
lives in Rome and Milan, where he works as
an editor. Balestrini has been the editor of the
magazine *Il Verri*, and has been a contributing editor for *Marcatré*, *Grammatica*, *Malebolge*, and *Il Caffé*. One of the principal
members of the avant-garde "Gruppo '63," he
edited the anthology of the same name with
Alfredo Giuliani. Balestrini was also included
in Giuliani's *I novissimi*. His work is characterized by a wry sense of humor, daring, and
a willingness to experiment in any form. He
has had shows of *poesia visiva* throughout
Italy, he has written a ballet that was produced at La Scala, and he has done extensive
experimentation with electronic and computer poetry. In 1963 he won the "Ferro di Cavallo" prize for the most experimental book of
the year.

His books of poetry are:

Il sasso appeso.
    Milano: Scheiwiller, 1961.
Come si agisce.
    Milano: Feltrinelli, 1963.
Altri procedimenti.
    Milano: Scheiwiller, 1966.
Ma noi facciamone un'altra.
    Milano: Feltrinelli, 1968.
Poesie practiche, 1954–1969.
    Torino: Einaudi, 1976.

In questo modo

Questi sono i nodi, queste le cicatrici,
gli abiti che hai indossato, la stagione inattesa
sull'asfalto dove ancora vivremo, quella nuvola
che abbastanza somiglia alla teiera già

fredda, con la faccia di uno che sta male,
azzurro come il ristorante, la distanza,
sebbene siano le nove, i preparativi
pressoché ultimati, papaveri distillati,

credendo ai miei occhi, sporgendo dal tetto
sulle cime di pini recisi, ma
inganni il titolo, garanzia ai passanti,
che quasi tutti se ne sono andati, si annidano

necessari e la barca che tu non trovi
mai, ma necessaria perché attraversiamo
quantunque noi non guardiamo e dove
vediamo se pure non c'è rimedio e passano

ancora incerti i luoghi dove
confini nettamente segnati ci rivelano . . .
Poi il cielo dovrà pur mutare. Come io potrei
cambiare di colpo argomento e pochi se ne

accorgerebbero, il tonfo che fruga ancora
sordo le ore del pomeriggio, e profondo
e i sassi che hai sotto la schiena o la fuga
di sostantivi corrosi dalle travolte strutture—

comunque niente di nuovo, la pomice
sui gomiti, se non c'è posto che per uno di noi
e appena uscito di casa s'imbatte,
tu t'imbatti, se hai capito quanto ti aspetto.

In This Manner

These are the lumps, these the scars,
the clothes you've put on, the unexpected season
on the asphalt where we'll always live, that cloud
which looks a lot like the teapot already

gone cold, with a sick man's face,
blue like the restaurant, the distance,
although it's nine o'clock, the preparations
almost finished, distilled poppies,

believing my eyes, leaning from the roof
over the tops of felled pines, but
you're cheating on the title, guarantee to passersby,
who almost all have gone, they stash away

necessaries and the boat you never
find, but necessary because we cross
even though we don't look around us and where
we see if there's still nothing to be done and still

uncertain places pass where
clearly marked boundaries reveal themselves to us . . .
Then even the sky will have to change. As I could
change my subject suddenly and few would

notice it, the splash which penetrates
the afternoon hours, still deep in their deafness,
and the rocks you have under your back or the escape
of corrosive substances from toppled structures—

however, nothing new, pumice
on the elbows, if there's a place for only one of us
and scarcely out of the house he runs into,
you run into, if you only knew how long I've been waiting for you.

L'istinto di conservazione

Qui conta come (può un pesce vivere
a lungo sulla sabbia secca? dormire
senza cuscino?) la vita dell'uomo è
tutta un tentativo (non ne ho la minima
idea, non sono mai stato cosí triste);

tuttavia una volta si era travestito
da lattaio, d'altra parte (cercai una posizione
piú comoda sulla sedia) non può vivere a lungo
(passammo il resto della notte seduti,
straziati dalla fame, aspettando l'alba).

Salí dunque fino all'ultimo piano,
come gli alberi piú alti nella neve
(descriveteci i luoghi che vi circondano se possibile),
e la lancetta sembrava girare troppo adagio;
nessuno lo vide, dormono tutti.

(La stessa sensazione, dunque state seduti,
dubitatene; sbottoniamo altre settimane,
e ancora la ferita, il raffreddore, mani
aperte che sporcano le acque, sempre che
non ci abbiano seguiti. Rossa come un cavallo.)

La febbre alta come la neve, un solo bottone
pensò. Un enorme risparmio di tempo.
Un cavillo—prego? galoppa (e
parliamone pure, il personaggio merita
di essere ricordato). Salí fino all'ultimo.

Perforata la sottile lamiera (potrei
avere qualcosa da bere?) nei ritagli
di tempo (non risponde) strappa i rami
ai boschi (una lisca nel palato) su una slitta
carica di neve (è scomparso) sbucato

The Instinct of Self-Preservation

What matters here is (can a fish live
for long on dry sand? sleep
without a pillow?) man's life is
just an attempt (I don't have the least idea
about it, I've never been so depressed);

anyway one time he disguised himself
as a milkman, on the other hand (I tried to find a more
comfortable position in the chair) he can't live long
(we spent the rest of the night sitting,
tortured by hunger, waiting for the dawn).

Then he walked up to the top floor,
like the highest trees in the snow
(describe your surroundings to us if possible),
and the hour hand seemed to move too slowly;
no one saw him, they're all asleep.

(The same feeling, so stay in your seat,
don't believe it; let's open up other weeks,
and even the wound, the headcold, open
hands which dirty the water, provided
they haven't followed us. Red like a horse.)

The fever high as the snow, just one button
he thought. An enormous saving of time.
A cavil—do you say? he gallops off (and so
let's talk about him, the character deserves
to be remembered). He walked up to the top.

Having made holes in the thin plate (could
I have something to drink?) in the odd
moments (he doesn't answer) he breaks branches
in the woods (a fish-bone in the palate) on a sled
loaded with snow (he disappeared) having appeared

Nanni Balestrini

da chissà dove (e ossicini sul pavimento
dappertutto) e la grandine sul prato spuntata
nel paesaggio pitturato; in forma di gocciola,
altissimo torreggiante campanaro, giacendo
in fondo alla torre, bevendo a grandi sorsi.

from who knows where (and little bones all over
the floor) and hail having sprouted on the meadow
in the painted landscape; in the form of a drop,
highest towering bell-ringer, lying
at the base of the tower, drinking with huge gulps.

De cultu virginis

Prima di posare sul sagrato si libra ad ali tese
negli specchi di luce bagnata, rotti da un piede verde;
al *Malcontento Bar* ferisce mortalmente uno sconosciuto
scambiandolo per il suo seduttore.

Altri esempi: torri nel pozzo di San Giminiano, l'amo
al luccio, la rossa in buca. Perciò se al diavolo di Cartesio
(riviviamo il brusco atterraggio che ci lasciò sabato tutti
confusi nelle nostre tenebre

con una gamba ingessata, la penna che macchiò in volo la giacca)
all'ultimo gioco si strappò la membrana—sul Palazzo della Ragione
rivola, proprio quando impugnando l'unica stecca buona
rivinsi al Duca di Sessa

l'abiura. Spesso preghiamo che Dio ci dia una mano
(un cilindro di carta d'amaretto, dateci fuoco in cima,
attenti! la cenere sale, su quasi fino al soffitto!)
e i bambini imparano che

sbocciano immobili giorni in cui non ricevono doni,
a non calpestare i fiori, strappare ali a gialle farfalle
o fidarsi di uomini che in tasca nascondono molte chiavi
e mutano in una fonte. Un uccello

bianco ogni tanto lacera aquiloni nel sole. TEOREMA:
Francesco Petrarca era forse infelice di non avere il caffè?

De Cultu Virginis

Before lying in the churchyard you poise on outstretched wings
in the mirrors of wet light, fragments from a green foot;
at the *Malcontent Bar* he fatally wounded a stranger,
mistaking him for her seducer.

Other examples: towers in the pit of San Giminiano, the hook
in the pike, red in its mouth. Therefore, if the Cartesian devil
(we relive Saturday's rough landing which left us all
lost in our shadows

with one leg in a cast, the pen that stained the jacket in flight)
he tore his membrane in the final game—he's flying on the Palace
of Reason again, just when he grabbed the only good stick I won back
the abjuration at the Duke

of Sessa. We often pray for God to give us a hand
(a cylinder made from a cookie wrapper, you light the top,
watch out! the ashes climb, almost to the ceiling!)
and children learn that

motionless days blossom when they don't get gifts,
not to trample on flowers, tear the wings off yellow butterflies
or trust men who hide many keys in their pockets
and change into a fountain. A white

bird occasionally tears up kites in the sun. THEOREM:
Could it be that Francesco Petrarcha was unhappy because he didn't have
coffee?

Nanni Balestrini   401

Apologo dell'evaso

La massima della mia azione difforme,
infausto al popolo il fiume
che al cinema videro spopolare

il delta, i fertilissimi campi
e i piú nocivi insetti (chiara
minaccia ai vizi dei governanti!).

Fra i pampini ovunque liberi
galleggiavano, gonfi—e si fa vano
l'ufficio dello storico. Ma saremo

a lungo preservati dal morso
del tafano azzurro, da iniezioni
di calciobromo, dall'unghie della zarina?

Lucenti strani corpi
violano il cielo; sbanda
il filo di formiche diagonale

nel cortile riemerso; ancora
il sole sorge dietro
la Punta Campanella incustodita

dai finanzieri corrotti e un argine
ultimo crolla. Lode
a un'estate di foco. S'io fossi

la piccola borghesia colata
nelle piazze fiorite e nei dí
di festa che salvi c'ignora

dalla droga e dalla noia per un po'
d'uva lavata in mare
presso la marcia catapulta; rifugiati

The Fugitive's Apologue

The principle behind my nonconformist action,
the river, a curse to the people,
at the movies they saw it destroy

the delta, the most fertile fields
and the nastiest insects (clear
threat to the vices of the ruling class!).

Wherever the bodies weren't tangled in the vines
they floated, swollen—and it makes the job
of the historian useless. Shall we be

protected a long time from the bite
of the blue-tailed fly, from injections
of calcium bromide, from the nails of the czarina?

Strange luminous bodies
violate the heavens; the diagonal
column of ants breaks up

in the resurfaced courtyard; the sun
still rises behind
Campanella Point, unguarded by

corrupt customs officials, and a last
dike collapses. Praised be
a summer of fire. If I were

the petite bourgeoisie filtered
into flowered piazzas and into festival
days which, saved, keep us from

drugs and boredom for a few
grapes washed in the sea
near the rotten catapult; taking refuge

Nanni Balestrini   403

al primo tuono nelle gelaterie—chi fuggirei?
Passato il temporalaccio d'agosto
i graspi giungono a riva

fra i remi ai contrabbandieri salpati
nel novilunio e anzitutto conviene
(usciti dal vico cieco chiamammo

e orme erano ovunque
dell'abominevole uomo delle nevi)
fare l'amore intanto

che sui ponti la Via Lattea dilata.
Il Po nasce dal Monviso;
nuvole . . . ma di ciò, altra volta.

at first thunder in ice cream bars—who would I run from?
The August shower having passed
grape stems reaching the shore

around the oars of the smugglers setting out
under the new moon and furthermore it's fitting
(having come out of the blind alley we shouted

and there were footprints all over the place,
the abominable snowman's)
to make love while

the Milky Way spreads on the bridges.
The Po is born in Monviso;
clouds . . . but that's another story.

Tape Mark

La testa premuta sulla spalla, trenta volte
piú luminoso del sole io contemplo il loro ritorno,
finché non mosse le dita lentamente e mentre la moltitudine
delle cose accade, alla sommità della nuvola
esse tornano tutte alla loro radice e assumono
la ben nota forma di fungo cercando di afferrare.

I capelli tra le labbra, esse tornano tutte
alla loro radice, nell'accecante globo di fuoco
io contemplo il loro ritorno, finché non muove le dita
lentamente, e malgrado che le cose fioriscano
assume la ben nota forma di fungo cercando
di afferrare mentre la moltitudine delle cose accade.

Nell'accecante globo di fuoco io contemplo
il loro ritorno quando raggiunge la stratosfera mentre la moltitudine
delle cose accade, la testa premuta
sulla spalla, trenta volte piú luminose del sole
esse tornano tutte alla loro radice, i capelli
tra le labbra assumono la ben nota forma di fungo.

Giacquero immobili senza parlare, trenta volte
piú luminosi del sole essi tornano tutti
alla loro radice, la testa premuta sulla spalla
assumono la ben nota forma di fungo cercando
di afferrare, e malgrado che le cose fioriscano
si espandono rapidamente, i capelli tra le labbra.

Mentre la moltitudine delle cose accade nell'accecante
globo di fuoco, esse tornano tutte
alla loro radice, si espandono rapidamente, finché non mosse
le dita lentamente quando raggiunse la stratosfera
e giacque immobile senza parlare, trenta volte
piú luminoso del sole cercando di afferrare.

Tape Mark

The head pressed against the shoulder, thirty times
brighter than the sun I contemplate their return,
until he slowly moved his fingers and while the multitude
of things go on, at the top of the cloud
they all return to their roots and assume
the well-known mushroom shape trying to grasp.

Hairs in the mouth, they all return
to their roots, in the blinding fireball
I contemplate their return until he slowly moves
his fingers, and even though things blossom
assumes the well-known mushroom shape trying
to grasp while the multitude of things go on.

In the blinding fireball I contemplate
their return when it reaches the stratosphere while the multitude
of things go on, the head pressed
against the shoulder, thirty times brighter than the sun
they all return to their roots, hairs
in the mouth assume the well-known mushroom shape.

They lie motionless without speaking, thirty times
brighter than the sun they all return
to their roots, the head pressed against the shoulder
they assume the well-known mushroom shape trying
to grasp, and even though things blossom
they rapidly expand, hairs in the mouth.

While the multitude of things go on in the blinding
fireball, they all return
to their roots, they rapidly expand, until he slowly
moved his fingers when he reached the stratosphere
and lay motionless without speaking, thirty times
brighter than the sun trying to grasp.

Io contemplo il loro ritorno, finché non mosse le dita
lentamente nell'accecante globo di fuoco,
esse tornano tutte alla loro radice, i capelli
tra le labbra e trenta volte piú luminosi del sole
giacquero immobili senza parlare, si espandono
rapidamente cercando di afferrare la sommità.

I contemplate their return, until he slowly moved
his fingers in the blinding fireball,
they all return to their roots, hairs
in the mouth and thirty times brighter than the sun
they lie motionless without speaking, they rapidly
expand trying to grasp the top.

Nanni Balestrini

Ma noi facciamone un'altra

1,1
non la riproduzione
con gli occhi del linguaggio
da qualsiasi parte ti metti
non mima niente
un varco incolmabile
un mare di ambiguità
dietro la pagina
gli anni della palude

            non la riproduzione
            nel paesaggio verbale
            dopo la confusione delle
            non c'è piú posto per loro
            la rivoluzione non è un
            si lamentano sempre
            mentre passiamo bruciando
            un'altra restaurazione
            la negazione di un modo di formare

     con gli occhi del linguaggio
     dopo la confusione delle
     il rifiuto della storia
     delle intenzioni e delle idee
     5,3
     senza lasciar tracce
     7,3
     questo tipo di montaggio
     non è un sentimento

But We'll Make Another One

1.1
not the reproduction
with the eyes of the language
whichever way you turn
he doesn't mime anything
an unfillable hole
a sea of ambiguity
behind the page
the years of the quagmire

                  not the reproduction
                  in the verbal landscape
                  after the confusion of the
                  there's no longer any place for them
                  the revolution isn't a
                  they're always groaning
                  while we walk by in flames
                  another restoration
                  the denial of a way to create

         with the eyes of the language
         after the confusion of the
         the rejection of history
         of the intentions and ideas
         5.3
         without leaving a trace
         7.3
         this kind of montage
         is not merely sentiment

Nanni Balestrini

da qualsiasi parte ti metti
non c'è piú posto per loro
delle intenzioni e delle idee
nel paesaggio verbale
l'amnistia ai fascisti
hanno fatto la ricostruzione
non c'è piú tempo da perdere
voi non lo avete trasformato
in altre parole

non mima niente
la rivoluzione non è un
3,5
l'amnistia ai fascisti
5,5
l'azione consiste nel confronto fra
il linguaggio del linguaggio
qui manca un verso
9,5

un varco incolmabile
si lamentano sempre
senza lasciar tracce
hanno fatto la ricostruzione
l'azione consiste nel confronto fra
il rifiuto della storia
sovrappone un'altra immagine
l'arte dell'impazienza
la parola come un oggetto

un mare di ambiguità
mentre passiamo bruciando
3,7
non c'è piú tempo da perdere
il linguaggio del linguaggio
sovrappone un'altra immagine
7,7
dopo un lungo silenzio
viene un verso piú lungo di tutti gli altri

whichever way you turn
there's no longer any place for them
of the intentions and ideas
in the verbal landscape
amnesty for the Fascists
they've carried out the reconstruction
there's no longer any time to lose
you haven't changed it
in other words

he doesn't mime anything
the revolution isn't a
3.5
amnesty for the Fascists
5.5
the action lies in the confrontation between
the language of the language
a line is missing here
9.5

an unfillable hole
they're always groaning
without leaving a trace
they've carried out the reconstruction
the action lies in the confrontation between
the rejection of history
it superimposes another image
the art of impatience
the word as an object

a sea of ambiguity
while we walk by in flames
3.7
there's no longer any time to lose
the language of the language
it superimposes another image
7.7
after a long silence
there comes a line which is longer than all the others

Nanni Balestrini   413

              dietro la pagina
              un'altra restaurazione
              questo tipo di montaggio
              voi non lo avete trasformato
              qui manca un verso
              l'arte dell'impazienza
              dopo un lungo silenzio
              nel paesaggio verbale
              l'aborto della resistenza

gli anni della palude
la negazione di un modo di formare
non è un sentimento
in altre parole
5,9
la parola come un oggetto
viene un verso piú lungo di tutti gli altri
l'aborto della resistenza
il rifiuto della storia

behind the page
another restoration
this kind of montage
you haven't changed it
a line is missing here
the art of impatience
after a long silence
in the verbal landscape
the failure of the resistance

the years of the quagmire
the denial of a way to create
is not merely sentiment
in other words
5.9
the word as an object
there comes a line which is longer than all the others
the failure of the resistance
the rejection of history

Senza lacrime per le rose
(1969)

> Infine, la grande industria e la sua scienza non sono
> il premio per chi vince la lotta di classe. Sono il terreno
> stesso di questa lotta. E finché il terreno è occupato dal
> nemico bisogna spararci sopra, senza lacrime per le
> rose.
>
> Mario Tronti, *Operai e capitale*

1

a
metà strada
nel buio ne
i
fitti alb
l'albero prefe
risce la cal
ma ma il vento non si pla
ca la lotta di
il
compito è di
eliminare il
di classe è un fa
tto oggettivo è in
dipendente dal
la volontà dell'uom
rovesciato
il
potere i
deologico della borghes
la situazione è tranquil
la a torino dopo le sedici or
e di guerriglia di
ieri
oggi tutto deve e
ssere subordinato a
gli alberi fanno troppo rumore
lla definizione d
i una strateg
la fiat non creò un al
tro uomo dicen
do tu sei i

Without Tears for the Roses
(1969)

> In conclusion, big industry and its science are not
> the prize for the one who wins the class struggle. They
> are the field of battle itself. And as long as the field is
> occupied by the enemy we must spray it with bullets,
> without tears for the roses.
>
> Mario Tronti, *Workers and Capital*

1

half
way
in the dark in
the
thick tr
the tree pre
fers the cal
m but the wind doesn't cal
m down the struggle of
the
task is to
eliminate the
of class it's an objec
tive fact it's in
dependent of the
will of manki
overturned
the
ideological p
ower of the bourgeol
the situation is peacefu
l in turin after the sixteen hou
rs of yesterday's
guerilla
today everything must b
e subordinated to
the trees make too much noise
at definition o
f a strateg
fiat didn't create ano
ther man sayi
ng you are m

Nanni Balestrini

417

l mio schiav
la grande
il
rovesciamento delle i
dee dominant

2

la grande
tra
sgression
e ideologica dell'epoc
con
le sue giustificazioni secolari
una realtà spro
fonda di colpo nel passat
a
lle fiamme automobili e co
struito barricate con
tavole di le
gno i
rrorate di carburante ma
n mano che le forze
di polizia si avv
icinano
avvicina
vano alle barricate ven
iva appiccato il
e gli alber
i intorno
oggi tutto dev
essere subordinato
la
verità della violenza la
violenza co
me ragione ultima di tutt
ormai afferma
ta scopertamente
la
realtà politica è
ormai
la realtà la violenza o nella
la
parola
di classe

y slav
the great
the
overthrow of do
minant ideas

2

the great
ideo
logica
l sin of the epoc
with
its secular justifications
a reality sin
ks suddenly in the pas
t
o the flames cars and barri
cades constructed with
wooden ta
bles the
ails of gasoline as
the police
forces app
roach
they approach
ed the barricades it was
going to start the
and the tre
es around there
today everything must
be subordinated
the
truth of violence
violence a
s the final reason for everythi
now open
ly declared
the
political reality is
now
reality violence or in
the
word
of classes

3

quindi
è per
questo che ci ribelliamo per
ché siamo sfruttati abbastanz
completamente la vecchia id
eologia
la cultura della b
orghesia o la cultura del va
lore di scambio
il
compito della parola
è di eliminar
logica la borghesia per
duta la sua egemonia
ideologica nella
quella
morte è
già avvenuta
rendere evidente che n
ella sostanza
e
la vecchia cultur
a e i vecchi u
si e i costum
sostenuti da tutte
le
classi sfruttatr
ici per miglia
ia di anni allo scopo d
i avvelenare
la
mente del
popolo
o l'u
topia culturale o
niente sarà piú
come prima

4

che
cosa vogliamo
tut

3

therefore
it's because
of this that we rebel be
cause we have been exploited enoug
completely the old id
eology
the bourgeois cul
ture or the culture of ca
sh value
the
word's task
is to eliminate
logic the bourgeois lo
st its ideological
hegemony in
that
death has
already occurred
to make clear that i
n the substance
and
the old cultur
e and the old w
ays and the custom
endured by all
the
exploited class
es for thousa
nds of years to the extent o
f poisoning
the
peoples'
minds
either cul
tural utopia or
nothing will any longer be
what it used to be

4

what
do we want
all

auto incendiate mezzi pesanti l
asciati di travers
o sulle massicciate
stradali resti di barri
cate legname sottra
tto ai cantieri edili
annerito dalle fiamme co
ntorti semafori divelti
un rullo compressore
tutto
se
non lo col
pisci il
nemico
rovesciato gruppi elettroge
ni bruciati vie disselc
iate e pietre sparse
un po'
ovunque vetrine insegne di
i negozi infrante carcasse
di
colpisci il nemico di classe
auto sfasciate o i
incendiate cristalli degl
i ingressi dei caseggiati
crollati per le sas
sate cantieri sconvolti e pa
lizzate incenerite
cumuli di pietre frammenti
di tubi di cement
o e gli alber
i intorn
il
nemico di classe non cadrà

5

a
la definizione di u
na stretagia
l'i
nversione di una linea p
olitica da vent'anni dominan
nel
momento in cui la
classe

cars set on fire heavy pieces l
eft crosswis
e on the road
beds remainders of barri
cades wood tak
en from the lumber yards
blackened by the flames co
ntorted traffic lights uprooted
a steamroller
everything
if
you don't stri
ke him the
overthrown
enemy generato
rs burnt streets ripp
ed up and scattered stones
all over
the place shopwindows signs from
the stores
shattered frames
of
you strike the enemy of class
wrecked cars or the
burnt plate glass of th
e entrances to arcades
broken down by the ston
ings torn up storage yards and fe
nces burnt to ashes
heaps of stones fragments
of cement pipe
s and the tree
s aroun
the enemy of class will not fall

5

to
the definition of
a stretagy
the i
nversion of a political l
ine of twenty years dominan
in the
moment in which the
working

operaia conquisterà una sua
organizzazion
e politica di lott
la parola
mentre
trasformata in istituto so
ciale compie disci
plinatamente le sue
gli a
lberi fanno troppo rumore
funzioni di equilibrio ga
rantisce l'ordine essa è tu
tta dentro questa
societ
ma cre
are formare e ne
lla lotta
una parola e una p
arola
pratica ma
teriale cre
ata nel
masse nella lotta
formare nell
e
nuovi u
si e
nuovi

class will its own
organizatio
and politics if struggl
the word
while
transformed into social in
stitution it accomplishes with disci
pline its
the t
rees make too much noise
balanced functions it gua
rantees order it is al
l inside this
societ
but tó cre
ate to shape and in
the struggle
a word and a w
ord
material pr
actice cre
ated in th
masses in the struggle
to form in th
e
new cus
toms and
new

Antonio Porta

Born Leo Paolazzi in Milan in 1935, Porta continues to live there, where he works as an editor in a publishing house. He was editor of *Malebolge* and was a contributing editor to *Il Verri*. Porta was a member of the "Gruppo '63" and "i novissimi." He has also been a major figure in *poesia visiva*, with exhibitions throughout Italy and the rest of Europe. Porta's poetry most often portrays a fallen world of sadism and violence, but not from the point of view of a nihilist or an anarchist. He is a Catholic and a humanist, and that makes him something of a rarity among the avant-garde. Porta believes in absolute truth and perhaps in absolute good, but he sees the road to those goals as a difficult one. Like the other members of the "Gruppo '63," Porta is extremely interested in developing a new poetics. His critical works, and his theoretical explanation of his poetry of "objects" and the function of meter and syntax, are among the most cogent and interesting discussions of contemporary Italian poetics.

His books of poetry are:

La palpebra rovesciata.
   Milano: Azimuth, 1960.
Aprire.
   Milano: Scheiwiller, 1964.
I rapporti.
   Milano: Feltrinelli, 1966.
Cara.
   Milano: Feltrinelli, 1969.
Metropolis.
   Milano: Feltrinelli, 1971.
Week-end.
   Roma: Cooperativa Scrittori, 1974.

Europa cavalca un toro nero

1

Attento, abitante del pianeta,
guardati! dalle parole dei Grandi
frana di menzogne, lassú
balbettano, insegnano il vuoto.
La privata, unica, voce
metti in salvo: domani sottratta
ti sarà, come a molti, oramai,
e lamento risuona il giuoco dei bicchieri.

2

Brucia cartucce in piazza, furente
l'auto del partito: sollevata la mano
dalla tasca videro forata.
Tra i giardini sterili si alza
altissimo angelo, in pochi
l'afferrano e il resto è niente.

3

In su la pancia del potente
la foresta prospera: chi mai
l'orizzonte oltre l'intrico scorgerà!
Fruscia la sottoveste sul pennone,
buone autorità viaggiano in pallone,
strade e case osservano dall'alto,
gli uomini sono utili formiche,
la folla ingarbugliata, buone
autorità, cervello di sapone,
sopra le case giuocando scivolate.

4

Un incidente, dicono, ogni ora,
una giornata che c'era scuola nell'aria
un odore di detriti, crescono
sulla piazza gli aranci del mercante.
Il pneumatico pesantissimo (tale
un giorno l'insetto sfarinò)

Europa Rides a Black Bull

1

Look out, inhabitants of earth,
beware! from the words of the Great Ones
comes a landslide of lies, they babble
up there, instructing the void.
Put the private, individual voice
in a safe place: tomorrow it will be
taken away, as with many already,
and lament echoes the clinking of glasses.

2

Bullets blaze in the piazza, the activist's
car drives madly; the hand was lifted
from the pocket I saw blown open.
Out of the sterile gardens the holiest
angel rises, in a few minutes
they seize him and it's all over.

3

The forest prospers on the belly
of the powerful, who can never see
the horizon for all their intrigue!
Underwear flutters on the flagpole,
goodly officials take a balloon ride,
they observe streets and houses from above,
men are such useful ants,
the confused mob, goodly
officials, brains made of soap,
sliding merrily over the houses.

4

An accident, they say, every hour,
one day when there was school in the air
an odor of garbage, the grocer's
oranges grow on the piazza.
The gigantic tire (the insect
once destroyed like this)

orecchie livella occhi voce,
le scarpe penzolano dal ramo,
evapora la gomma della frenata.

5

Il treno, il lago, gli annegati,
i fili arruffati. Il ponte nella notte:
di là quella donna. Il viola
nasce dall'unghia e il figlio
adolescente nell'ora prevista dice:
« Usa il tuo sesso, è il comando. »
Dentro la ciminiera, gonfio di sonno
precipita il manovale, spezzata la catena.

6

Cani azzannano i passanti, uomini
raccomandabili guidano l'assassino,
fuori, presto, scivoli.
Negri annusano il vento.
Ambigua è la sciagura,
le sentinelle, i poliziotti.
I due voltarono le spalle.
Rete, sacco: volati
in basso come pompieri.
Spari. Vibra l'asfalto,
alla porta di una casa, il tonfo.

7

Con le mani la sorella egli
spinge sotto il letto. Un piede
slogato dondola di fuori.
Dalla trama delle calze sale
l'azzurro dell'asfissía. Guarda,
strofina un fiammifero, incendia
i cappelli bagnati d'etere
luminoso. Le tende divampano
crepitando. Li scaglia nel fienile
il cuscino e la bottiglia di benzina.
Gli occhi crepano come uova.
Afferra la doppietta e spara
nella casa della madre. Gli occhi
sono funghi presi a pedate.
Mani affumicate e testa
grattugiata corre alla polveriera,
inciampa, nel cielo lentamente

levels ears eyes voice,
the shoes dangle from the branch,
the rubber from the skid mark smokes.

5

The train, the lake, the drowned bodies,
the tangled wires. The bridge in the night:
beyond that woman. The violet
grows from the nail and the adolescent
son says, as was prophesied:
"Make sex pay, it's the Commandment."
Inside the smokestack, swollen with sleep,
the worker plummets, having broken the chain.

6

Dogs seize passersby, men
of integrity direct the assassin,
outside, quickly, you slip.
Negroes sniff the wind.
The disaster is ambiguous,
the sentries, the police.
Those two turn their backs.
Net, bag: hurling
to the ground fireman style.
Shots. The thud shakes
the asphalt, right up to the door.

7

With his hands he shoves his sister
under the bed. A dislocated
foot is dangling out.
From the knot of dirty stockings
the blue of asphyxia. Look,
he strikes a match, he lights up
her hair soaked in luminous ether.
The curtains go up in flames
crackling. There in the hovel, the kitchen
and the propane bottle blow sky high.
Her eyes crack like eggs.
He grabs the double-barreled shotgun
and shoots into his mother's house.
The eyes are mushrooms which have been
kicked to bits. Smoked hands and grated
head run to the powder magazine,
he stumbles, the explosion rises

Antonio Porta   431

s'innalza l'esplosione e i vetri
bruciano infranti d'un fuoco
giallo; abitanti immobili
il capo basso, contano le formiche.

8

Osserva l'orizzonte della notte,
inghiotte la finestra il gorgo del cortile,
l'esplosione soffiò dal deserto
sui capelli, veloce spinta al terrore:
tutto male in cucina, il gas
si espande, l'acqua scroscia,
la lampada spalanca il vuoto.
Richiude la porta dietro a sé,
e punge gli occhi il vento dell'incendio,
corre sugli asfalti, cosparso d'olio:
saltati i bottoni alla camicia estiva,
la ferita si colora, legume
che una lama rapida incide.

9

Vide dal suo posto le case
roventi incenerirsi e in fondo alla città
i denti battono sotto le lenzuola
e guizzano i corvi dall'ombelico.
L'A è finestra e oltre
s'agita la pianura di stracci.
L'O si apre e si chiama
lago ribollente fango.
« Galoppate a cammello nel deserto! »
Fa acqua l'animale sventrato
dal taxi furibondo: si ricordò
d'avere atteso tanto, la gola
trapassa il sapore dei papaveri:
cala veloce nelle acque dentro
l'auto impennata, volontario
palombaro, con un glú senza ricambio.

10

Un coro ora sono, ondeggianti
nel prato colmo di sussulti.
« Lo zoccolo del cavallo tradisce,
frana la ragione dei secoli. »
Urla una donna, partorisce,

slowly into the sky and the shattered
windows burn with a yellow
fire; immobile citizens
heads lowered, count the ants.

8

He observes the night horizon,
the window swallows the vortex of the courtyard,
the explosion blew from the desert
onto his hair, instantly slammed into terror:
total chaos in the kitchen, the gas
spreads, the water comes down in torrents,
the lamp rips open the emptiness.
He recloses the door behind him,
and the wind of the fireball stings his eyes,
runs along the asphalt, scattered with oil;
the buttons jump off the summer shirt,
the wound gushes its color, legume
cut open by a quick blade.

9

From his spot he sees the fiery
houses burn to ashes and down in the city
teeth chatter under the sheets
and ravens dart from the navel.
The A is a window and out there
the plain of rags stirs.
The O bursts open and is called
a lake of boiling mud.
"Gallop into the desert on a camel!"
The animal gutted by the wild taxi
leaks urine: he remembered
having waited for so long, his throat
gives off the smell of poppies:
he slips quickly into the water inside
the pitching car, volunteer
diver, with a final gurgle.

10

Now they are a chorus, rocking
in the meadow full of tremors.
"Some trust in chariots, and some in horses,
They are brought down and fallen."
A woman screams, she gives birth

per un bambino percosso.
Con un colpo di uncino mette a nudo
l'escavatrice venose tubature,
e radici cariche di schiuma
nel vento dell'albero antico,
spasimano, gigante abbattuto.
Quattromila metri di terriccio
premono le schiene, e un minatore
in salvo ha mormorato:
« Là è tutto pieno di gas. »
Un attimo, prima di scivolare
nella fogna gridò: Sí.

to a mangled baby boy.
With a blow from its scoop the power shovel
strips bare veinlike pipelines,
and roots laden with scum
in the wind of the ancient tree,
they suffer agonies, gigantic slaughter.
Four hundred thousand meters of dirt
press down on their backs, and a miner
in a safe place murmured:
"It's just loaded with gas over there."
An instant before sliding
into the sewer, he shouted: Yes!

Antonio Porta   435

Dialogo con Herz

« Fui preso dal terrore divenendo lepre,
e accettare, poi, entrò nelle abitudini. »
« Fosse vero potrei uccidermi. » « Qual è
il destino delle lepri? » « La morte semplice. »
« Mi possedeva una paura rivoltante, squittivo,
di notte, e brucavo le foglie, di cavolo
e di tabacco. D'inverno consumai le riserve. »

« Non voglio divenire lepre, ma uccello
e impigliarmi tra le spine. » « La lepre muore
di freddo, di fame, di vecchiaia o fucilata.
Basta agli uccelli, spesso, un forte
vento notturno, tramontana tra le anitre
congelate. » « Herz, disse sulla terrazza,
verremo risucchiati da una grondaia in un giorno
di pioggia, emblema di violenze. »

« Desideravo da tempo muovermi
tra gli alberi: divenire uccello e nel
fogliame estivo scoprire il cunicolo,
giungere al fondamento. » « Toccare le radici
e leccare sostanze nutritive. » « La vecchia
abbaia, hai detto, e lo scemo ha urtato
il muro, con la ruota. Stizzito solleva
la maschera dalle pietre e ricade nell'incertezza
di un universo in furioso divenire. »

« Scivolo nuotando tra alghe pericolose.
Affondo in fitte vegetazioni, ricoperto
di formiche e di foglie. Mastico piume,
è quasi la conoscenza: con la luce
del giorno tra le fessure e la polvere
che si alza in un formicolío di protezione
e di salvezza. »

Dialogue with Herz

"I was seized by the terror of turning into a rabbit,
and then accepting, I got used to it."
"If it were true I could kill myself." "What
happens to rabbits?" "A simple death."
"A revolting fear possessed me, I shrieked,
in the night, and nibbled leaves, cabbage and
tobacco leaves. I used the leftovers that winter."

"I don't want to be a rabbit, but a bird
and get tangled in the thorns." "A rabbit dies
from the cold, from hunger, from old age or a gunshot.
For birds a strong night wind is often
enough, a northern blast among the frozen
ducks." "Herz," he said on the terrace,
"we shall be sucked down a sewer on a rainy
day, emblem of violence."

"For a long time I've wanted to fly
through the trees: to become a bird and
discover a tunnel in the summer foliage,
to reach solid earth." "To hit the roots
and lick up nutritive juices." "The old bitch
barks, you said, and the idiot ran his
wheel into the wall. Irritated he strips the mask
from the stones and falls once more into the uncertainty
of a universe in a fury to become."

"I slip along swimming through dangerous seaweed.
I plunge into tons of vegetation, covered
with ants and leaves. I chew on feathers,
it's almost knowledge: with daylight
streaming through the fissures and the dust
which rises into a swarm of protection
and salvation."

Antonio Porta

437

Per i capelli ci afferra il vento, è vero,
dietro la nuvola si arresta un cielo specchiante:
nell'ombra maculata lo raggiunse la voce di Herz.
La sera, in terrazza, continuarono, felici:
« Avrà mai fine l'arbitrio del giorno e della notte? »

The wind seizes us by the hair, it's true,
a resplendent sky lingers behind the cloud:
Herz's voice reached him in the tarnished shadow.
The evening, on the terrace, they will remain happy:
"Will the power of day and night never end?"

Antonio Porta

Il vento soffia sul limite

Buca la curva e muore. Ma il corpo nel verde
frigorifero pietosamente vien disposto e avvolto
nel pesante lenzuolo. La donna corse con affanno
"Dov'è lui!" "Lí." fu indicato con il dito
starnutendo. Guardò la tavola di ghiaccio, l'occhio
cristallino. Le alte gambe di scatto ripiegò
con il capo, oscillando, segnò "Sí."

Le gonfie rane ingoiarono, si sa, le ceneri
calanti nel laghetto. Rimane, tuttavia,
sotto il lenzuolo impietrito e gli uccelli ascolta
levarsi a volo sopra gli occhi. Alberi liberi
frusciano nello spazio e un fiume furioso
piomba giú dall'alto. Siede sulla riva.

Legato accanto, il lenzuolo sbatte nel vento.
Caddero i lunghi denti ed i capelli, stopposa
parrucca, richiudono le tempie. Inciampa,
assorta, nelle case, ad incidere si ostina
una porta con le unghie. In breve, si pensa,
verrà posta al riparo. Ma cosí non è.

Domandò, piú tardi, una scala sulla quale
lenta arrampicasse fino a lui. "Bella
giornata, oggi, nevvero?" risposero fuggendo.
Il tempo segna pioggia. S'arresta dietro gli occhi.

Al limite nuvole soffiano sugli alberi,
stridendo ruotano montagne; aggrappati
uomini dormono tra le rocce. Luci,
abetaie verso

The Wind Blows on the Border

He breaks through the curve and dies. But the body in the green
refrigerator is mercifully laid out and wrapped up
in the heavy sheet. The woman ran breathlessly
"Where is he?" "There" he pointed with his finger,
sneezing. She looked at the table of ice, the crystalline
eye. His long legs knocking together, he bowed
his head, shaking, he motioned "Yes."

The swollen frogs will swallow up, we know, the ashes
which sink in the pond, yet he remains
petrified under the sheet and hears the birds
rise up in flight over his eyes. Free standing trees
rustle in space and a rushing stream
plummets down from above. He sits on the bank.

Tied close by, the sheet flaps in the wind.
The long teeth fall out and the hair, stringy
wig, encloses the temples. She stumbles,
absorbed, in the houses, she keeps trying to carve out
a door with her fingernails. In brief, you'd think
somebody would take care of her. But that's not the way it is.

She asked, later, for a ladder on which
she slowly climbed up to him. "Nice
day today, isn't it?" they replied running away.
It looks like rain. Everything comes to a stop behind her eyes.

At the border clouds blow on the trees,
screeching mountains wheel; huddled
men sleep in the rocks. Lights,
stands of fir toward

Antonio Porta   441

La pelliccia del castoro

1

La zebra scatta e s'avvicina,
la coscia allunga le strisce
lucide e accorcia, fa esplodere
lo zoccolo cartucce di sabbia,
fa un rombo di gola penetrata
da una mano abile che nuota
agitando le dita e stringe
la lingua disciolta nella saliva
bollente tra i denti alla deriva.

In gola penetra scuotendo
le anche l'animale impellicciato,
dilata la bocca dell'esofago,
lo stomaco si distende, in attesa
d'essere venduto e lavorato
come pelle per guanti.

2

La caccia alla balena ha inizio
sul mare innestato di vele
che l'incavo del vento carica di mare.
Stiamo vigili al comando, i ghiacci
inviano bagliori circondando la rotta.
Scoppia la bufera e la nave capriola,
la vista indebolisce, la gola
si torce, rigagnoli scendono sulle gambe,
la schiena del cetaceo splende
all'improvviso, incalziamo con gli arpioni
e primi si bucano i seni
gonfi e teneri, seconde
le coscie lucide, e rovescia
il ventre, le braccia
allunga all'indietro: « Issiamola
a bordo, divoriamo! »

Beaver Skin

1

The zebra jumps up and approaches,
the thigh stretches its bright
stripes and contracts, the hoof makes
cartridges of sand explode,
it makes a throat roar, penetrated
by a skillful hand that swims
wriggling the fingers and seizes
the tongue dissolved in boiling
saliva hanging from the teeth.

He penetrates into the throat, stirring
the haunches of the skin-wrapped animal,
the mouth of the esophagus dilated,
the stomach distends, waiting
to be sold and worked
as hide for gloves.

2

The whale hunt begins
on a sea grafted with sails
that the tunnel of wind charges with sea.
We are watchful at our posts, ice floes
send off gleams of light encircling the wake.
The hurricane explodes and the ship dances,
visibility grows poorer, our throats
tighten, torrents of water fall on our legs,
the whale's back suddenly
glistens, we give chase with harpoons
and the first ones pierce her swollen
and tender breasts, the second ones
her shiny flanks, and it turns her
belly up, arms
reaching backwards: "Let's hoist 'er
on board, let's eat 'er up!"

3

Veloce s'avvicinò e strinse piano
con le dita i rami carichi di frutti,
la dura scorza dell'albero feriva
la guancia e le piume, in vortice cadendo,
innumerevoli impedivano il respiro:
il succo stillava sugli occhi e nella gola
e fu costretto, infine!, a strangolare il serpente
imbecille accorso a impedire la raccolta:
ora che l'albero si faceva tenero
e abbracciato cedeva piegando le sue fibre!

4

Nel canneto penetra in corsa
perché le colombacce schiamazzino
in fuga: prima alla zampa
della gru cerca d'afferrarsi,
e si piega, poi, stretta
all'albero cedevole: finché
non scoppino in gola liti
e squittire di castori che forzano
l'uscita del singhiozzo lacrimoso.

Le gambe, intanto, scavano
le talpe e le mele dei seni
gratta la zampa dell'orso:
il fango di palude dove affonda,
sospinto dal vento che l'increspa,
sopra gli occhi si placa arrovesciati,
filtra nella chiostra del denti.

3

He approached quickly and with his fingers
softly grasped the fruit-laden branches,
the hard bark of the tree wounded
his cheek, and the feathers, falling in a vortex,
thousands of them, snatched away his breath:
the juice dripped into his eyes and down his throat
and he was forced, at last! to strangle the idiotic
serpent who had come to prevent the harvest:
now that the tree had made herself tender
embraced and submissive she surrendered her fibers!

4

Because the stupid doves thunder up
in flight he penetrates the canebrake
at full speed: first he tries to seize
the crane's leg,
and then it submits, backed
against the yielding tree: until
scoldings and yelps burst from the throats
of beavers who force the escape
of a tearful moan.

Meanwhile, bear legs dig up
moles and the bear claw scratches
the plump breast apples:
the marsh mud where he sinks,
driven by the wind which ripples it,
over the torn up eyes he calms down,
he sucks through his teeth.

Antonio Porta   445

DA Zero

sí, no, sí, no, sí, no, sí, no, sí, no, sí, no, sí, no, sí,
diverse, acute e gravi, lento, il battere dei trampolieri,
raro, schioccanti, occhi, non lo ricordano per nulla, come
viene il momento di dormire, corse attorno all'ostacolo, se
con l'unghia, stacca le squame dal muro, e in su: polvere

cammelli, come si immagina sarà la collina, azzoppati, perduto o
pioggia, potranno incontrarla, comincia la melodia, come una melo
merda, pieno di pappagalli, la nebbia dilegua, sbarcano, corallo
sferica, recidono una mano per l'offerta, sigilla la scatola nera, acqua
ruotano, confuse percezioni, nera lacca su nera lacca, limpide

come una collana, cade, tra le finestre, le ossa sono polvere e
il busto eretto, scendono rampicanti lungo il muro, oblique fendi
ieri, lombrichi, tra l'erba, e sta fermo, dietro la luce, rinchiuso
sclerotica estenuata, nel giardino brulicano, siede per aspettarla
e ha mosso una mano, si allontana, punta il dito di marmo, il naso

tante agita la sua coda, gli occhi fissi nell'ipnosi, roteando le gambe
tato, dilatati e richiusi, franato con un muro di mattoni, sotto le finestre di
per salire gli scalini, riprese a scavare sotto la torre, le ossa ripulite gli av
schizzò nella pianura, con una coda di scintille, annottando, gola palpi

. . . .

verde, è certamente verde, questo è il conflitto del verde, perde
tamente, il piú e il meno, entrambi sono accentuati, entrambi cupi,
lano, le anatre si impigliano lassú, si posano quando vedono un'acqua
assolutamente, dice, l'uomo no, si devono classificare, nasce il subl
finitamente, variabile, è sempre verde, sente aumentare la tensione
incerto, continuano a salire, contare, perdere, scoprire, fuggire, di

FROM Zero

yes, no, yes, no, yes, no, yes, no, yes, no, yes, no, yes, no, yes
various, sharp and heavy, slow, the beating of the stilt-birds,
rare, snapping, eyes, they don't remember it at all, as
the moment of sleep comes, he runs around the obstacle, if
with his fingernail, he takes scales off the wall, and above: dust

camels, as one imagines the hill will be, lame, lost or
rain, they should be able to find it, the melody begins, like an apple tree
shit, full of parrots, the fog disperses, they put ashore, coral
spherical, they cut off a hand as an offering, he seals the black box, water
they roll, confused perceptions, black lacquer on black lacquer, limpid

like a necklace, it falls, through the windows, the bones are dust and
the upright bust, climbing they descend along the wall, oblique splits
yesterday, earthworms, in the grass, and he stands still, behind the light, closed
up,
sclerotic worn out, they swarm in the garden, he sits and waits for her
and he moved a hand, he goes away, he points the marble finger, the nose

many he wags his tail, eyes in a hypnotic stare, swinging the legs
ted, dilated and closed up, collapsed with a brick wall, under the windows of
in order to walk up the stairs, he started to dig under the tower again, the
cleaned up bones, the adv
he sketched on the plain, with a tail of sparks, growing dark, you touch throat

. . . .

green, it's certainly green, this clash of the green, he loses
ainly, the long and short of it, both are stressed, both dark,
lain, the ducks get tangled up there, they light when they see water
absolutely, he says, not man, they must classify, it gives birth to the subl
perfectly, variable, it's always green, he feels the tension build
uncertain, they continue to climb, count, lose, discover, flee of

Antonio Porta   447

argento, comportamenti inappropriati, socialità deforme, minzioni da confli
l'ora, risponde, ciò determina l'ansia, stimolo inconsueto, che non mangia
orco, paralogismi, neografismi, neomorfismi, nudi ardenti, dice, senza occhi

senza concezione, senza misura, senza forma
senza metro, senza progetto, senza costruzio
ne, senza matrice, senza materia, senza mat
eriale, senza spazio, senza vuoto, senza st
abilità, ciò che congiunge, ciò che separa,
che raccoglie acqua in un setaccio, con una
concezione, con una misura, con una forma,
con un metro, con un progetto, con una cost
ruzione, con la matrice, con la materia, con
il materiale, poiché ha spazio, ha vuoto, è
stabilità, poiché è instabile, è vuoto, ciò
che è l'acqua, senza vuoto, senza pieno, se
nza congiunzioni, un numero come l'altro o

silver, inappropriate manners, deformed sociality, urinations from confli
the time, he answers, that determines the anxiety, unusual stimulus, that
                                                            doesn't eat
ogre, paralogisms, neographisms, neomorphisms, burning nudes, he says,
                                                            without eyes

without conception, without measure, without form
without meter, without plan, without construc
tion, without matrix, without matter, without mat
erial, without space, without emptiness, without st
ability, that which joins, that which separates,
which gathers water in a sieve, with a
conception, with a measure, with a form,
with a meter, with a plan, with a const
ruction, with the matrix, with the matter, with
the material, since it has space, has emptiness, is
stability, since it's unstable, is empty, that
which is water, without emptiness, without fullness, wi
thout connections, one number like another or

Aprire

1

Dietro la porta nulla, dietro la tenda,
l'impronta impressa sulla parete, sotto,
l'auto, la finestra, si ferma, dietro la tenda,
un vento che la scuote, sul soffitto nero
una macchia piú oscura, impronta della mano
alzandosi si è appoggiato, nulla, premendo,
un fazzoletto di seta, il lampadario oscilla,
un nodo, la luce, macchia d'inchiostro,
sul pavimento, sopra la tenda, la paglietta che raschia,
sul pavimento gocce di sudore, alzandosi,
la macchia non scompare, dietro la tenda,
la seta nera del fazzoletto, luccica sul soffitto,
la mano si appoggia, il fuoco nella mano,
sulla poltrona un nodo di seta, luccica,
ferita, ora il sangue sulla parete,
la seta del fazzoletto agita una mano.

2

Le calze infila, nere, e sfila, con i denti,
la spaccata, il doppio salto, in un istante, la calza maglia,
all'indietro, capriola, poi la spaccata, i seni
premono il pavimento, dietro i capelli, dietro la porta,
non c'è, c'è il salto all'indietro, le cuciture,
l'impronta della mano, all'indietro, sul soffitto,
la ruota, delle gambe e delle braccia, di fianco,
dei seni, gli occhi, bianchi, contro il soffitto,
dietro la porta, calze di seta appese, la capriola.

3

Perché la tenda scuote, si è alzato,
il vento, nello spiraglio la luce, il buio,
dietro la tenda c'è, la notte, il giorno,
nei canali le barche, in gruppo, i quieti canali,
navigano, cariche di sabbia, sotto i ponti,
è mattina, il ferro dei passi, remi e motori,
i passi sulla sabbia, il vento sulla sabbia,
le tende sollevano i lembi, perché è notte,

To Open

1

Behind the door, nothing, behind the curtain,
the mark printed on the wall, down there,
the car, the window, it stops, behind the curtain,
a breeze that stirs it, on the black ceiling,
an even darker stain, a hand print,
it was put there by reaching up, nothing, pressing,
a silk handkerchief, the lamp shudders,
a knot, the light, ink stain,
on the floor, above the curtain, the scrubbing rag,
drops of sweat on the floor, rising up,
the strain doesn't go away, behind the curtain,
the black of the handkerchief, shines on the ceiling,
the hand leans on it, fire in the hand,
a knot of silk on the armchair, it shines,
wounded, now blood on the wall,
the silk of the handkerchief waves its hand.

2

She puts on the stockings, black, and takes them off, with her teeth,
splits, double somersault, in an instant, tights,
backwards, tumble, then the splits, breasts
pressing against the floor, behind her hair, behind the door,
it isn't there, only the backwards flip, the seams,
the handprint, backwards, on the ceiling,
the cartwheel, of legs and arms, sideways,
of breasts, eyes, whites, against the ceiling,
behind the door, hanging silk stockings, tumble.

3

Because the curtain stirs, it rises,
the wind, light through the vent, darkness,
behind the curtain there is, night, day,
boats in the canals, in a string, quiet canals,
navigate, loaded with sand, under the bridges,
it's morning, the iron of the steps, cars and motors,
footsteps on the sand, wind on the sand,
the curtains lift their hems, because it's night,

giorno di vento, di pioggia sul mare,
dietro la porta il mare, la tenda si riempie di sabbia,
di calze, di pioggia, appese, sporche di sangue.

4

La punta, la finestra alta, c'era vento,
si è alzato adagio, stride, in un istante,
ovale, un foro nella parete, con la mano,
in frantumi, l'ovale del vetro, sulle foglie,
è notte, mattina, fitta, densa, chiara,
di sabbia, di diamante, corre sulla spiaggia,
alzato e corso, la mano premuta, a lungo,
fermo, contro il vetro, la fronte, sul,
il vetro sulla mattina, premette, oscura,
la mano affonda, nella terra, nel vetro, nel ventre,
la fronte di vetro, nubi di sabbia,
nella tenda, ventre lacerato, dietro la porta.

5

Ruota delle gambe, la tela sbatte nel vento,
quell'uomo, le gambe aderiscono alla corsa,
la corda si flette, verso il molo, sulla sabbia,
sopra le reti, asciugano, le scarpe di tela,
il molo di cemento, battono la corsa,
non c'è che mare, sempre piú oscuro, il cemento,
nella tenda, sfilava le calze con i denti,
la punta, ha premuto un istante, a lungo,
le calze distese sull'acqua, sul ventre.

6

Di là, stringe la maniglia, verso,
non c'è, né certezza, né uscita, sulla parete,
l'orecchio, poi aprire, un'incerta, non si apre,
risposta, le chiavi tra le dita, il ventre aperto,
la mano sul ventre, trema sulle foglie,
di corsa, sulla sabbia, punta della lama,
il figlio, sotto la scrivania, dorme nella stanza.

day of wind, of rain on the sea,
the sea behind the door, the curtains filled with sand,
stockings, rain, hanging, filthy with blood.

4

The knife points, the high window, it was windy,
he rose slowly, screeches, in an instant,
oval, a hole in the wall, with the hand,
in fragments, glass oval, on the leaves,
it's night, morning, sharp, dense, clear,
of sand, of diamond, she runs on the beach,
he gets up and runs, the hand presses, a long time,
he stops, against the glass, the forehead, against,
the glass on the morning, it pressed, dark,
the hand plunges, into the ground, into the glass, into her stomach,
glass forehead, clouds of sand,
in the curtain, splintered glass, behind the door.

5

Cartwheel, the cloth flaps in the wind,
that man, his legs are fixed in motion,
the rope curves, toward the pier, on the sand,
on the nets, they dry, cloth shoes,
cement pier, he breaks into a run,
there isn't anything but sea, always darker, cement,
in the curtain, she took off her socks with her teeth,
the knife point, it pressed an instant, a long time,
stockings stretched out on the water, on her stomach.

6

Away, squeezes the handle, towards,
there isn't, either certainty, or escape, on the wall,
the ear, then to open, an uncertainty, it doesn't open,
reply, keys in hand, stomach open,
hand on the stomach, shaking on the leaves,
on the run, on the sand, tip of the blade,
the son, under the writing desk, sleeps in the room.

Antonio Porta   453

7

Il corpo sullo scoglio, l'occhio cieco, il sole,
il muro, dormiva, il capo sul libro, la notte sul mare,
dietro la finestra gli uccelli, il sole nella tenda,
l'occhio piú oscuro, il taglio nel ventre, sotto l'impronta,
dietro la tenda, la fine, aprire, nel muro,
un foro, ventre disseccato, la porta chiusa,
la porta si apre, si chiude, ventre premuto,
che apre, muro, notte, porta.

7

The body on the rock, blind eye, the sun,
the wall, he was sleeping, head on a book, night on the sea,
birds behind the window, sun in the curtain,
the eye darker now, the slash in the stomach, under the mark,
behind the curtain, the end, to open, in the wall,
a hole, withered stomach, the closed door,
the door opens, closes, pressed stomach,
which opens, wall, night, door.

DA Rapporti umani

XII

Camminare diviene intollerabile, è passato
un altro anno, con i piedi incollati ai pavimenti,
prima o dopo, con le gambe ridotte all'osso,
miele dei muscoli, piú che un'antica verità,
rinchiuso nella stanza, non ti sa dire, e poi non c'è.

Sulle strade di ghiaccio, pattinando, con la sciarpa
verde e un berretto scuro, per un complesso di colpe,
breve felicità, non s'incontrano mai, cosí t'infurii,
gratti il muro con l'unghia e te la spezzi, disteso
sulla panchina, anitre imbalsamate galleggiano sul lago,
"mi raccontava una storia"—"sí, ma soltanto la fine."

XIII

Comincia la sete aumenta, l'ha sollevata, la fa
impazzire, gli uccelli covano tra i massi rotola-
ti dalla montagna, raccontandole storie, una mano
sulle ginocchia, apparizioni, bulbi di crisantemi,
la testa tra le gambe, per ciò piangono tutti,
è la fame, per trent'anni d'amore, spine nella
barba multicolore, la casa brucia con gli anni, gli
occhi non sai dove guardano, se è l'ora, non ci
credono piú, ancora

XIV

Sono biglie di vetro, ricordati di quegli anni, e li
fa schizzare via, né inquietudini né incertezze, con
il mantello rosso, con le piume, rimbalzano sul pavimento, sciolgono nell'acqua la miscela dell'iride,
dilaga, pisciata di cavallo, orecchie che macerano ne
la terra, tibia percorsa dalle formiche, un angolo di
giardino, ai fori delle narici

FROM Human Relations

XII

Walking becomes unbearable, another year
has gone by, feet stuck to the floor,
sooner or later, legs shrunk down to the bone,
muscles turned to honey, shut away in the room,
I can't give you anything but an old saying, there's nothing else.

On icy streets, skating along, with a green scarf
and a dark beret, because of all my guilt,
fleeting happiness, no one ever says hello, so you get mad,
scratch the wall with your nail and break it, stretched out
on the park bench, stuffed ducks floating on the lake,
"he was telling me a story"—"yeah, but only the ending."

XIII

The thirst begins and increases, it has risen, it
drives you crazy, the birds nest among the mountain's
rolling boulders, telling them stories of
ghosts, hand on knees, chrysanthemum bulbs,
head between the legs, they all cried about that,
it's hunger, for thirty years of love, thorns in the multi-
colored beard, the house burning for years, you don't
know where the eyes are looking, the time has come it seems
when they no longer believe us, still

XIV

They're glass marbles, remember those years, and
neither apprehension nor uncertainty, with its red cloak,
with its feathers, makes them scatter, they rebound
off the sidewalk, in water they dissolve into a rainbow,
it spreads, horse piss, ears grimy with
dirt, shinbone covered with ants, a corner of
garden, at the holes of the nostrils

XV

I due stanno abbracciati, con un mazzo di crisantemi,
bevono alla loro tazza, le unghie nella schiena, la
candela gli brucia le mani, continua a camminare in
ginocchio, tenero pallone, curva del ventre, partorirà
un gatto, sotto la tenda, nuotando nell'ossigeno,
rana piena di latte, scivola lontano e la guardava,
sulla coperta di pelo, muoversi nella piazzetta, le
dita a O, il cagnolino alle calcagna, le impronte

XV

They're embracing, with a bunch of chrysanthemums,
sipping from their cups, her fingernails down his back,
he burns his hands on the candle, she keeps walking around
on her knees, tender balloon, the curve of her stomach, she'll
give birth to a cat, under the curtain, swimming in the oxygen,
frog full of milk, it slides away and she watches it go,
on top of the fur comforter, moving around in the piazza,
fingers at 0, the puppy at her heels, footprints

Antonio Porta

Utopia del nomade

Movimenti

1

si muove nella stagione lo consente
ogni luogo ha regole dettate dal clima
nella stagione inclemente dispone le sue difese
si sposta per sopravvivere o vivere
l'inverno lavorerà al coperto
conoscendo gli usi di molti luoghi
il cibo gli verrà dato in compenso

2

ricchezza prima sono mani e intelligenza
la seconda ricchezza avvicina l'altro da sé
può ritornare in luoghi uguali transumante
mutare itinerario ripetere il giro della terra
torna verso la fine in un luogo stabilito al principio

3

avrà figli da una o più donne
il tempo necessario passa ad insegnare loro
quello che sa la donna o le donne provvedono finché il padre
non torni a raccontare se i figli non seguono il padre
parlano senza ruoli

4

lascia alle spalle una terra predata
circondato da uomini disossati dicendo
la ricchezza altrove senza mentire

5

appena fermo in forma di saluto
spuntano affondano radici dai piedi
strappano senza male alla partenza

Nomad's Utopia

Movements

1

he moves as the season permits
every place has laws dictated by the climate
in inclement weather he sets up his defenses
he moves from place to place to survive or live
in winter he'll work undercover
knowing the uses of many places
food will be given to him in return

2

hands are the first wealth and intelligence
the second wealth the rest comes by itself
he can return to the same grazing places
change itinerary and repeat his circuit of the land
at the end he comes back to a place agreed on from the start

3

he will have children by one or more women
he spends the time necessary to teach them
what he knows the woman or women provide until the father
comes back to see if the children follow the father
they speak without roles

4

he turns his back on a plundered land
surrounded by boneless men saying
without lying that the wealth is elsewhere

5

I barely pause to say hello
roots from the feet sprout and sink in
upon parting they rip up without harm

6

la città si chiama Immagine non ha limiti
né centri può specchiarsi in sé stessa
luogo dove incontrarsi non è dunque
una città ma punto di protezione
porticati o tende luogo vegetale e animale
luogo di acque e coltivazioni uomini
vi s'incontrano o lasciano come vogliono si manifesta
il pensiero linguaggio che va preso alla lettera
sistema di piani e curve per scendere e salire
dietro a donne dietro a figli e animali
non esiste proprietà del suolo

7

si allontanano dalla pianura occupate dall'Industria
uomini senza farsi contare non è un capo
territori abbandonati montagnosi abitabili
imparano a farne a meno di quella la Ricca
che scompaia razzìa buco della terra
Cattedrale Chimica

6

the city named Image has neither boundaries
nor centers it can model itself on itself
place where you meet it is not therefore
a city but a point of protection
porches or tents vegetable and animal place
place of waters and human cultivation
they meet there or leave as they wish they show their
thoughts language which is taken literally
systems of planes and curves for going down and coming up
behind women behind children and animals
ownership of the soil doesn't exist

7

they leave the plain occupied by Industry
men without being big shots he's no boss
abandoned territories mountainous habitable
they learn to do without what the Rich One has
the one that disappears plunder hole in the earth
Chemical Cathedral

Adriano Spatola

Born in Fiume in 1941, Spatola currently lives in Bologna. He has been editor of *Malebolge* and *Il Verri*. Spatola was also a member of the "Gruppo '63." He has been especially active in the field of *poesia visiva*. The power of his poetry lies in the combination of surrealist technique and a wry sense of humor. But, like most of the rest of his contemporaries, he sees poetry as a means for exploring serious social and political issues.

His books of poetry are:

L'oblò.
    Milano: Feltrinelli, 1964.
Poesia da montare.
    Bologna: Sampietro, 1965.
Zeroglifico.
    Milano: Edizioni Geiger, 1966.
Majakovskiiiiiij.
    Milano: Edizioni Geiger, 1971.

Il boomerang

1

arma che torna contro se stessa, il pesce s'arpiona nel
ventre fra i flutti dello champagne

e: imbandita e: luccicante—cristalli—e ritorno (in
giacca bianca) a togliere le briciole

noi tutti cosí bene accomodati, nudi, sopra l'erba, per
la foto-ricordo

decidendo d'amarci in articulo mortis, suicidio: modalità decise per telefono

essendo ormai in protesto la cambiale che ci siamo aval-
lati l'un con l'altra

pieghe lucide, grasso: lampo azzurro, l'impianto che si
squaglia

frutto maturo l'ascensore appeso e come il verme nella
mela dentro eccomi assiso a battere spondei

2

mi guadagno la paga stando in bagno due ore, scrivendo
versi galanti per le vecchie signore

ma questi morti di fame invadono le piazze, rovinano il
selciato, si bagnano con l'acqua degli idranti

vado a prendere l'aperitivo—ghiaccio, possibilmente—
in mezzo alla mia razza, in mezzo alla mia gente

ma questi morti di fame invadono le piazze, rovinano il
selciato, si bagnano con l'acqua degli idranti

con un gesto tranquillo della mano ecco fermo un tassí:
insieme a lei m'allontano

The Boomerang

1

weapon that turns on itself, the fish spears itself
in the gut in waves of champagne

and: table set out and: glittering—crystal—and I return
(in a white jacket) to pick up the crumbs

we've arranged ourselves so nicely, nude, here on the grass,
for our souvenir photograph

deciding to make love *in articulo mortis*, suicide:
formalities were arranged by telephone

by now the check had bounced, so we wrote another one
to cover it

brilliant envelopes, fat: blue lightning, the melting
factory

ripe fruit hanging elevator and like the worm
in the apple, here I am inside banging out spondees

2

I earn my pay by sitting in the bath for two hours, writing
elegant verse for old ladies

but these starving people are invading the piazzas, messing
up the pavement, taking baths in the water from fire hydrants

I go out for an aperitif—ice, possibly—
in the midst of my race, in the midst of my people

but these starving people are invading the piazzas, messing
up the pavement, taking baths in the water from fire hydrants

with a casual gesture of my hand I stop a taxi:
she and I split the scene together

Adriano Spatola   467

ma questi morti di fame invadono le piazze, rovinano il
selciato, si bagnano con l'acqua degli idranti

e un altro che ormai li conosceva tutti, anche quelli in
borghese, l'han pestato: soprattutto sull'occhio tesserato

3

necropoli di dodge, di carriole, di tralicci sventrati,
di rimorchi-giardino nei quali tra la pioggia cresce l'erba

necropoli: tombe-macerie che l'autocarro scarica sulla
riva del fiume, tumuli-detriti che la piena corrode e porta
al mare

quando gira l'impastatrice—sabbia, ghiaia e cemento—
nella piazza scavata per le fondamenta due metri sotto
il livello del piano stradale, sopra la carne viva della
città

e nello scantinato la tomba di famiglia per macchine da
scrivere, scaffali fitti di urne sopra le quali polvere cade
dai nuovi modelli

ma sotto la tettoia, nell'area della fabbrica, necropoli
di biciclette—ciechi manubri, sellini

con rastrello-bulldozer che devasta negli orti le lattughe,
sulla terrazza gerani dentro il vaso calpestati dall'uomo
dell'antenna

necropoli-posteggi: visitarli nel tardo tramonto nel giorno dei morti, dentro la nebbia, novembre, fari opachi, la-
pidi illeggibili

le date di N e di M si accendono e si spengono, variabile commossa intensità

4

ah! quello che scava nella strada, trapano nel dente

e proprio dentro il buco del dente si posa la nicotina

secrezioni benzoliche, sudori metaniferi

but these starving people are invading the piazzas, messing
up the pavement, taking baths in the water from fire hydrants

and another person who by now knew them all, even the ones
in civies, they smashed him: above all on the official eye

3

necropolis of Dodges, wheelbarrows, gutted mattress ticking,
garden trailers—in which grass grows in the rain

necropolis: tomb-ruins which the truck dumps on the
banks of the river, tumulus-detritus that the highwater
corrodes and carries out to sea

when the mixer turns—sand, gravel and cement—
in the piazza excavated for the foundations two meters
below street level, above the city's living
flesh

and the family crypt for typewriters in the basement,
shelves filled with urns, dust falls from the
newer models above

but under the corrugated roof, in the area by the factory,
a necropolis of bicycles—blind handlebars, seats

with the tractor-bulldozer which destroys lettuce in the
kitchen gardens, on the terrace inside a vase, geraniums
trampled by the antenna man

necropolis-parking lots: to visit them in the late twilight
on the Day of Death, inside the fog, November, opaque
headlights, illegible tombstones

the dates of N and M light up and then go out, variable
and moving intensity

4

yeah! the guy who digs up the road, drill in your tooth

and the nicotine settles right inside the cavity

benzol secretions, methane sweats

e sotto l'epidermide s'annida l'arabesco dei rami che al profondo pompano pus, rivoltano le scorie di petrolio conciato—gas di scappamento che colorano il sangue

cristo! voglio proprio vederli galleggiare, sull'acqua an-guilliforme di piscina: sputi, carogne: mentre mi si spezza

and nestling under the epidermis the arabesque of branches
which pump pus up from the depths, they push up the
scum of filthy kerosene—exhaust gases which color the blood

Christ! I really want to see them swim on the writhing
water of the swimming pool: spittle, carrion: while
it breaks me down

Sterilità in metamorfosi

per Corrado Costa, Bologna 6 maggio 1964

1

persino è della pietra far vermi questa notte
dentro la pietra sono i suoi capelli
grumo nero impastato con bianchissima calce
e la roccia sta nel mezzo del lago
le sue dita irte di radici sono formiche
grumi neri impastati con bianchissima calce
le cinque dita sono cinque radici nel mondo che si solleva
perché persino la pietra fa vermi questa notte
fondamento del quale purtroppo qui non è luogo
radice comune dalla quale rampollano essi stanotte
è lama di coltello che taglia tra le dita

2

è lama di coltello che taglia tra le dita
si fa sabbia pietra rossa e della sabbia fango
e la roccia sta nel mezzo del lago
la mano a cinque dita che fu dentro la fogna
perché la roccia nel mezzo del lago si carica d'acqua
occhio del pesce arpionato che fissa il nero stivale che luccica d'acqua
è lama di coltello che fende la tua mano
e il mondo che si solleva si chiude a pugno
guarda nel centro della mano
ogni radice è dentro la tua carne
non risalgono piú dal baratro giallo di sabbia

3

non risalgono piú dal baratro giallo di sabbia
grumi neri impastati con bianchissima calce
è la tua mano che s'apre tra le dita come un fiore nell'alba
rana squartata che frigge nell'olio della cucina sul fiume
e i funghi tra le dita seminati ora vedono il sole
radice inchiodata allo scafo della roccia sommersa
come s'alza nell'aria il pesce che l'aria consuma
e i funghi gonfiati dal sole producono pus
perché dentro la pietra sono i suoi capelli

Sterility in Metamorphosis

for Corrado Costa, Bologna, May 6, 1964

1

even the stone produces worms tonight
inside the stone are her hairs
black clot filled with the whitest lime
and the rock sits in the middle of the lake
its fingers bristling with roots are ants
black clots filled with the whitest lime
the five fingers are five roots in the world which rises
because even the stone produces worms tonight
foundation of which unfortunately here isn't the place
common roof from which they shoot up tonight
it's a knife blade which cuts between the fingers

2

it's a knife blade which cuts between the fingers
becomes sand red stone and from the sand mud
and the rock sits in the middle of the lake
the five-fingered hand which was in the sewer
because the rock in the middle of the lake is loaded with water
eye of the speared fish which stares at the black root glittering with water
it's a knife blade which cuts through your hand
and the world which rises closes to a fist
look in the center of the hand
every root is inside your flesh
they don't rise again from the yellow chasm of sand

3

they don't rise again from the yellow chasm of sand
black clots filled with the whitest lime
it's your hand which opens between the fingers like a flower at dawn
cut up frog which fries in the oil in the kitchen on the river
and the mushrooms scattered between the fingers now they see the sun
root riveted to the hull of the submerged rock
as the fish rises in the air which the air consumes
and the mushrooms swollen from the sun produce pus
because inside the stone is her hair

Adriano Spatola   473

perché il mondo che si solleva si chiude a pugno
perché non risalgono piú dal baratro giallo di sabbia
e il sole li gonfia perché producano pus

4

perché ho preso i capelli di colei che mi fece
al lento ruotare dell'occhio dentro la testa
sepolti tra le mie dita essi che terra ricopre
questa mano medusa schiacciata dal piede di marmo
quando dentro il tuo ventre semino dita di mani e di piedi
perché con la pietra si salda la torre di carne
lama di sabbia rossa che fende la sterile acqua
e il mondo che si solleva si chiude a pugno
al lento ruotare dell'occhio dentro la testa
radice inchiodata allo scafo della roccia sommersa
pesce che s'alza nell'aria e che l'aria consuma

5

è la tua colpa colomba rossa che sale dall'intestino
come la mano che tengo nell'acqua che bolle
e il ventre è questa parete che scivola sopra di me
mentre distesa sul fianco la città s'addormenta
in mezzo alla piazza di marmo gonfio di pus
e come sappiamo da tempo da sempre bambini gridano in piazza
quando mi levo dal letto sopra la valle
e la sua mano aperta sotto la gonfia radice si chiude con la radice
perché non risalgono piú dal baratro giallo di sabbia
avendo già appeso il cappello alla torre dell'orologio
corpo di luce che dentro alimento e distruggo
gonfie di vermi radici le sbarre in rugoso cemento

6

lascio la lingua che affondi dentro la pietra scheggiata
mentre mi spezzo le unghie contro la tenera carne
perché ho preso i capelli di colei che mi fece
perché persino la pietra fa vermi questa notte
al lento ruotare dell'occhio dentro la testa
quando su dal tuo ventre sorgono dita di mani e di piedi
denti del ventre che strappo con l'unghia affilata
affinché il piede dell'uomo conosca la morsa delle radici
tra i funghi gonfiati dal sole che semina pus
corpo di luce che dentro alimento e distruggo
qui dentro lamiera contorta della sua casa
perché la roccia nel mezzo del lago si carica d'acqua

because the world which rises closes to a fist
because it doesn't rise again from the yellow chasm of sand
and the sun swells them so they can produce pus

4

because I grabbed the hair of the woman who made me
to the slow rolling of the eye in the head
buried between my fingers those which earth covers
this medusa hand crushed by the marble foot
when inside your chest I scatter fingers and toes
because you heal the tower of flesh with the stone
blade of red sand which cuts through the sterile water
and the world which rises closes into a fist
to the slow rolling of the eye in the head
root riveted to the hull of the submerged rock
fish which rises in the air and which the air consumes

5

it's your fault red dove which rises from the intestine
like the hand I hold in the boiling water
and the womb is this wall which slides over me
while stretched out on its side the city sleeps
in the middle of the piazza of pus swollen marble
and as we have known for a long time children have always cried in the piazza
when I get up from the bed above the valley
and her open hand under the swollen root closes with the root
because they no longer rise from the yellow chasm of sand
having already hung the hat from the clocktower
body of light which I feed and destroy inside
swollen with worms roots the bars in rutted cement

6

I leave the tongue which you plunge inside the chipped stone
while I break my fingernails against the tender flesh
because I seized the hair of the woman who made me
because even the stone produces worms tonight
to the slow rolling of the eye in the head
when fingers and toes spout from your womb
teeth of the womb which I tear with a sharp fingernail
so that the man's foot might know the grip of the roots
between the mushrooms swollen by the sun which sows pus
body of light which I feed and destroy inside
here inside twisting metal sheet from his house
because the rock in the middle of the lake is loaded with water

Adriano Spatola   475

7

perché la roccia nel mezzo del lago si carica d'acqua
grumo nero impastato con bianchissima calce
tela bianca che strappo con l'unghia affilata
qui dentro lamiera contorta della sua casa
scende la pressa rugosa che schiaccia la dura mano
è la tua colpa colomba rossa che ruota dentro la testa
piedi di marmo che tarlo corrode nel mezzo del prato
ora che il tempo equivale a ciò che sarà
unghia che taglia contorta lamiera del ponte
al lento nuotare del pesce dentro la roccia

8

semino capelli e dita nel ventre che arai
perché con la pietra si salda la torre di carne
ed è calda la cera che scende a riempire la bocca
ora che il tempo equivale a ciò che sarà
radice inchiodata allo scafo della roccia sommersa
e lungo disteso sul pavimento il quadro dell'impiccato
perché ho preso i capelli di colei che mi fece
radice comune dalla quale rampollano essi stanotte
perché il mondo che si solleva si chiude a pugno
quando nel sonno degli abitanti si brucia la vera città
scoppiano sassi nel fuoco sotto la pelle
riga che cresce e che sale sul foglio
verso ritmato nel luogo dell'insolita lama
e il ventre è questa parete che scivola sopra di me
sui denti che l'unghia affilata strappa dall'alveo

9

e dentro qui questa pietra capelli di questa colei
ah che prendo le dita e i capelli di questa colei
come s'alza nel pesce lamiera contorta del ponte
affinché il piede dell'uomo conosca la morsa delle radici
e come sappiamo da tempo da sempre bambini gridano in piazza
sepolti tra le tue dita essi che terra ricopre
pesce che frigge nell'olio della cucina sul fiume
mondo che si solleva nel chiudersi a pugno
raccolgo polvere e sassi sotto la pelle
mentre chino sul foglio annoto gli effetti dell'esplosione
per questa ripugnanza tra me chino e me chino in avanti
e il nodo che lega alle cose divampa sul collo dell'impiccato

7

because the rock in the middle of the lake is loaded with water
black clot filled with the whitest lime
white wire I cut with a sharp fingernail
here inside twisted metal sheet from her house
it goes down the rutted press which crushes the hard hand
it's your fault red dove which rolls inside the head
marble which wood-worm corrodes in the middle of the field
now that the time is equivalent to that which will be
fingernail which cuts a twisted metal sheet from the bridge
to the slow swimming of the fish inside the rock

8

I sow hair and fingers in the womb I plow
because you heal the tower of flesh with the stone
and the wax which comes down to fill the mouth is hot
now that the time is equivalent to that which will be
root riveted to the hull of the submerged rock
and stretched out along the floor the painting of the hanged man
because I seized the hair of the woman who made me
common root from which they sprout tonight
because the world which rises closes to a fist
when the true city burns in the sleep of the inhabitants
rocks explode in the fire under the skin
line which grows and which rises on the sheet
rhythmical line in the remarkable blade's place
and the womb is this wall which slides over me
on the teeth which the sharp fingernail tears from the riverbed

9

and here in this stone hair of the one who
ah that I seize the fingers and hair of this one who
as it rises in the fish a twisted metal sheet from the bridge
so that the man's foot might know the grip of the roots
and as we have known for a long time children have always cried in the piazza
buried between your fingers those which earth covers
fish which fries in the oil in the kitchen on the river
world which rises closing into a fist
I gather dust and stones under the skin
while I stoop on the metal sheet I take note of the explosion's effects
for this disgust between I stoop and I stoop forward
and the knot which ties things bursts into flame on the hanged man's neck

Adriano Spatola   477

10

io siedo sopra me stesso
rosea medusa che brucio la mia libertà
è la mia pelle conciata il muro che incido con l'unghia
fuoco che danza nel volto contro se stesso
corpo di luce che dentro alimento e distruggo
s'accumula cera che frigge tra l'unghia e la carne
la roccia sommersa divampa dentro la sterile acqua
al lento nuotare dell'occhio dentro la testa
nel ventre di questa parete che scivola sopra di me
sabbia che si fa pietra
l'erba che cresca in mezzo ai capelli
ruggine sopra le unghie
ora che il tempo equivale a ciò che sarà
pressa rugosa che schiaccia nell'occhio la testa
gonfia di vermi radice la sbarra in rugoso cemento
la mano le cinque dita già dentro la fogna

11

perché si degna colei che mi fece
radice inchiodata allo scafo della roccia sommersa
e scoppiano sassi nel fuoco sotto la pelle
è questa la mia sapienza è la sapienza che parlo
nodo che lega alle cose divampo nel collo dell'impiccato
perché si degna colei che mi fece
e io siedo sopra me stesso
mentre ruota la notte nell'occhio del chiuso spazio
mentre scivola sopra di me nel suo ventre la bianca parete
con questa sapienza che il sole gonfia di pus
perché si degna colei che mi fece
roccia sommersa divampo dentro la sterile acqua
tela bianca che strappo con l'unghia affilata
polvere e sassi raccolti sotto la pelle
cinque dita cinque radici nel mondo che si solleva
perché si degna colei che mi fece

12

è lama di coltello che fende la mia mano
mentre la roccia nel mezzo del lago si carica d'acqua
né piú risale dal baratro giallo di sabbia
là dentro lamiera contorta della mia casa
mentre chino sul foglio annoto gli effetti dell'esplosione
è la mia pelle conciata il muro che incido con l'unghia
nel ventre di questa parete che scivola sopra di me

10

I sit on myself
rose-colored medusa who burns my freedom
it's my tanned skin the wall I carve with a fingernail
fire which dances against itself in the face
body of light which I feed and destroy inside
it accumulates wax which fries between the fingernail and flesh
the submerged rock bursts into flame in the sterile water
to the slow swimming of the eye in the head
in the womb of this wall which slides over me
sand which becomes stone
the grass which grows in the midst of the hair
rust on top of the fingernails
now that the time is equivalent to that which will be
rutted press that crushes the eye in the head
swells with worms root the bar in the rutted cement
the hand the five fingers already in the sewer

11

because the woman who made me graces me
root riveted to the hull of the submerged rock
and rocks explode in the fire under the skin
this is my knowledge it's knowledge that I speak
knot that ties things I burst in the hanged man's neck
because the woman who made me graces me
and I sit on myself
while the night rolls in the eye of the closed space
while the white wall slides over me in her womb
with this knowledge that the sun swells with pus
because the woman who made me graces me
submerged rock I burst in the sterile water
white wire I tear with the sharp fingernail
dust and rocks gathered under the skin
five fingers five roots in the world which rises
because the woman who made me graces me

12

it's a knife blade which cuts through my hand
while the rock in the middle of the lake is loaded with water
nor does it any longer rise again from the yellow chasm of sand
there inside a twisted metal sheet from my house
while I stoop on the metal sheet I take note of the explosion's effects
it's my tanned skin the wall I carve with my fingernail
in the womb of this wall which slides over me

Adriano Spatola   479

grumo nero impastato con bianchissima calce
cinque dita cinque radici nel mondo che si solleva
sui denti che l'unghia affilata strappa dall'alveo
fuoco che danza nel volto contro se stesso
rosea medusa che brucia la mia libertà
s'accumula cera che frigge tra l'unghia e la carne
gonfia di vermi radice la sbarra in rugoso cemento
e come sappiamo da tempo da sempre bambini gridano in piazza
quando nel sonno degli abitanti si brucia la vera città
al lento nuotare del pesce dentro la roccia
e i funghi gonfiati dal sole producono pus

13

poiché persino la pietra fa vermi questa notte
casa avvampante nello spazio chiuso dai chiodi della roccia
rana squartata che frigge nell'olio della cucina sul fiume
e l'erba ricresce tra i suoi capelli
è la tua mano che s'apre come un fiore nell'alba
è la radice inchiodata allo scafo della roccia sommersa
è la mia colpa dispersa nel ventre di alcune madri
ah giuoco che mi moltiplica
ah freccia feconda
ah torre feconda
poiché persino la pietra fa vermi questa notte
trascina la pelle che pende sopra la ghiaia del nostro giardino
piede che fango ricopre al salire del mondo
riga che cresce e che sale sul foglio

14

riga che cresce e che sale sul foglio
fuoco che danza nel vuoto contro se stesso
mentre distesa sul fianco la città s'addormenta
e semino capelli e dita nel ventre che arai
e il ventre è questa parete che scivola sopra di me
e come sappiamo da sempre da tempo bambini gridano in piazza
luce che si consuma nel pesce che ruota dentro la testa
tela bianca che strappo con l'unghia affilata
unghie spezzate contro la tenera carne
la tua colpa colomba rossa che sale dall'intestino
è la mia colpa dispersa nel ventre di alcune madri
e nel tuo ventre il nodo che lega alle cose
pesce che s'alza nell'aria e che l'aria consuma

black clot filled with the whitest lime
five fingers five roots in the world which rises
on the teeth which the sharp fingernail tears from the riverbed
fire which dances against itself in the face
rose-colored medusa who burns my freedom
wax accumulates which burns between the fingernail and flesh
swells with worms root the bar in rutted cement
and as we have known for a long time children have always cried in the piazza
when the true city burns in the sleep of the inhabitants
to the slow swimming of the fish inside the rock
and the mushrooms swollen by the sun produce pus

13

because even the stone produces worms tonight
house blazing in the space closed by the rock's nails
cut up frog which fries in the oil in the kitchen on the river
and grass grows again in her hair
it's your hand which opens like a flower at dawn
it's the root riveted to the hull of the submerged rock
it's my guilt spread in the wombs of several mothers
ah game which multiplies me
ah fertile arrow
ah fertile tower
because even the stone produces worms tonight
she drags the skin which hangs over the gravel of our garden
foot which mud covers at the rising of the world
line which grows and which rises on the sheet

14

line which grows and which rises on the sheet
fire which dances against itself in the emptiness
while stretched out on its side the city falls asleep
and I sow hair and fingers in the womb I plow
and the womb is the wall which slides over me
and as we have known for a long time children have always cried in the piazza
light consumed in the fish which rolls inside the head
white wire I tear with the sharp fingernail
fingernails broken against the tender flesh
your guilt red dove which rises from the intestine
it's my guilt spread in the wombs of several mothers
and in your womb the knot which ties all things
fish which rises in the air and which the air consumes

Adriano Spatola   481

15

è lama di sabbia rossa che fende la sterile acqua
questa mano medusa schiacciata dal piede di marmo
nel ventre di questa parete che scivola sopra di me
pressa di marmo che scende con cinque radici sopra la testa
cinque radici nel mondo che si solleva chiudendosi a pugno
siringa che inietta bacilli alla radice del naso
perché a quel tempo tra gli occhi non c'era la morte
non c'era a quel tempo tra gli occhi una cosa immortale
ma sono le grida dei bimbi che giocano in piazza
nel ventre di questa parete le cinque radici
lame di sabbia rossa che fendono sterili acque
e collo dell'impiccato
di ciò che è stato detto
si sa che è stato detto perché bruci nel mondo

16

a cui ci sono dati gli oggetti quando sono pensati
per questa ripugnanza tra me chino e chino in avanti
radice comune dalla quale rampollano essi stanotte
posizione imperfetta che con lo sguardo riacquisto cosí
perché cosí si trascende nell'onda che gonfia stanotte
in cui ci sono dati gli oggetti quando sono pensati
e precedono quelli che oggetti hanno pure un motivo
fondamento del quale purtroppo qui non è luogo
radice comune dalla quale rampollano essi stanotte
in cui ci sono dati gli oggetti quando sono pensati
e precedono quelli che oggetti hanno pure un motivo
fondamento del quale purtroppo qui non è luogo
radice comune dalla quale rampollano essi stanotte
per questa ineguaglianza tra me chino e me chino in avanti
perché sia necessario notare soltanto la condizione
perché non solo essenziali si appare secondo la divisione

15

it's a blade of red sand which cuts through the sterile water
this hand medusa crushed by the marble foot
in the womb of this wall which slides over me
marble press which comes down on the head with five roots
five roots in the world which rises closing itself into a fist
syringe which injects bacilli at the root of the nose
because at that time there was no death between the eyes
there was no immortal thing at that time between the eyes
but they are the cries of the children who play in the piazza
in the womb of this wall the five roots
blades of red sand which cut through sterile waters
and the hanged man's neck
of that which has been said
you know that it has been said so it can burn in the world

16

who are the objects given to when they're thought
for this disgust between I stoop and I stoop forward
common root from which they sprout tonight
imperfect position which I thus recover with the look
because thus one transcends in the wave which swells tonight
in which the objects are given to us when they're thought
and they precede those the objects which also have a motive
foundation of which unfortunately here isn't the place
common root from which they sprout tonight
in which the objects are given to us when they're thought
and they precede those the objects which also have a motive
foundation of which unfortunately here isn't the place
common root from which they sprout tonight
for this inequality between I stoop and I stoop forward
because it is necessary to note only the condition
because not only essential it appears according to the division

Designer: Al Burkhardt
Compositor: G & S Typesetters
Printer: Vail-Ballou Press
Binder: Vail-Ballou Press
Text: VIP Optima
Display: Typositor Optima
Cloth: Joanna Arrestox A 14550
Paper: 50 lb eggshell cream